HARBRACE
ESSENTIALS

WITH RESOURCES FOR
WRITING IN THE DISCIPLINES

CHERYL GLENN
The Pennsylvania State University

LORETTA GRAY
Central Washington University

WADSWORTH
CENGAGE Learning

Australia • Brazil • Japan • Korea • Mexico • Singapore • Spain • United Kingdom • United States

WADSWORTH
CENGAGE Learning

Harbrace Essentials with Resources for Writing in the Disciplines
Cheryl Glenn, Loretta Gray

Senior Publisher: Lyn Uhl

Publisher: Monica Eckman

Acquiring Sponsoring Editor: Kate Derrick

Development Editor: Michell Phifer

Editorial Assistant: Marjorie Cross

Media Editor: Cara Douglass-Graff

Executive Marketing Manager: Stacey Purviance

Marketing Coordinator: Brittany Blais

Marketing Communications Manager: Linda Yip

Content Project Manager: Rosemary Winfield

Art Director: Marissa Falco

Manufacturing Buyer: Betsy Donaghey

Rights Acquisition Specialist: Alexandra Ricciardi

Production Service: Lifland et al., Bookmakers

Text and Cover Designer: Anne Bell Carter

Compositor: PreMediaGlobal

Library of Congress Control Number: 2012932084

ISBN-13: 978-1-133-59088-0

ISBN-10: 1-133-59088-8

Wadsworth
20 Channel Center Street
Boston, MA 02210
USA

Cengage Learning is a leading provider of customized learning solutions with office locations around the globe, including Singapore, the United Kingdom, Australia, Mexico, Brazil, and Japan. Locate your local office at **international.cengage.com/region**.

Cengage Learning products are represented in Canada by Nelson Education, Ltd.

For your course and learning solutions, visit **www.cengage.com**.

Purchase any of our products at your local college store or at our preferred online store **www.cengagebrain.com**.

Instructors: Please visit **login.cengage.com** and log in to access instructor-specific resources.

Printed in the United States of America
1 2 3 4 5 6 7 16 15 14 13 12

Contents

v

S **PART 2** **EFFECTIVE SENTENCES**

M   PART 5   MECHANICS

W   PART 6   WRITING

Preface

Welcome to *Harbrace Essentials with Resources for Writing in the Disciplines.* Whether you are a high school student, a college student, or a professional, you will find in this book all the practical information and strategies you need to make your writing voice heard. If you are like many of our students or colleagues, you want a portable handbook that provides answers to all your questions about writing—one that you can carry in a purse, briefcase, or backpack. We have answered this need with a concise handbook that includes only essential topics so that you can always have the information you need at your fingertips.

What are the essentials? When we ask this question of both students and composition instructors, they tell us they want information on grammar, style, punctuation, and mechanics, as well as strategies for writing paragraphs and essays, conducting research, and documenting sources. Their response is reflected in this book's contents.

Part 1 Grammar

Part 2 Effective Sentences

Part 3 Effective Language

Part 4 Punctuation

Part 5 Mechanics

Part 6 Writing

Part 7 Research

Part 8 Writing in the Disciplines

You will find samples of student writing throughout this book. Full papers are presented and discussed in chapters 26, 28, 32, 33, 34, 35, 36, and 38. It is our hope that wherever you are in the writing process, you will be able to access information quickly and easily.

Here are a few suggestions for using this book most efficiently:

▪ **Brief Table of Contents.** If you have a topic in mind, such as writing a thesis statement or using commas correctly, check the brief contents list inside the front cover of this book.

▪ **Index.** You can also find information quickly by consulting the index at the back of the book. There you will find chapter and section numbers as well as page numbers.

▪ **MLA, APA, CMS, and CSE Documentation Directories.** If you have a specific question about citing a source you have used or listing the source in a bibliography, refer to one of these style- and discipline-specific directories: MLA (Modern Language Association), generally used in writing about literature; APA (American Psychological Association), used in writing in the social sciences; CMS (*Chicago Manual of Style*), used in writing in the humanities; and CSE (Council of Scientists and Engineers), used in writing in the natural sciences. The chapter on MLA documentation is preceded by a tabbed divider for quick access.

▪ **Writing in the Disciplines.** Because writing in college occurs in courses beyond the first-year writing course, part 8 of this handbook includes chapters on writing about literature, in the social sciences, in the humanities, in the natural sciences, and in business. Each of these chapters covers the types of writing and document design used in the particular discipline and provides fresh, interesting examples of professional and student writing; the coverage reflects current practices and theories of specialized writing and presentations. These chapters will help you connect the writing and presentations you do in your classes with the realities of writing and presenting on the job and in the world.

- **Revision Symbols**. Inside the back of the book is a list of revision symbols. If you are taking a writing course and receive feedback that includes these symbols, you can look at this list to find the sections of the book where pertinent guidelines or strategies are discussed.

- **Glossary of Usage**. This glossary includes definitions of words that are commonly confused or misused (such as *accept* and *except*). It is organized like a dictionary, so you can just look up words you have questions about and find not only common meanings but also sample sentences showing appropriate usage.

Although we believe that *Harbrace Essentials with Resources for Writing in the Disciplines* will help you answer any question you have about writing, if you have suggestions for improving the next edition or if we can assist you in any way, don't hesitate to write to us c/o Cengage Learning, English Editorial, 20 Channel Center Street, Boston, MA 02210.

Cheryl Glenn
Loretta Gray
January 2012

Teaching and Learning Resources

Enhanced InSite™

Printed Access Card (1 semester):
978-1-133-59612-7
Instant Access Code (1 semester):
978-1-133-59614-1

Printed Access Card (2 semesters): 978-1-133-59599-1
Instant Access Code (2 semesters): 978-1-133-59600-4

From a single, easy-to-navigate site, you and your students can manage the flow of papers online, check for originality, and conduct peer reviews. Students can access a multimedia eBook with text-specific workbook, private tutoring options, and resources for writers that include anti-plagiarism tutorials and downloadable grammar podcasts. Enhanced InSite™ provides the tools and resources you and your students need *plus* the training and support you want. Learn more at **www.cengage .com/insite**. *(Access card/code is required.)*

Multimedia eBook

Printed Access Card: 978-1-133-59605-9
Instant Access Code: 978-1-133-59604-2

Harbrace Essentials with Resources for Writing in the Disciplines is available as a multimedia eBook! Now students can do all of their reading online or use the eBook as a handy reference while they're completing other coursework. The eBook includes the full text of the print version with interactive exercises, an integrated text-specific workbook, user-friendly navigation, search, and highlighting tools, and links to videos that enhance the handbook content. *(Access card/code is required.)*

Online College Workbook

A great companion to the handbook, the Online College Workbook covers grammar, punctuation, usage, style, and writing. Also included are exercises with clear examples and explanations that supplement the exercises found in the handbook.

The workbook is available as part of the Multimedia eBook (see above) or as a password-protected, downloadable PDF for instructors at the companion Web site. The Answer Key is in the Online Instructor's Resource Manual.

Online Instructor's Resource Manual

Available for easy download at the companion Web site, the password-protected Online Instructor's Resource Manual is designed to provide maximum flexibility in planning and customizing a course. Materials include a variety of pedagogical questions (and possible solutions) to use when teaching a course with this handbook, sample syllabi with possible assignments for a semester-long course and for a quarter-long course, sample in-class collaborative learning activities, technology-oriented activities, and critical thinking and writing activities.

English Composition CourseMate

Harbrace Essentials with Resources for Writing in the Disciplines is complemented by English Composition CourseMate. This set of resources includes an interactive eBook; interactive teaching and learning tools, including quizzes, flashcards, videos, workbook, and more; and Engagement Tracker, a first-of-its-kind tool that monitors student engagement in the course. Go to **www.login.cengage.com** to access these resources, and look for the icon 🖳, which denotes a resource available within CourseMate.

InfoTrac® College Edition with InfoMarks™

Printed Access Card: 978-0-534-55853-6
This online research and learning center offers over twenty million full-text articles from nearly six thousand scholarly and popular periodicals. The articles cover a broad spectrum of disciplines and topics—ideal for every type of researcher. Learn more at **www.cengage .com/infotrac**. *(Access code/card is required.)*

Turnitin®
Printed Access Card (1 semester):
978-1-4130-3018-1
Printed Access Card (2 semesters):
978-1-4130-3019-8

This proven, online plagiarism-prevention software promotes fairness in the classroom by helping students learn to correctly cite sources and allowing instructors to check for originality before reading and grading papers. *(Access code/card is required.)*

Additional Resources

Merriam-Webster's Collegiate® Dictionary, 11th Edition
Casebound: 978-0-8777-9809-5 *(not available separately)*

Merriam-Webster's Dictionary, 2nd Edition
Paperbound: 978-0-8777-9930-6 *(not available separately)*

Acknowledgments

We would like to thank our colleagues who reviewed this handbook during the course of its development. Their astute comments and thoughtful suggestions helped shape this first edition.

Susan Achziger, *Community College of Aurora*; William Allegrezza and Anne Balay, *Indiana University Northwest*; Chris Allen and Kristin Gardner, *Piedmont Technical College*; Andrew Andermatt, *Clinton Community College*; Heidi Anderson and Susan Perala-Dewey, *University of Minnesota Duluth*; Martha Bachman, *Camden County College*; Ned Bachus and Joseph Kenyon, *Community College of Philadelphia*; Joy Barta, *California State University–San Bernardino*; Ann Bliss, *University of California–Merced*; Christel Broady, *Georgetown College*; Susan Butterworth and Timothy Quigley, *Salem State College*; Anthony Cavaluzzi, *Adirondack Community College*; Cindy Cochran, *Illinois College*; Anita Cook, *Bridgewater College*; Patricia Cullinan, *Truckee Meadows Community College*; Susan Dalton, *Alamance Community College*; Joshua Dickinson, *Jefferson Community College*; Clark Draney, *College of Southern Idaho*; Jeannine Edwards, *University of Memphis*; Tahmineh Entessar, *Webster University*; Daniela Falco and Patricia Taylor, *University of Connecticut*; Eugene Flinn and Patricia Flinn, *New Jersey City University*; Jennifer Garcia, *Ventura College*; Susan Garrett, *Goucher College*; Marivel Gonzales-Hernandez and Sara Kaplan, *Del Mar College*; Carl Herzig, *St. Ambrose University*; Monica Hogan, *Johnson County Community College*; Martha Holder, *Wytheville Community College*; Michelle Holt, *University of Montana–Helena*; Nancy Hull, *Calvin College*; Brian Jackson and Brett McInelly, *Brigham Young University*; Geri Jacobs, *Jackson Community College*; Peter Jacoby, *San Diego Mesa College*; Joseph Justice, *South Plains College*; Christy Kinnion, *Wake Technical Community College*; Edis Kittrell,

Montana State University–Bozeman; Patti Kurtz, *Minot State University*; Angela Laflen, *Marist College*; Jeanette Lukowski, *Bemidji State University*; Kara Lybarger-Monson, *Moorpark College*; Christopher Manley, *University of Notre Dame*; Kevin McKelvey, *University of Indianapolis*; Timothy Messick, *Mohawk Valley Community College*; Kevin Miller, *Emerson College*; Robert Mellin, *Purdue University–North Central*; Edwin Miner, *Utah Valley University*; Lyle Morgan, *Pittsburg State University*; Susana Morris, *Auburn University*; David Mulry, *Schreiner University*; Joanna Murray, *Heald College*; Dana Nkana, *Illinois Central College*; Karen O'Donnell, *Finger Lakes Community College*; Dave Page, *Inver Hills Community College*; Callie Palmer, *Linn Benton Community College*; Twila Papay, *Rollins College*; Marjorie Pitts, *Ohio Northern University*; Bridget Pool, *Northern Virginia Community College*; Cheryl Renee, *Brevard Community College*; Jennifer Richardson, *State University of New York–Potsdam*; Heather Rodgers, *Saint Charles Community College*; Anne Schmit, *North Platte Community College*; Stacy Waddoups, *Utah Valley University*; Mary Williams, *Midland College*; Robert Williams, *Grossmont College*; and Paul Wise, *University of Toledo*.

G

GRAMMAR

1 Sentence Essentials

The second you decide to write, you are making a decision. You will make many more before you lift your hands from the keyboard and say, "Finished." Whether you are choosing a word, connecting thoughts, or crafting an essay, you will find it easier to make decisions if you have a clear purpose in mind. The purposeful use of language is called **rhetoric.** Throughout this book, you will be encouraged to *think rhetorically*—to consider how to achieve your purpose with a given audience and within a specific context. This chapter covers concepts of grammar that will help you write clear, convincing sentences.

1a Parts of speech

When you look up a word in the dictionary, you will often find it followed by one or more of these labels: *adj., adv., conj., interj., n., prep., pron.,* and *v.* (or *vb.*). These are the abbreviations for the traditional eight parts of speech: *adjective, adverb, conjunction, interjection, noun, preposition, pronoun,* and *verb.*

(1) Verbs
Verbs that indicate action (*walk, drive, study*) are called **action verbs.** Verbs that express being or experiencing are called **linking verbs;** they include *be, seem,* and *become* and the sensory verbs *look, taste, smell, feel,* and *sound.* Both action verbs and linking verbs are frequently accompanied by **auxiliary** or **helping verbs** that add shades of meaning, such as information about time (*will* study this afternoon), ability (*can* study), or obligation (*must* study).

THINKING RHETORICALLY

VERBS

Decide which of the following sentences evokes a clearer image:

The team captain **was** absolutely ecstatic.

Grinning broadly, the team captain **shot** both her arms into the air.

You probably chose the sentence with the action verb *shot* rather than the sentence with *was*. Most writers avoid using the verb *be* in any of its forms (*am, is, are, was, were,* or *been*) when their goal is vibrant imagery. Instead, they use vivid action verbs.

(2) Nouns

Nouns usually name people, places, things, and ideas. **Proper nouns** are specific names: *Bill Gates, Redmond, Microsoft Corporation*. **Common nouns** refer to any member of a class or category: *person, city, company.* There are three types of common nouns.

- **Count nouns** refer to people, places, things, and ideas that can be counted. They have singular and plural forms: *boy, boys; park, parks; car, cars; concept, concepts.*
- **Noncount nouns** refer to things or ideas that cannot be counted: *furniture, information.*
- **Collective nouns** are nouns that can be either singular or plural, depending on the context: *The **committee** published its report* [singular]. *The **committee** disagree about their duties* [plural].

THINKING RHETORICALLY

NOUNS

Nouns like *entertainment* and *nutrition* that refer to concepts are called **abstract nouns.** In contrast, nouns like *guitar* and *apple* that refer to things perceivable by the senses are called **concrete nouns.** When your rhetorical situation calls for the use of abstractions, balance them with tangible details conveyed through concrete nouns.

(3) Pronouns

Most pronouns (*it, he, she, they,* and many others) replace antecedents—nouns that have already been mentioned.

Dan thinks **he** will have the report done by Friday.

An antecedent may also be a noun and the words modifying it.

My parents bought the cheap, decrepit house because they

thought **it** had charm.

The pronouns in the preceding examples are **personal pronouns.** For a discussion of other types of pronouns, see chapter 5.

(4) Adjectives

Adjectives most commonly modify nouns: *spicy* food, *special* price. Sometimes they modify pronouns: *blue* ones, anyone *thin.* Adjectives usually answer one of these questions: Which one? What kind of . . . ? How many? What color or size or shape (and so on)? Although adjectives usually precede the nouns they modify, they occasionally follow them: *enough* time, time *enough.* Adjectives may also follow linking verbs such as *be, seem,* and *become*:

The moon is **full** tonight.   He seems **shy.**

Articles are a subclass of adjectives because, like adjectives, they are used before nouns. There are three articles: *a, an,* and *the.* The article *a* is used before a consonant sound (**a** yard, **a** university, **a** VIP); *an* is used before a vowel sound (**an** apple, **an** hour, **an** NFL team).

MULTILINGUAL WRITERS

ARTICLE USAGE

English has two types of articles: indefinite and definite. The **indefinite articles** *a* and *an* indicate that a singular noun is used in a general way.

- Use an indefinite article when you introduce a singular noun for the first time.

  Pluto is **a** dwarf <u>planet</u>.

- When you are defining a word, use an indefinite article.

  A <u>planet</u> is a celestial body orbiting a star such as our sun.

The **definite article,** *the,* is used before a noun that has already been introduced or when a reference is obvious.

- Once a noun has been introduced, use the definite article to refer to it a second time.

  Scientists distinguish between planets and <u>dwarf planets</u>. One of **the** <u>dwarf planets</u> in our solar system is Pluto.

- Subsequent mention does not always include exact repetition of a noun. However, the noun chosen must be close in meaning to a word already introduced.

  Scientists are not sure how to <u>classify</u> some celestial bodies. **The** <u>classification</u> of Pluto proved to be controversial.

- Use the definite article before a noun that everyone in the audience considers unique, such as *moon, universe,* and *sky.*

  The <u>moon</u> is full tonight.

(5) Adverbs

Adverbs most frequently modify verbs. They provide information about time, manner, place, and frequency, thus answering one of these questions: When? How? Where? How often?

The conference <u>starts</u> **tomorrow.** [time]

I **rapidly** <u>calculated</u> the cost. [manner]

We <u>met</u> **here.** [place]

They **often** <u>work</u> late on Thursdays. [frequency]

Adverbs that modify verbs can often move from one position in a sentence to another.

He **carefully** removed the radio collar.

He removed the radio collar **carefully.**

Adverbs also modify adjectives and other adverbs by intensifying or otherwise qualifying the meanings of those words.

I was **extremely** <u>curious</u>. [modifying an adjective]

The team played **surprisingly** <u>well</u>. [modifying an adverb]

THINKING RHETORICALLY

ADVERBS

What do the adverbs add to the following sentences?

The scientist **delicately** places the slide under the microscope.

"You're late," he whispered **vehemently.**

She is **wistfully** hopeful.

Adverbs can help you portray an action, indicate how someone is speaking, and add detail to a description.

(6) Prepositions

A **preposition** is a word that combines with a noun and any of its modifiers to provide additional detail—often answering one of these questions: Where? When?

> <u>**In** the early afternoon</u>, we walked **through** <u>our old neighborhood</u>. [answers the questions *When?* and *Where?*]

A preposition may also combine with a pronoun.

> We walked **through** it.

A grammar rule that has caused much controversy over the years is the one that advises against ending a sentence with a preposition. Most professional writers now follow this rule only when they adopt a formal tone. If their rhetorical situation calls for an informal tone, they will not hesitate to place a preposition at the end of a sentence.

> He found friends **on** whom he could depend. [formal]
>
> He found friends he could depend **on**. [informal]

SOME COMMON PREPOSITIONS

about	behind	for	of	to
above	between	from	on	toward
after	by	in	out	under
as	despite	into	past	until
at	during	like	since	up
before	except	near	through	with

Phrasal prepositions consist of more than one word.

Except for the last day, it was a wonderful trip.

SOME COMMON PHRASAL PREPOSITIONS		
according to	due to	in spite of
as for	except for	instead of
because of	in addition to	with regard to

(7) Conjunctions

Conjunctions are connectors; they fall into four categories: coordinating, correlative, subordinating, and adverbial. A **coordinating conjunction** connects similar words or groups of words; that is, it generally links a word to a word, a phrase to a phrase, or a clause to a clause. There are seven coordinating conjunctions. Use the made-up word *fanboys* to help you remember them.

F	A	N	B	O	Y	S
for	and	nor	but	or	yet	so

tired **yet** excited [*Yet* joins two words and signals contrast.]

in the boat **or** on the pier [*Or* joins two phrases and marks them as alternatives.]

We did not share a language, **but** somehow we communicated. [*But* joins two independent clauses and signals contrast.]

In the example sentence above, *but* links two independent clauses and thus is preceded by a comma. A coordinating conjunction such as *but* may also link independent clauses that stand alone as sentences.

The momentum in the direction of globalization seems too powerful to buck, the economic logic unmatchable. **But** in a region where jobs are draining away, and where an ethic of self-reliance remains a dim, vestigial, but honored memory, it seems at least an outside possibility.   —**BILL MCKIBBEN**, "Small World"

A **correlative conjunction** (or **correlative**) consists of two parts. The most common correlatives are *both . . . and, either . . . or, neither . . . nor,* and *not only . . . but also.*

Not only did they run ten miles, **but** they **also** swam twenty laps. [*Not only . . . but also* joins two independent clauses and signals addition.]

Generally, a correlative conjunction links similar structures. The following sentence has been revised because the correlative conjunction was linking a phrase to a clause.

Not only ₍did he save₎ ~~saving~~ the lives of the accident victims, **but** he **also** prevented many spinal injuries.

A **subordinating conjunction** introduces a dependent clause. It also carries a specific meaning; for example, it may indicate cause, concession, condition, purpose, or time. A dependent clause that begins a sentence is followed by a comma.

Unless the project receives funding, the research will stop. [*Unless* signals a condition.]

She studied Spanish **when** she worked in Costa Rica. [*When* signals time.]

SUBORDINATING CONJUNCTIONS

after	before	once	unless
although	even if	since	until
as if	even though	so that	when
as though	if	than	whether
because	in that	though	while

Adverbial conjunctions—such as *however, nevertheless, then,* and *therefore*—link independent clauses. These conjunctions, also called **conjunctive adverbs,** signal relationships such as cause, condition, and contrast. Adverbial conjunctions are set off by commas. An independent clause preceding an adverbial conjunction may end in a semicolon or a period.

The senator thought the plan was reasonable**; however,** the voters did not.

The senator thought the plan was reasonable. **However,** the voters did not.

The senator thought the plan was reasonable. The voters, **however,** did not.

The senator thought the plan was reasonable. The voters did not**, however.**

ADVERBIAL CONJUNCTIONS

also	indeed	moreover	still
finally	instead	nevertheless	then
furthermore	likewise	nonetheless	therefore
however	meanwhile	otherwise	thus

---

(8) Interjections

Interjections most commonly express an emotion such as surprise or dread. Interjections that come before a sentence end in a period or an exclamation point.

Oh. Now I understand.

Wow! Your design is astounding.

Interjections that begin or interrupt a sentence are set off by commas.

Hey, what are you doing?

The solution, **alas,** was not as simple as I had hoped it would be.

EXERCISE 1

Identify the part of speech for each word in the sentences below.

1. The hike to Lake Ann was short but quite challenging.

2. Neither Lee nor I expected trouble; nonetheless, we packed gear for emergencies.

3. After we unpacked at our campsite, we swam slowly across the lake.

 Subjects and predicates

A sentence consists of two parts:

$$\boxed{\text{SUBJECT + PREDICATE}}$$

The **subject** is generally someone or something that either performs an action or is described. The **predicate** expresses the action initiated by the subject or gives information about the subject.

> The <u>landlord</u> + <u>renovated</u> the apartment.
> [The subject performs an action; the predicate expresses the action.]

> <u>They</u> + <u>had sounded</u> reasonable.
> [The subject is described; the predicate gives information about the subject.]

The central components of the subject and the predicate are often called the **simple subject** (the main noun or pronoun) and the **simple predicate** (the main verb and any auxiliary verbs). They are underlined in the examples above.

Compound subjects and **compound predicates** include a connecting word (conjunction) such as *and, or,* or *but.*

The Republicans **and** the Democrats are debating this issue.
[compound subject]

The candidate stated his views on abortion **but** did not discuss stem-cell research. [compound predicate]

1c   Complements

Complements are parts of the predicate required by the verb to make a sentence complete. A complement is generally a pronoun, a noun, or a noun with modifiers.

The chair of the committee introduced —

    her. [pronoun]

    Sylvia Holbrook. [noun]

    the new member. [noun with modifiers]

There are four different complements: direct objects, indirect objects, subject complements, and object complements.

The **direct object** either receives the action of the verb or shows the result of the action.

I. M. Pei designed **the East Building of the National Gallery.**

Steve McQueen invented **the bucket seat** in 1960.

Indirect objects typically name the person(s) receiving or benefiting from the action indicated by the verb. Verbs that often take indirect objects include *buy, give, lend, sell, send,* and *write.*

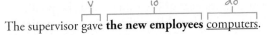

    v   io   do

The supervisor gave **the new employees** computers.

[*To whom* were the computers given?]

    v io   do

She wrote **them** recommendation letters.

[*For whom* were the recommendation letters written?]

The **subject complement** follows a linking verb. The most common linking verb is *be* (*am, is, are, was, were, been*). Other linking verbs are *become, seem,* and *appear* and the sensory verbs *feel, look, smell, sound,* and *taste.* A subject complement can be a pronoun, a noun, or a noun with modifiers. It can also be an adjective.

The winner was—

you. [pronoun]

Harry Solano. [noun]

the <u>person</u> with the highest score. [noun with modifiers]

ecstatic. [adjective]

The **object complement** helps complete the meaning of a verb such as *call, elect, make, name,* or *paint.* The object complement can be a noun or an adjective, along with any modifiers.

Reporters called the rookie **the best <u>player</u>.** [noun with modifiers]

The strike left the fans **somewhat <u>disappointed</u>.** [adjective with modifier]

EXERCISE 2

Identify the subject and the predicate in each sentence. Then, looking at just the predicate, identify the type of complement the sentence contains.

1. Octopuses and their relatives have been living in our oceans for millions of years.

2. They can change color or shape.

3. These shape-changers are often frightening.

4. The blue-ringed octopus can give an unsuspecting diver an unpleasant surprise.

5. Researchers consider the poison of the blue-ringed octopus one of the deadliest in the world.

Phrases

A **phrase** is a sequence of grammatically related words without a subject, a predicate, or both. A phrase is categorized according to its most important word.

(1) Noun phrases

A noun phrase consists of a main noun and its modifiers. It can serve as a subject or as a complement. It can also be the object of a preposition such as *in, of, on, at,* or *to.*

> **The heavy frost** killed **many fruit trees.** [subject and direct object]

> **My cousin** is **an organic farmer.** [subject and subject complement]

> **His farm** is in **eastern Oregon.** [subject and object of the preposition *in*]

MULTILINGUAL WRITERS

NUMBER AGREEMENT IN NOUN PHRASES

Some words must agree in number with the nouns they precede. The words *a, an, this,* and *that* are used before singular nouns; *some, few, these, those,* and *many* are used before plural nouns:

> **an/that** opportunity [singular noun]
> **some/few/those** opportunities [plural noun]

The words *less* and *much* precede nouns representing abstract concepts or masses that cannot be counted (noncount nouns):

> **less** freedom, **much** water [noncount nouns]

(2) Verb phrases

A verb is essential to the predicate of a sentence. It generally expresses action or a state of being. Besides a main verb, a verb phrase includes one or more **auxiliary verbs,** sometimes called *helping verbs,* such as *be, have, do, will,* and *should.*

The passengers **have deplaned.** [auxiliary verb + main verb]

(3) Verbal phrases

A **verbal phrase** differs from a verb phrase in that the verb form in a verbal phrase serves as a noun or a modifier rather than as a verb.

He <u>was</u> **reading** the story aloud. [*Reading* is part of the verb phrase *was reading.*]

Reading is fundamental to academic success. [*Reading* serves as a noun. COMPARE: **It** is fundamental to academic success.]

The student **reading** aloud is an education major. [*Reading aloud* modifies *the student.*]

Verbal phrases are divided into three types: gerund phrases, participial phrases, and infinitive phrases.

Gerund phrases include a verb form ending in *-ing.* A gerund phrase serves as a noun, usually functioning as the subject or object in a sentence.

<u>**Writing a bestseller**</u> was her only goal. [subject]

My neighbor enjoys <u>**writing about distant places.**</u> [object]

Because gerund phrases act as nouns, pronouns can replace them.

That was her only goal.   My neighbor enjoys **it.**

THINKING RHETORICALLY

GERUNDS

What is the difference between the following sentences?

They bundle products together, which often results in higher consumer costs.

Bundling products together often results in higher consumer costs.

In the first sentence, the actor, *they,* is the focus. In the second sentence, the action of the gerund phrase, *bundling products together,* is the focus. As you revise, ask yourself whether you want to emphasize actors or actions.

Participial phrases include either a present participle (a verb form ending in *-ing*) or a past participle (a verb form ending in *-ed* for regular verbs or another form for irregular verbs). Participial phrases function as modifiers.

Fearing a drought, the farmers used less irrigation water.

All the farmers in the area, **plagued by drought,** used less irrigation water.

Farmers conserved water, **fearing a drought in late summer.**

Remember that gerund and participial phrases differ in function. A gerund phrase functions as a noun; a participial phrase functions as a modifier.

Working together can spur creativity. [gerund phrase]

Working together, the students designed their own software. [participial phrase]

A present participle (*-ing* form) cannot function alone as the main verb in a sentence. It must be accompanied by a form of *be* (*am, is, are, was,* or *were*).

They ^are^ **thinking** about the future.

THINKING RHETORICALLY

PARTICIPIAL PHRASES

If some of your sentences sound monotonous or choppy, try combining them by using participial phrases.

> Fans crowded along the city streets. They were celebrating their team's first state championship.
>
> REVISED
>
> **Crowded along the city streets,** fans celebrated their team's first state championship.

Infinitive phrases serve as nouns or as modifiers. The form of the infinitive is distinct—the infinitive marker *to* followed by the base form of the verb.

The company intends **to hire** twenty new employees. [noun]

We discussed his plan **to use** a new packing process. [modifier of the noun *plan*]

To attract customers, the company changed its advertising strategy. [modifier of the verb *changed*]

Some instructors advise against putting words between the infinitive marker *to* and the base form of the verb.

Under the circumstances, the
^The~~ jury was unable to, ~~under the circumstances,~~ convict the defendant.

This is good advice to remember if the intervening words create a cumbersome sentence. However, most writers today recognize that a single word splitting an infinitive can provide emphasis.

He did not expect to actually publish his work.

MULTILINGUAL WRITERS

VERBS FOLLOWED BY GERUNDS AND/OR INFINITIVES

Some verbs in English can be followed by a gerund, some can be followed by an infinitive, and some can be followed by either.

Verbs Followed by a Gerund

admit   consider   dislike   finish   avoid   deny   enjoy

Example: She **enjoys playing** the piano.

Verbs Followed by an Infinitive

agree   decide   deserve   hope   need   plan   promise   seem

Example: She **promised to play** the piano for us.

Verbs Followed by Either a Gerund or an Infinitive

begin   continue   like   prefer   remember   stop   try

Examples: She **likes to play** the piano. She **likes playing** the piano.

Although either a gerund phrase or an infinitive phrase can follow these verbs, the resulting sentences may differ in meaning.

We **stopped discussing** the plan. [The discussion has ended.]

We **stopped to discuss** the plan. [The discussion has not yet started.]

(4) Prepositional phrases

Prepositional phrases provide information about time, place, cause, manner, and so on. They can also answer one of these questions: Which one? What kind of . . . ?

> **With great feeling,** Martin Luther King expressed his dream **of freedom.**
> [*With great feeling* describes the way the speech was delivered, and *of freedom* specifies the kind of dream.]

> King delivered his most famous speech **at a demonstration in Washington, DC.**
> [Both *at a demonstration* and *in Washington, DC* provide information about place.]

A **prepositional phrase** consists of a **preposition** (a word such as *at, of,* or *in*) and a pronoun, noun, or noun phrase (called the **object of the preposition**). A prepositional phrase modifies another element in the sentence.

> Everyone **in class** went to the play. [modifier of the pronoun *everyone*]

> Some students met the professor **after the play.** [modifier of the verb *met*]

(5) Appositives

An **appositive** is most often a noun or a noun phrase that refers to the same person, place, thing, or idea as a preceding noun or noun phrase but in different words. When the appositive simply specifies the referent, no commas are used.

> Cormac McCarthy's novel ***The Road*** won a Pulitzer Prize.
> [The appositive specifies which of McCarthy's books won the award.]

When the appositive provides extra details, commas set it off.

> *The Road***, a novel by Cormac McCarthy,** won a Pulitzer Prize.
> [The appositive provides an extra detail about the book.]

(6) Absolute phrases

An **absolute phrase** is usually a noun phrase modified by a prepositional phrase or a participial phrase.

Her guitar in the front seat, she pulled away from the curb.

More vaccine having arrived, the staff scheduled its distribution.

The first absolute phrase provides details; the second expresses cause.

EXERCISE 3

Label the underlined phrases in the following sentences as noun, verb, prepositional, verbal, appositive, or absolute phrases. For verbal phrases, specify the type: gerund, participial, or infinitive. When a long phrase includes a short phrase, identify just the long phrase.

1. <u>Dedicated to the collection and diffusion of knowledge</u>, the Smithsonian comprises <u>over a dozen museums</u>.

2. People come <u>from every state</u> <u>to visit the museums</u>.

3. Scientists and scholars <u>visiting a Smithsonian museum</u> <u>can use its outstanding facilities</u>.

4. <u>Receiving a Smithsonian fellowship</u> is <u>the dream</u> <u>of many students</u>.

5. The Smithsonian owes <u>its existence</u> <u>to James Smithson</u>, <u>a scientist from Great Britain</u>.

6. <u>His bequest firmly rooted in the Enlightenment ideals of democracy and education</u>, James Smithson left the citizens <u>of the United States</u> <u>an unsurpassable legacy</u>.

1e   Clauses

(1) Independent clauses

A **clause** is a group of related words that contains a subject and a predicate. An **independent clause,** sometimes called a *main clause,* has the same grammatical structure as a simple sentence: both contain a subject and a predicate.

S　　　　pred

The students earned high grades.

An independent clause can stand alone as a complete sentence. Other clauses can be added to independent clauses to form longer, more detailed sentences.

(2) Dependent clauses

A **dependent clause** also has a subject and a predicate. However, it cannot stand alone as a complete sentence because of the word introducing it—usually a relative pronoun or a subordinating conjunction.

S　　pred

The athlete **<u>who</u> placed first** grew up in Argentina. [relative pronoun]

S　　　　pred

She received the gold medal **<u>because</u> she performed flawlessly.** [subordinating conjunction]

Noun clauses are dependent clauses that serve as subjects or objects. They are introduced by *if, that,* or a *wh-* word such as *why, what,* or *when.* Notice the similarity in usage between noun phrases and noun clauses.

What the witness said may not be true. [subject]

We do not understand **why they did it.** [direct object]

When no misunderstanding would result, the word *that* can be omitted from the beginning of a clause.

The scientist said **she was moving to Australia.** [*that* omitted]

However, *that* should always be retained when there are two noun clauses.

The scientist said **that she was moving to Australia** and **that her research team was planning to accompany her.** [*that* retained in both noun clauses]

An **adjectival clause,** or **relative clause,** follows a pronoun, noun, or noun phrase and answers one of these questions: Which one? What kind of . . . ? Such clauses, which nearly always follow the words they modify, usually begin with a **relative pronoun** (*who, whom, that, which,* or *whose*) but sometimes start with a **relative adverb** (*when, where,* or *why*).

Nobody likes news reports **that pry into someone's private life.** [answers the question *What kind of news reports?*]

Students **who have good study habits** begin their research early. [answers the question *Which students?*]

A relative pronoun can be omitted as long as the meaning of the sentence is still clear.

Mother Teresa was someone **the whole world admired.** [*Whom,* the direct object of the clause, has been omitted: the whole world admired *whom.*]

She was someone **who cared more about serving than being served.** [*Who* cannot be omitted because it is the subject of the clause.]

An **adverbial clause** usually answers one of the following questions: Where? When? Why? How? How frequently? In what manner? Adverbial clauses are introduced by subordinating conjunctions such as *because, although,* and *when.*

When the need arises, the company hires new writers. [answers the question *How frequently does the company hire new writers?*]

She acted **as though she cared only about herself.** [answers the question *How did she act?*]

THINKING RHETORICALLY

ADVERBIAL CLAUSES

In an adverbial clause that refers to time or establishes a fact, both the subject and any form of the verb *be* can be omitted. Using such **elliptical clauses** will make your writing more concise.

> **Though tired,** they continued to study for the exam.
> [COMPARE: **Though they were tired,** they continued to study for the exam.]

Be sure that the omitted subject of an elliptical clause is the same as the subject of the independent clause. Otherwise, revise either the adverbial clause or the main clause.

I was
While reviewing your report, a few questions occurred to me.

OR

I thought of
While reviewing your report, a few questions occurred to me.

EXERCISE 4

1. Identify the dependent clauses in the following paragraph.
2. Identify the underlined words as coordinating, correlative, subordinating, or adverbial conjunctions.

¹<u>If</u> you live by the sword, you might die by the sword. ²<u>However</u>, <u>if</u> you make your living by swallowing swords, you will not necessarily die by swallowing swords. ³At least, this is the conclusion Brian Witcombe and Dan Meyer reached <u>after</u> they surveyed forty-six professional sword swallowers. ⁴(Brian Witcombe is a radiologist, <u>and</u> Dan Meyer is a famous sword swallower.) ⁵Some of those surveyed mentioned <u>that</u> they had experienced <u>either</u> "sword throats" <u>or</u> chest pains, <u>and</u> others who let their swords drop to their stomachs described perforation of their innards, <u>but</u> the researchers could find no listing of a sword-swallowing mortality in the medical studies they reviewed. ⁶The researchers did not inquire into the reasons for swallowing swords in the first place.

TECH SAVVY

Using a Grammar Checker

Most word-processing programs have features that help writers identify grammar errors as well as problems with usage and style, but these grammar checkers have significant limitations. A grammar checker will usually identify

- fused sentences, sometimes called run-on sentences (chapter 3),
- wordy or overly long sentences (chapter 14), and
- missing apostrophes in contractions (17b).

However, a grammar checker can easily miss

- sentence fragments (chapter 2),
- dangling or misplaced modifiers (chapter 6),
- problems with pronoun-antecedent agreement (5c),
- errors in subject-verb agreement (4f), and
- misused or missing commas (chapter 15).

Because these omissions can weaken your credibility as a writer, you should never rely solely on a grammar checker to find them. Furthermore, grammar checkers can mark as wrong words or phrases that you have chosen deliberately to suit your rhetorical situation (chapter 24).

Used carefully, a grammar checker can be a helpful tool, but keep the following advice in mind:

- Use a grammar checker only in addition to your own editing and proofreading.
- Always evaluate any sentences flagged by a grammar checker to determine whether there is, in fact, a problem.
- Adjust the settings on your grammar checker to look for specific types of errors. If you are using Microsoft Word, select Tools; then select either Spelling and Grammar or Options to customize your settings.
- Carefully review the revisions proposed by a grammar checker before accepting them. Sometimes the proposed revisions create new errors.

2 Sentence Fragments

As its name suggests, a **sentence fragment** is only a piece of a sentence; it is not complete.

2a Recognizing sentence fragments

A sentence is considered a fragment when it is incomplete in one of three ways.

- It is missing a subject *or* a verb.

  I stared at the blank screen. **Wondering where to begin.** [no subject]

  Alternative medical treatment may include hypnosis. **The placement of a patient into a sleeplike state.** [no verb]

- It is missing both a subject *and* a verb.

  They slept soundly. **Despite the noise from the party upstairs.**

- It is a dependent clause.

  Ultimate Frisbee is a popular sport. **Because it can be played almost anywhere.**

2b Phrases as sentence fragments

A phrase is a group of words without a subject and/or predicate. When punctuated as a sentence (that is, with a period, a question mark, or an exclamation point), it becomes a fragment. You can revise such a fragment by attaching it to a related sentence, usually the one preceding it.

Verbal phrase as a fragment

Early humans valued color. ~~Creating~~ , *creating* permanent colors with **natural pigments.**

Prepositional phrase as a fragment

For years, the Scottish have dyed sweaters with soot. ~~Originally~~ , *originally* **from the chimneys of peat-burning stoves.**

Appositive phrase as a fragment

During the Renaissance, one of the most highly valued

pigments was ultramarine. ~~An~~ —*an* **extract from lapis lazuli.**

Absolute phrase as a fragment

The deciduous trees of New England are known for their brilliant

autumn color. ~~Sugar~~ , *sugar* **maples dazzling tourists with their**

orange and red leaves.

Instead of attaching a fragment to the preceding sentence, you can recast the fragment as a complete sentence.

Fragment	Humans painted themselves for a variety of purposes. **To attract a mate, to hide themselves from game or predators, or to signal aggression.**
Revision	Humans used color for a variety of purposes. For example, they painted themselves to attract a mate, to hide themselves from game or predators, or to signal aggression.

2c Dependent clauses as sentence fragments

A dependent clause is a group of words with both a subject and a predicate, but because it begins with a subordinating conjunction or a relative pronoun, it cannot stand alone as a sentence. To revise such a fragment, attach it to a related sentence, usually the sentence preceding it.

The iceberg was no surprise. ~~Because~~ the *Titanic*'s wireless operators had received reports of ice in the area.

More than two thousand people were aboard the *Titanic*. ~~Which~~ *, which* was the largest ocean liner in 1912.

You can also recast the fragment as a complete sentence by removing the subordinating conjunction or relative pronoun and supplying any missing elements.

The iceberg was no surprise. The *Titanic*'s wireless operators had received reports of ice in the area.

More than two thousand people were aboard the *Titanic*. In 1912, this ocean liner was the world's largest.

THINKING RHETORICALLY

FRAGMENTS

When used judiciously, fragments—like short sentences—emphasize ideas or add surprise. However, fragments are generally permitted only when the rhetorical situation allows the use of a casual tone.

May. When the earth's Northern Hemisphere awakens from winter's sleep and all of nature bristles with the energies of new life. My work has kept me indoors for months now. I'm not sure I'll ever get used to it.

—KEN CAREY, *Flat Rock Journal: A Day in the Ozark Mountains*

EXERCISE 1

Locate and revise the fragments in the following paragraph.

[1]Folklore from around the world contains references to wild men in the woods. [2]Such as the Greek satyrs, the Russian *leshiy*, and the Yetis of the Himalayas. [3]In North America, many people, including normally skeptical citizens and scientists, are fascinated by stories of Sasquatch. [4]A name originating in the Salish word *saskehavas*. [5]Another name commonly used is Big Foot. [6]An allusion to the size of the footprints reportedly belonging to a giant apelike creature. [7]That smells bad. [8]Most sightings of Sasquatch occur in the Pacific Northwest. [9]From northern California to central Alaska. [10]Although reports have come from almost every state. [11]During the settlement of the United States, stories of hairy ape-men were told by Native Americans. [12]And later on by trappers. [13]Teddy Roosevelt recorded one such story.

A **comma splice,** or **comma fault,** refers to the incorrect use of a comma between two independent clauses.

Most stockholders favored the merger,ᵇᵘᵗ the management did not.

A **fused sentence,** or **run-on sentence,** consists of two independent clauses run together without any punctuation at all.

The first section of the proposal was approved; however, the budget will have to be resubmitted.

To revise a comma splice or a fused sentence, include appropriate punctuation and any necessary connecting words.

3a   Locating comma splices and fused sentences

You can find comma splices and fused sentences by remembering that they commonly occur in certain contexts.

■ With transitional words and phrases such as *however, therefore,* and *for example*

Comma splice: The director is unable to meet you this week, however, next week she has time on Tuesday.

- When an explanation or an example is given in the second sentence

  Fused sentence: The cultural center has a new collection of spear points ~~many~~ *. Many* of them were donated by a retired anthropologist.

- When a positive clause follows a negative clause, or vice versa

  Comma splice: A World Cup victory is not just an everyday sporting event ~~it~~ *. It* is a national celebration.

- When the subject of the second clause is a pronoun whose antecedent is in the preceding clause

  Fused sentence: Lake Baikal is located in southern Russia ~~it~~ *. It* is 394 miles long.

> ### 3b   Revising comma splices and fused sentences

If you find comma splices or fused sentences in your writing, try one of the following methods to revise them.

(1) Linking independent clauses with a comma and a coordinating conjunction

By linking clauses with a comma and a coordinating conjunction (such as *and* or *but*), you signal the relationship between the clauses (addition or contrast, for example).

Fused sentence: Joseph completed the first experiment *, and* he will complete the other by Friday.

Comma splice: Some diplomats applauded the treaty, *but* others opposed it vehemently.

(2) Linking independent clauses with a semicolon or a colon or separating them with a period

When you link independent clauses with a semicolon, the semicolon usually indicates addition or contrast. When you link clauses with a colon, the second clause serves as an explanation or an elaboration of the first. A period indicates that each clause is a complete sentence, distinct from surrounding sentences.

Comma splice: Our division's reports are posted on our Web page, hard copies are available by request.

Revision 1: Our division's reports are posted on our Web page; hard copies are available by request.

Revision 2: Our division's reports are posted on our Web page. Hard copies are available by request.

Fused sentence: His choice was difficult ‸ he would either lose his job or betray his ethical principles.

(3) Recasting an independent clause as a dependent clause or as a phrase

A dependent clause includes a subordinating conjunction such as *although* or *because,* which indicates how the dependent and independent clauses are related (in a cause-and-effect relationship, for example). A prepositional phrase includes a preposition such as *in, on,* or *because of* that may also signal a relationship directly. Verbal, appositive, and absolute phrases suggest relationships less directly because they do not include connecting words.

Comma splice: The wind had blown down trees and power lines, the whole city was without electricity for several hours.

Revision 1: Because the wind had blown down power lines, the whole city was without electricity for several hours. [dependent clause]

Revision 2: Because of the downed power lines, the whole city was without electricity for several hours. [prepositional phrase]

Revision 3: The wind having blown down power lines, the whole city was without electricity for several hours. [absolute phrase]

(4) Integrating one clause into the other

When you integrate clauses, you will generally retain the important details but omit or change some words.

> **Fused sentence:** The proposal covers all but one point it does not describe how the project will be assessed.

> **Revision:** The proposal covers all the points except assessment procedures.

(5) Using transitional words or phrases to link independent clauses

Another way to revise fused sentences and comma splices is to use transitional words and phrases such as *however, on the contrary,* and *in the meantime.*

> **Fused sentence:** Sexual harassment is not just an issue for
> women *. After all,* men can be sexually harassed too.

> **Comma splice:** The word *status* refers to relative position
> within a group *; however,* it is often used to indicate only positions of prestige.

EXERCISE 1

Revise each comma splice or fused sentence in the following paragraph. Some sentences may not need revision.

[1] In the introduction to his book of true stories, *I Thought My Father Was God*, Paul Auster describes how he was able to collect these accounts of real and sometimes raw experience. [2] In October 1999, Auster, in collaboration with National Public Radio, began the *National Story Project*, during an interview on the radio program *Weekend All Things Considered*, he invited listeners to send in their stories about unusual events—"true stories that sounded like fiction." [3] In just one year, over four thousand stories were submitted Auster read every one of them.

[4]"Of the four thousand stories I have read, most have been compelling enough to hold me until the last word," Auster affirms, "most have been written with simple, straightforward conviction, and most have done honor to the people who sent them in." [5]Some of the stories Auster collected can now be read in his anthology choosing stories for the collection was difficult, though. [6]"For every story about a dream or an animal or a missing object," explains Auster, "there were dozens of others that were submitted, dozens of others that could have been chosen."

3c   Divided quotations

When dividing quotations with attributive tags such as *he said* or *she asked,* use a period between independent clauses.

Comma splice: "Beauty brings copies of itself into being," states Elaine Scarry, "it makes us draw it, take photographs of it, or describe it to other people."

Both parts of the quotation are complete sentences, so the attributive tag is attached to the first, and the sentence is punctuated with a period.

4   Verbs

Choosing verbs to convey your message precisely is the first step toward writing clear sentences.

4a   Verb forms

Regular verbs have four forms: a base form, an -*s* form (third-person singular in the present tense), an -*ing* form (present participle), and an -*ed* form (past participle).

VERB FORMS OF REGULAR VERBS

Base Form	-s Form (Present Tense, Third Person, Singular)	-ing Form (Present Participle)	-ed Form (Past Form or Past Participle)
work	works	working	worked
watch	watches	watching	watched
apply	applies	applying	applied
stop	stops	stopping	stopped

CAUTION

When verbs are followed by words with similar sounds, you may find their endings (-*s* or -*ed*) difficult to hear. In addition, these verb endings may seem unfamiliar because your dialect does not have them. Nonetheless, you should use -*s* and -*ed* when you write for an audience that expects you to include these endings.

                seems
She seem satisfied with the report.
     ^

                   supposed
We were suppose to receive the results yesterday.
        ^

Irregular verbs have from three to eight forms. Most irregular verbs, such as *write,* have forms similar to some of those for regular verbs: base form (*write*), -*s* form (*writes*), and -*ing* form (*writing*). However, the past form (*wrote*) and the past participle (*written*) vary from the regular forms. The following list includes the base form, the past-tense form, and the past participle for irregular verbs.

VERB FORMS OF IRREGULAR VERBS

Base Form	Past Form	Past Participle
arise	arose	arisen
awake	awaked, awoke	awaked, awoken
be	was/were	been
begin	began	begun
break	broke	broken
bring	brought	brought
buy	bought	bought
choose	chose	chosen
come	came	come
dive	dived, dove	dived
do	did	done
dream	dreamed, dreamt	dreamed, dreamt
drink	drank	drunk
drive	drove	driven
eat	ate	eaten
forget	forgot	forgotten
forgive	forgave	forgiven
get	got	gotten, got

(Continued on page 36)

(Continued from page 35)

Base Form	Past Form	Past Participle
give	gave	given
go	went	gone
hang (suspend)	hung	hung
hang (execute)	hanged	hanged
keep	kept	kept
know	knew	known
lay (to place)	laid	laid
lead	led	led
lie (to recline)	lay	lain
lose	lost	lost
pay	paid	paid
rise	rose	risen
say	said	said
see	saw	seen
set	set	set
sink	sank	sunk
sit	sat	sat
speak	spoke	spoken
stand	stood	stood
steal	stole	stolen
swim	swam	swum
take	took	taken
tell	told	told
throw	threw	thrown
wear	wore	worn
write	wrote	written

MULTILINGUAL WRITERS

OMISSION OF FORMS OF *BE* IN OTHER LANGUAGES

Forms of the verb *be* can be omitted in some languages.
In English, however, they are necessary.

Sentence without an auxiliary verb: The population ᵢₛ growing.

Sentence without a linking verb: It ᵢₛ quite large.

A **phrasal verb** is a combination of a verb and a particle
such as *up, out,* or *on.* A **particle** resembles an adverb or
a preposition, but it is so closely associated with a verb that
together they form a unit of meaning that often cannot be
deduced from the common meanings of the individual words.
For example, the phrasal verb *blow up* means "to enlarge": She
blew up the photograph so that she could see the faces better.

The verb and particle in most phrasal verbs may be separated by a short noun phrase or by a pronoun.

She **called** the meeting **off**.

The student **turned** it **in** yesterday.

Some phrasal verbs are not separable, however.

The group **went over** the proposal.

Particles that add little meaning are often deleted.

I **sent** ~~out~~ the invitations.

The **auxiliary verbs** *be, do,* and *have* combine with main
verbs, both regular and irregular.

be	*am, is, are, was, were surprised*
	am, is, are, was, were writing
do	*does, do, did call*
	doesn't, don't, didn't spend

have	*has, have, had prepared*
	has, have, had read

Another type of auxiliary verb is called a **modal auxiliary**. There are nine modal auxiliaries: *can, could, may, might, must, shall, should, will,* and *would*. The following box provides examples of common meanings conveyed by modal auxiliaries.

COMMON MEANINGS OF MODAL AUXILIARIES

Meaning	Modal Auxiliary	+	Main Verb	Example
Ability	can, could		afford	They *can afford* to buy a small house.
Certainty	will		leave	We *will leave* tomorrow.
Obligation	must		return	You *must return* your books soon.
Advice	should		talk	He *should talk* with his counselor.
Permission	may		use	You *may use* the computers in the library.

CAUTION

When a modal auxiliary occurs with the auxiliary *have* (*must have forgotten, should have known*), *have* frequently sounds like the word *of*. When you proofread, be sure that modal auxiliaries are not followed by *of*.

They **could of taken** another route.
     have

Writers generally do not combine modal auxiliaries unless they want to portray a regional dialect.

We **might could** plan the meeting for after the holidays.
     be able to

MULTILINGUAL WRITERS

PHRASAL MODALS

English also has **phrasal modals**, which consist of more than one word. They have meanings similar to those of one-word modals.

be able to (ability): We **were able to** find the original document.

have to (obligation): You **have to** report your test results.

Other common phrasal modals are *be going to, be supposed to, had better, used to,* and *ought to.* Most phrasal modals have more than one form (*am able to, is able to, were able to*). Only *had better, ought to,* and *used to* have a single form.

EXERCISE 1

Revise the following sentences. Explain any changes you make.

1. Any expedition into the wilderness suffer its share of mishaps.

2. The Lewis and Clark Expedition began in May 1804 and end in September 1806.

3. Fate must of smiled on Meriwether Lewis and William Clark, for there were no fatalities under their leadership.

4. Lewis and Clark lead the expedition from St. Louis to the Pacific Ocean and back.

5. By 1805, the Corps of Discovery, as the expedition was call, included thirty-three members.

6. The Corps might of lost all maps and specimens had Sacajawea, a Native American woman, not fish them from the Missouri River.

4b **Verb tenses**

Providing information about time, verb tenses are labeled as present, past, or future and as simple, progressive, perfect, or perfect progressive.

VERB TENSES

	Present	Past	Future
Simple	walk, walks	walked	will walk
Progressive	am, is, are walking	was, were walking	will be walking
Perfect	has, have walked	had walked	will have walked
Perfect progressive	has, have been walking	had been walking	will have been walking

(1) Simple tenses

Simple present	I, you, we, they *work* he, she, it *works*
Simple past	*worked* (only one form)
Future	*will work* (only one form)

The **simple present tense** is used to indicate a current state, a habitual action, or a general truth.

We **are** ready. [current state]

Dana **uses** common sense. [habitual action]

The sun **rises** in the east. [general truth]

It is also commonly used to add a sense of immediacy to historical actions and to discuss literary and artistic works.

In 1939, Hitler's armies **attack** Poland. [historical present]

Joseph Conrad **writes** about what he sees in the human heart. [literary present]

On occasion, the simple present tense is used to refer to future time.

The festival **begins** next month.

The **simple past tense** refers to completed past actions or events.

He **traveled** to the Philippines. [past action]

The accident **occurred** several weeks ago. [past event]

The **simple future tense** refers to future actions or states.

I **will call** you after work today. [future action]

The video **will be** ready by Friday. [future state]

(2) Progressive tenses

Present progressive	I *am working*
	he, she, it *is working*
	you, we, they *are working*
Past progressive	I, he, she, it *was working*
	you, we, they *were working*
Future progressive	*will be working* (only one form)

The **present progressive tense** signals an activity in progress or a temporary situation.

The doctor **is attending** a conference. [activity in progress]

We **are living** in a yurt right now. [temporary situation]

The present progressive tense can also refer to a future event when it occurs with an expression indicating time.

> They **are leaving** for Alaska next week. [*Next week* indicates a time in the future.]

The **past progressive tense** signals an action or event that occurred in the past and was repeated or ongoing.

> The new member **was** constantly **interrupting** the discussion. [repeated past action]

> We **were eating** dinner when we heard the news. [ongoing past action]

The **future progressive tense** refers to actions that will occur over some period of time in the future.

> She **will be giving** her report at the end of the meeting. [future action]

MULTILINGUAL WRITERS

VERBS NOT USED IN THE PROGRESSIVE FORM

Some verbs that do not express actions but rather mental states, emotions, conditions, or relationships are not used in the progressive form. These verbs include *believe, belong, contain, cost, know, own, prefer,* and *want.*

> The book ~~is containing~~ contains many Central American folktales.

(3) Perfect tenses

Present perfect	I, you, we, they *have worked* he, she, it *has worked*
Past perfect	*had worked* (only one form)
Future perfect	*will have worked* (only one form)

The **present perfect tense** signals a time prior to the present. It can refer to a situation originating in the past but continuing into the present. It can also refer to a past action that has current relevance.

> They **have lived** in New Zealand for twenty years. [situation originating in the past and still continuing]
>
> I **have read** that book already, but I could certainly read it again. [past action that is completed but currently relevant]

The **past perfect tense** refers to an action completed at a time in the past prior to another past time or past action.

> Before 1990, he **had worked** in a shoe factory. [past action prior to a given time in the past]
>
> I **had studied** geology before I transferred to this school. [past action prior to another past action]

The **future perfect tense** refers to an action that is to be completed prior to a future time.

> By this time next year, I **will have finished** medical school.

(4) Perfect progressive tenses

Present perfect progressive	I, you, we, they *have been working* he, she, it *has been working*
Past perfect progressive	*had been working* (only one form)
Future perfect progressive	*will have been working* (only one form)

The **present perfect progressive tense** signals that an action, state, or event originating in the past is ongoing or incomplete.

> I **have been feeling** tired for a week. [ongoing state]
>
> We **have been organizing** the conference since April. [incomplete action]

The **past perfect progressive tense** refers to a situation or an action occurring over a period of time in the past and prior to another past action or time.

> She **had been living** so frugally all year that she saved enough money for a new car. [past situation prior to another action in the past]

The **future perfect progressive tense** refers to an action that is occurring in the present and will continue to occur for a specific amount of time.

> In one more month, I **will have been working** on this project for five years.

4c   Verb tense consistency

By using verb tenses consistently, you help your readers understand when the actions or events you are describing took place. Every verb tense can be discussed in terms of time frame and aspect. *Time frame* refers to whether the tense is present, past, or future. *Aspect* refers to whether it is simple, progressive, perfect, or perfect progressive. (See the chart on page 40.) Consistency in the time frame of verbs, though not necessarily in their aspect, ensures that sentences reporting a sequence of events link together logically. In the following paragraph, notice that the time frame remains in the past, but the aspect may be either simple, perfect, or progressive.

past perfect

In the summer of 1983, I **had** just **finished** my third year of

simple past

architecture school and **had** to find a six-month internship.

past perfect (compound predicate)

I **had grown** up and **gone** through my entire education in the

past perfect

Midwest, but I **had been** to New York City once on a class field

simple past *simple past*

trip and I **thought** it **seemed** like a pretty good place to live. So,

armed with little more than an inflated ego and my school portfolio,

simple past

I **was** off to Manhattan, oblivious to the bad economy and the fact

past progressive

that the city **was overflowing** with young architects.

—PAUL K. HUMISTON, "Small World"

If you do need to shift to another time frame, you can use
a time marker:

now, then, today, yesterday
in two years, during the 1920s
after you finish, before we left

For example, in the following paragraph, the time frame shifts
back and forth between present and past. The time markers
are bracketed.

simple present *simple past*

These woods **are** not wild; indeed, they **were** not wild [in Thoreau's

day]. [Today], the beach and trails of Walden Pond State Reservation

simple present *simple present*

draw about 500,000 visitors a year. Few of them **hunt** ants, however.

simple present   simple past

Underfoot and under the leaf litter there **is** a world as wild as it **was**

simple past

[before human beings **came** to this part of North America].

—JAMES GORMAN, "Finding a Wild, Fearsome World Beneath Every Fallen Leaf"

On occasion, a shift in time is indicated implicitly—that is, without an explicit time marker. A writer may change tenses, without including time markers, (1) to explain or support a general statement with information about the past, (2) to compare and contrast two different time periods, or (3) to comment on a topic. In the following pair of sentences, the second sentence provides evidence from the past to support the claim in the first sentence.

Thomas Jefferson, author of the Declaration of Independence, **is** considered one of our country's most brilliant citizens. His achievements **were** many, as **were** his interests.

EXERCISE 2

Revise the following paragraph so that it contains no unnecessary shifts in verb tense.

I **had** already **been walking** for a half hour in the semidarkness of Amsterdam's early-morning streets when I **came** to a red light. I **am** in a hurry to get to the train station and no cars **were** out yet, so I **cross** over the cobblestones, passing a man waiting for the light to change. I never **look** back when he **scolds** me for breaking the law. I **had** a train to catch. I **was** going to Widnau, in Switzerland, to see Aunt Marie. I **have** not **seen** her since I **was** in second grade.

Voice indicates the relationship between a verb and its subject. When a verb is in the **active voice,** the subject is generally a person or thing performing an action. When a verb is in the **passive voice,** the subject is usually the *receiver* of the action.

Jen Wilson **wrote** the essay. [active voice]

The essay **was written** by Jen Wilson. [passive voice]

Notice that the actor, Jen Wilson, appears in a prepositional phrase beginning with *by* in the passive sentence. Some sentences, however, do not include a *by* phrase because the actor is unknown or unimportant.

Jen Wilson's essay **was published** in the student newspaper.

The best way to decide whether a sentence is in the passive voice is to examine its verb phrase.

(1) Verbs in the passive voice

The verb phrase in a sentence written in the passive voice consists of a form of the auxiliary verb *be* (*am, is, are, was, were, been*) and a past participle. Depending on the verb tense, other auxiliaries such as *have* and *will* may appear as well. The following sentences include common forms of *call* in the passive voice:

Simple present	The meeting *is called* to order.
Simple past	The recruits *were called* to duty.
Present progressive	The council *is being called* to act on the proposal.
Past perfect	Ms. Jones *had been called* to jury duty twice last year, but she was glad to serve again.

If a verb phrase does not include both a form of the auxiliary verb *be* and a past participle, it is in the active voice.

(2) Choosing between the active and passive voice

To use the active voice for emphasizing an actor and an action, first make the actor the subject of the sentence; then choose verbs that will help your readers see what the actor is doing.

A group of students **planned** the graduation ceremony.

Use the passive voice when you want to stress the recipient of the action, rather than the actor, or when the actor's identity is unimportant or unknown.

Tuition increases **were discussed** at the board meeting.

Writers of scientific prose often use the passive voice to highlight the experiment rather than the experimenter. The following is an excerpt from a lab report by student Heather Jensen:

First, the slides **were placed** on a compound microscope under low

power, a 40× magnification level. The end of the root tip **was located**;

then the cells immediately behind the root cap **were examined**.

EXERCISE 3

Identify the voice in each sentence as active or passive.

1. In a *National Geographic* report, Tom O'Neill describes the discovery of ancient art in Guatemala.

2. Archaeologist William Saturno recently discovered the oldest known Maya mural.

3. The mural was found in a tunnel used by looters.

4. The tunnel was actually a small room attached to a pyramid.

5. The mural was dated to about 150 years before the beginning of the Maya Classic period.

4e   Mood

The **mood** of a verb expresses the writer's attitude toward the factuality of what is being expressed. The **indicative mood** is used for statements and questions regarding fact or opinion. The **imperative mood** is used to give commands or directions. The **subjunctive mood** is used to state requirements, make requests, and express wishes.

Indicative	We will be on time.
Imperative	Be on time!
Subjunctive	The director insists that we be on time.

The subjunctive mood is also used to signal hypothetical situations (situations that are not real or not currently true—for example, *If I were president, . . .*).

Verb forms in the subjunctive mood serve a variety of functions. The **present subjunctive** is the base form of the verb. It is used to express necessity.

> The doctor recommended that he **go** on a diet. [active voice]

> We demanded that you **be reimbursed**. [passive voice]

The **past subjunctive** has the same form as the simple past (for example, *had, offered, found,* or *wrote*). However, the past subjunctive form of *be* is *were,* regardless of person or number. This form is used to present hypothetical situations.

> If they **offered** me the job, I would take it. [active voice]

> Even if he **were promoted**, he would not change his mind. [passive voice]

The **perfect subjunctive** verb has the same form as the past perfect tense: *had* + past participle. The perfect subjunctive signals that a statement is not factual.

I wish I **had known** about the scholarship competition.
[active voice]

If she **had been awarded** the scholarship, she would have quit
her part-time job. [passive voice]

The following guidelines should help you avoid pitfalls
when using the subjunctive.

TIPS FOR USING THE SUBJUNCTIVE

- In clauses beginning with *as if* and *as though*, use the past
  subjunctive or the perfect subjunctive:

  He acts as if he ~~was~~ *were* the owner.

  She looked at me as though she **heard** *had* this story before.

- In nonfactual dependent clauses beginning with *if*, use the past
  subjunctive or the perfect subjunctive. Avoid using *would have* in
  the *if* clause.

  If I ~~was~~ *were* rich, I would buy a yacht.

  If the driver ~~would have~~ **checked** *had* his rearview mirror, the
  accident would not have happened.

- In dependent clauses following verbs that express wishes, requirements, or requests, use the past subjunctive or the perfect
  subjunctive.

  I wish I ~~was~~ *were* taller.

  My brother wishes he **studied** *had* harder years ago.

EXERCISE 4

Use subjunctive verb forms to revise the following sentences.

1. The planners of Apollo 13 acted as if the number 13 was a lucky number.

2. Superstitious people think that if NASA changed the number of the mission, the astronauts would have had a safer journey.

3. They also believe that if the lunar landing would have been scheduled for a day other than Friday the Thirteenth, the crew would not have encountered any problems.

4. The crew used the lunar module as though it was a lifeboat.

5. If NASA ever plans a space mission on Friday the Thirteenth again, the public would object.

4f   Subject-verb agreement

To say that a verb *agrees* with a subject means that the form of the verb (*-s* form or base form) is appropriate for the subject. For example, if the subject refers to one person or thing (*an athlete, a computer*), the *-s* form of the verb (*runs*) is appropriate. If the subject refers to more than one person or thing (*athletes, computers*), the base form of the verb (*run*) is appropriate. Notice in the following examples that the singular third-person subjects in the first line take a singular verb (*-s* form) and all the other subjects take the base form.

He, she, it, Joe, a student	has, looks, writes
I, you, we, they, the Browns, the students	have, look, write

The verb *be* has three different present-tense forms and two different past-tense forms:

I	am/was
He, she, it, Joe, a student	is/was
You, we, they, the Browns, the students	are/were

(1) Words between the subject and the verb

When phrases such as the following occur between the subject and the verb, they do not affect the number of the subject or the form of the verb:

along with	in addition to	not to mention
as well as	including	together with

Her **salary,** together with tips, **is** just enough to live on.

Tips, together with her salary, **are** just enough to live on.

(2) Subjects joined by *and*

A compound subject (two nouns joined by *and*) that refers to a single person or thing takes a singular verb.

The **founder <u>and</u> president** of the art association **was** elected to the board of the museum.

(3) Subjects joined by *or* or *nor*

When singular subjects are linked by *or, either . . . or,* or *neither . . . nor,* the verb is singular as well.

The **provost <u>or</u>** the **dean** usually **presides** at the meeting.

<u>**Either**</u> his **accountant <u>or</u>** his **lawyer has** the will.

If the linked subjects differ in number, the verb agrees with the subject closer to the verb.

Neither the basket nor the **apples were** expensive. [plural]

Neither the apples nor the **basket was** expensive. [singular]

(4) Inverted order

In most sentences, the subject precedes the verb.

The large **cities** of the Northeast **were** the hardest hit by the winter storms.

The subject and verb can sometimes be inverted for emphasis; however, they must still agree.

The hardest hit by the winter storms **were** the large **cities** of the Northeast.

When *there* begins a sentence, the subject and verb are always inverted; the verb still agrees with the subject, which follows it.

There **are** several **cities** in need of federal aid.

(5) Clauses with relative pronouns

In an adjectival (relative) clause, the subject is generally a relative pronoun (*that, who,* or *which*). To determine whether the relative pronoun is singular or plural, you must find its antecedent (the word or words it refers to). When the antecedent is singular, the relative pronoun is singular; when the antecedent is plural, the relative pronoun is plural. In essence, the verb in the adjectival clause agrees with the antecedent.

The person who reviews proposals is out of town this week.

The director met with the **students who are** studying abroad next quarter.

The Starion is one of the new **models that include** a DVD player as standard equipment.

(6) Indefinite pronouns

The indefinite pronouns *each, either, everybody, everyone,* and *anyone* are considered singular and so require singular verb forms.

Either of them **is willing** to lead the discussion.

Everybody in our apartment building **has** a parking place.

All, any, some, none, half, and *most* can be either singular or plural, depending on whether they refer to a unit or quantity (singular) or to individuals (plural).

My sister collects antique **jewelry;** <u>some</u> of it **is** quite valuable.

My sister collects comic **books;** <u>some</u> **are** quite valuable.

When an indefinite pronoun is followed by a prepositional phrase beginning with the preposition *of,* the verb agrees in number with the object of the preposition.

<u>None</u> of **those are** spoiled.

<u>None</u> of the **food is** spoiled.

(7) Collective nouns and measurement words

Collective nouns and measurement words require singular verbs when they refer to groups or units. They require plural verbs when they refer to individuals or parts.

Singular (regarded as a group or unit)	**Plural (regarded as individuals or parts)**
The **majority rules.**	The **majority** of us **are** in favor.
Ten million gallons of oil **is** more than enough.	**Ten million gallons** of oil **were spilled.**

(8) Words ending in -s

Titles of works that are plural in form (for example, *Star Wars* and *Dombey and Son*) are treated as singular because they refer to a single book, movie, recording, or other work.

> ***Julie & Julia* is** one of the films she discussed in her paper.

Some nouns ending in *-s* are singular: *linguistics, news,* and *Niagara Falls.*

> The **news is** encouraging.

Nouns such as *athletics, politics,* and *electronics* can be either singular or plural, depending on their meanings.

> **Statistics is** an interesting subject. [singular]
>
> **Statistics are** often misleading. [plural]

(9) Subjects and subject complements

Some sentences may have a singular subject and a plural subject complement, or vice versa. In either case, the verb agrees with the subject.

> Her primary **concern is** rising health-care **costs.**
>
> **Croissants are** the bakery's **specialty.**

THINKING RHETORICALLY

AGREEMENT OF RELATED SINGULAR AND PLURAL NOUNS

When a sentence has two or more nouns that are related, use either the singular form or the plural form consistently.

> The **student** raised her **hand.**   The **students** raised their **hands.**

Occasionally, you may have to use a singular noun to retain an idiomatic expression or to avoid ambiguity.

> **They** kept their **word.**

(10) Subjects beginning with *what*

When *what* may be understood as "the thing that," the verb in the main clause is singular.

> What we need **is** a new policy. [*The thing that* we need is a new policy.]

If *what* is understood as "the things that," the verb in the main clause is plural.

> What we need **are** new guidelines. [*The things that* we need are new guidelines.]

EXERCISE 5

Choose the correct form of the verb in parentheses.

1. There (is/are) at least two good reasons for changing motor oil: risk of contamination and danger of additive depletion.

2. Reasons for not changing the oil (include/includes) the cost to the driver and the inconvenience of the chore.

3. What I want to know (is/are) the number of miles I can drive before changing my oil.

4. But my brother says three thousand miles (is/are) not long enough.

5. Each of the car manuals I consulted (recommends/recommend) five-thousand-mile intervals.

6. Neither the automakers nor the oil station attendants (know/knows) how I drive, however.

5 Pronouns

When you use pronouns effectively, you add clarity and coherence to your writing.

5a Recognizing pronouns

A **pronoun** is commonly defined as a word used in place of a noun that has already been mentioned—its antecedent.

John said **he** would guide the trip.

Most pronouns refer to nouns, but some modify nouns.

This man is our guide.

Pronouns are categorized as personal, reflexive/intensive, relative, interrogative, demonstrative, or indefinite.

(1) Personal pronouns
Personal pronouns are like nouns: they refer to people, places, things, ideas, and so on.

Singular	I, me, you, he, him, she, her, it
Plural	we, us, you, they, them

(2) Possessive pronouns

Possessive pronouns are personal pronouns that indicate ownership and similar relationships.

Singular   my, mine, your, yours, his, her, hers, its

Plural   our, ours, your, yours, their, theirs

Avoid confusing possessive forms with common contractions: *it's (it is), they're (they are),* and *who's (who is).*

(3) Reflexive/intensive pronouns

Reflexive pronouns direct the action back to the subject (*I saw myself*); intensive pronouns are used for emphasis (*I myself questioned the judge*).

Singular   myself, yourself, himself, herself, itself

Plural   ourselves, yourselves, themselves

Avoid using a reflexive pronoun as a subject.

Ms. Palmquist and ~~myself~~ discussed our concern with the senator.

Hisself, themself, and *theirselves* are inappropriate in college or professional writing. Instead, use *himself* and *themselves.*

(4) Relative pronouns

An adjectival clause (or relative clause) ordinarily begins with a relative pronoun: *who, whom, which, that,* or *whose.* To provide a link between this type of dependent clause and the main clause, the relative pronoun corresponds to a word or words in the main clause called the **antecedent.**

The students talked to **a reporter who** had just returned from overseas.

Who, whose, and *whom* ordinarily refer to people; *which* refers to things; *that* refers to things and, in some contexts, people. The possessive *whose* (used in place of the awkward *of which*) usually refers to people but sometimes refers to things.

The poem, **whose** author is unknown, has recently been set to music.

Knowing the difference between an essential clause and a nonessential clause will help you decide whether to use *which* or *that*. A clause that a reader needs in order to identify the antecedent correctly is an **essential clause.**

ant   ess cl
The person who presented the award was last year's winner.

If the essential clause were omitted from this sentence, the reader would not know which person was last year's winner.

A **nonessential clause** is *not* needed for correct identification of the antecedent and is thus set off by commas. A nonessential clause often follows a proper noun (a specific name).

ant   noness cl
Andrea Bowen, who presented the award, was last year's winner.

If the nonessential clause were removed from this sentence, the reader would still know the identity of last year's winner.

According to a traditional grammar rule, *that* is used in essential adjectival clauses, and *which* is used in nonessential adjectival clauses.

I need a job **that** pays well.

For years, I have had the same job, **which** pays well enough.

However, some professional writers use *which* in essential clauses. Nonetheless, if you are following APA guidelines, use *which* only in nonessential clauses.

(5) Interrogative pronouns

The interrogative pronouns *what, which, who, whom,* and *whose* are question words.

Who won the award?   **Whom** did you see?

(6) Demonstrative pronouns

The demonstrative pronouns *this* and *these* indicate that someone or something is close by in time, space, or thought. *That* and *those* signal remoteness.

These are important documents; **those** can be thrown away.

(7) Indefinite pronouns

Indefinite pronouns usually do not refer to specific persons, objects, ideas, or events.

anyone	anybody	anything
everyone	everybody	everything
someone	somebody	something
no one	nobody	nothing
each	either	neither

Indefinite pronouns do not refer to an antecedent. In fact, some indefinite pronouns *serve* as antecedents.

Someone forgot **her** purse.

5b **Pronoun case**

To understand the uses of pronouns, you must first be able to recognize person and number. **Person** indicates whether a pronoun refers to the writer (**first person**), to the reader (**second person**), or to another person, place, thing, or idea (**third person**). **Number** reveals whether a pronoun is singular or plural.

Case refers to the form a pronoun takes to indicate its relationship to other words in a sentence. There are three cases: subjective, objective, and possessive.

He [subjective] wants **his** [possessive] legislators to help **him** [objective].

CASE:	Subjective		Objective		Possessive	
NUMBER:	Singular	Plural	Singular	Plural	Singular	Plural
First person	I	we	me	us	my mine	our ours
Second person	you	you	you	you	your yours	your yours
Third person	he, she, it	they	him, her, it	them	his, her, hers, its	their theirs

(1) Pronouns in the subjective case

A pronoun that is the subject of a sentence is in the subjective case. To determine which pronoun form is correct in a compound subject (a noun and a pronoun joined by *and*), say the sentence using the pronoun alone, omitting the noun. For the following sentence, notice that "*Me* solved the problem" sounds strange, but "*I* solved the problem" sounds fine.

~~Me and~~ Marisa~~,~~ solved the problem.
and I

Place the pronoun *I* last in the sequence. If the compound subject contains two pronouns, test each one by itself.

He
~~Him~~ and I joined the club in July.

Pronouns following a *be* verb (*am, is, are, was, were, been*) should also be in the subjective case.

The first to arrive were Kevin and ~~me~~.
I

MULTILINGUAL WRITERS

NOUN OR PRONOUN AS SUBJECT

In some languages, a noun in the subject position may be followed by a pronoun. In Standardized English, though, such a pronoun should be omitted.

My roommate ~~he~~ works in the library for three hours a week.

---

(2) Pronouns in the objective case

Whenever a pronoun follows an action verb or a preposition, it takes the **objective case**.

Direct object	The whole staff admired **him**.
Indirect object	The staff sent **him** a card.
Object of a preposition	The staff depended on **him**.

Pronouns in compound objects are also in the objective case.

They will appoint you or ~~I~~ me. [direct objects]

They lent Tom and ~~I~~ me money for tuition. [indirect objects]

Janice sat between my brother and ~~I~~ me. [objects of the preposition]

To determine whether to use the subjective or objective case, remember to say the sentence with just the pronoun. Notice that "They will appoint *I*" does not sound right.

(3) Possessive forms

Possessives can be divided into two groups based on whether they are followed by nouns. *My, your, his, her, its, our,* and *their* are all followed by nouns; *mine, yours, his, hers, ours,* and *theirs* are not. (Note that *his* is in both groups.)

Their budget is higher than **ours.**
[*Their* is followed by a noun; *ours* is not.]

(4) Appositive pronouns

Appositive pronouns are in the same case as the nouns they rename.

The red team—Rebecca, Leroy, and ~~me~~ I —won by only one point.

A trophy was presented to the red team—Rebecca, Leroy, and ~~I~~ me.

EXERCISE 1

Revise the following paragraph, using appropriate pronouns. Some sentences may not require editing.

¹When I was twelve, my family lived in Guatemala for a year. ²My parents taught English at a university; me and my younger brother went to a local school. ³Although the Spanish language was new to both Sam and I, we learned to speak it quickly. ⁴At first, we couldn't understand much at all, but with the help of a tutor, who we met every day after school, we started learning "survival" Spanish. ⁵After we learned to ask and answer some basic questions, we started making friends, whom eventually introduced us to they're own version of Spanish.

(5) Who/whoever and whom/whomever

To choose between *who* and *whom* or between *whoever* and *whomever,* you must first determine whether the word is functioning as a subject or an object. A pronoun functioning as the subject takes the subjective case.

Who won the award? [COMPARE: **She** won the award.]

The teachers know **who** won the award.

The student **who** won the award was quite surprised.

Whoever won the award deserves it.

When the pronoun is an object, use *whom* or *whomever*.

Whom did they hire? [COMPARE: They hired **him.**]

I do not know **whom** they hired.

The student **whom** they hired graduated in May.

Whomever they hired will have to work hard this year.

Whom may be omitted in sentences when no misunderstanding would result.

> The friend he relied on moved away.
> [*Whom* has been omitted after *friend*.]

(6) Pronouns with infinitives and gerunds

A pronoun grouped with an infinitive (*to* + the base form of a verb) takes the objective case.

> The director wanted **me** to help **him.**

A gerund (*-ing* verb form functioning as a noun) is preceded by a possessive pronoun.

> I appreciated **his** helping Denise. [COMPARE: I appreciated **Tom's** helping Denise.]

Notice that a possessive pronoun is used before a gerund but not before a present participle (*-ing* verb form functioning as an adjective).

> I saw **him** helping Luke.

(7) Pronouns in elliptical constructions

The words *as* and *than* frequently introduce **elliptical constructions**—clauses in which the writer has intentionally omitted words. To check whether you have used the correct case in an elliptical construction, read the written sentence aloud, inserting any words that have been omitted from it.

> She admires Clarice as much as **I.** [subjective case]
> Read aloud: She admires Clarice as much as *I do.*

> She admires Clarice more than **me.** [objective case]
> Read aloud: She admires Clarice more than *she admires me.*

EXERCISE 2

Correct the pronoun errors in the following sentences.

1. The board of directors has asked you and I to conduct a customer survey.

2. They also recommended us hiring someone with extensive experience in statistical analysis.

3. Whomever understands statistics should take the lead on this project.

4. Although the board asked me to be in charge, I would like you to recruit and interview candidates.

5c   Pronoun-antecedent agreement

A pronoun and its antecedent (the word or word group to which it refers) agree in number (both are singular or both are plural).

The **supervisor** said **he** would help.
[Both antecedent and pronoun are singular.]

My **colleagues** said **they** would help.
[Both antecedent and pronoun are plural.]

MULTILINGUAL WRITERS

POSSESSIVE PRONOUNS

A possessive pronoun (*his, her, its, their, my, our,* or *your*), also called a **possessive determiner,** agrees with its antecedent, not with the noun it precedes.

Ken Carlson brought ~~her~~ his young daughter to the office today.

[The possessive pronoun *his* agrees with the antecedent, *Ken Carlson*, not with the following noun, *daughter*.]

(1) Indefinite pronouns

An indefinite pronoun such as *everyone, someone,* or *anybody* takes a singular verb form.

Everyone **has** [not *have*] the right to an opinion.

Difficulties arise, however, because words like *everyone* and *everybody* seem to refer to more than one person even though they take a singular verb. Thus, the definition of grammatical number and our everyday notion of number conflict. In conversation and informal writing, a plural pronoun (*they, them,* or *their*) is often used with the singular *everyone.* Nonetheless, when you write for an audience that expects you to follow traditional grammar rules, make sure to use a third-person singular pronoun.

Everyone has the combination to <u>their</u> private locker. *(his or her)*

You can avoid the awkwardness of using *his* or *her* by using an article instead, making both the antecedent and the possessive pronoun plural, or rewriting the sentence using the passive voice (the *be* auxiliary + the past participle).

Everyone has the combination to **a** private locker. [article]

Students have combinations to **their** private lockers. [plural antecedent and plural possessive pronoun]

The combination to a private locker **is issued** to everyone. [passive voice]

(2) Two antecedents joined by *or* or *nor*

If a singular and a plural antecedent are joined by *or* or *nor,* place the plural antecedent second and use a plural pronoun.

Either Jennifer **or** her <u>roommates</u> will explain how <u>they</u> chose their majors.

Neither the president **nor** the <u>senators</u> stated that <u>they</u> would support the proposal.

(3) Collective nouns

When an antecedent is a collective noun such as *team, faculty,* or *committee*, determine whether you intend the noun to be understood as singular or plural. Then, make sure that the pronoun agrees in number with the noun.

it

The choir decided that ~~they~~ would tour during the winter.
[Because the choir decided as a group, *choir* should be considered singular.]

they

The committee may disagree on methods, but ~~it~~ must agree on basic aims.
[Because the committee members are behaving as individuals, *committee* is regarded as plural.]

EXERCISE 3

Revise each sentence in the way indicated so that pronouns and antecedents agree.

1. Everyone should have the right to participate in a study only if they feel comfortable doing so. (Make the antecedent plural.)

2. A team of researchers should provide its volunteers with consent forms, in which they describe to the volunteers the procedures and risks involved in participation. (Make sure all pronouns are plural.)

3. Every participant should be guaranteed that the information they provide will remain confidential. (Make the antecedent plural.)

5d   Clear pronoun reference

The meaning of each pronoun in a sentence should be immediately obvious. In the following sentence, the pronoun *he* clearly refers to the antecedent, *Jack*.

Jack has collected shells since **he** was eight years old.

(1) Ambiguous or unclear pronoun references

When a pronoun can refer to either of two antecedents, the ambiguity may confuse readers. To make the antecedent clear, replace the pronoun with a noun or rewrite the sentence.

Mr. Anderson told Mr. Eggers that _^he [*Mr. Eggers*] would be in charge of the project.

OR

Mr. Anderson put Mr. Eggers in charge of the project.

(2) Remote or awkward pronoun references

To help readers understand your meaning, place pronouns as close to their antecedents as possible. The following sentence needs to be revised so that the relative pronoun *that* is close to its antecedent, *poem*. Otherwise, the reader would wonder how a new book could be written in 1945.

The **poem** [*that was originally written in 1945*] has been published in a new book ~~that was originally written in 1945~~.

Notice, however, that a relative pronoun does not always have to follow its antecedent directly. In the following example, there is no risk of misunderstanding.

We slowly began to notice **changes** in our lives **that** we had never expected.

(3) Broad or implied pronoun references

Pronouns such as *it, this, that,* and *which* sometimes refer to the sense of a whole clause, sentence, or paragraph.

Large corporations may seem stronger than individuals, but **that** is not true. [*That* refers to the sense of the whole first clause.]

In academic rhetorical situations, revise sentences that do not have specific antecedents.

When class attendance is compulsory, some students feel that

education is being forced on them. This~perception~is unwarranted.

[In the original sentence, *this* had no clear antecedent.]

In addition, remember to express an idea explicitly rather than merely implying it.

My father is a music teacher. ~Teaching music~ ~It~ is a profession that requires

much patience.

[In the original sentence, *it* had no expressed antecedent.]

Be especially careful to provide clear antecedents when you are referring to the work or possessions of others. The following sentence requires revision because *she* can refer to someone other than Jen Norton.

In~her~ ~Jen Norton's~ new book, ~Jen Norton~ ~she~ argues for election reform.

(4) The use of *it* without an antecedent

The expletive *it* does not have a specific antecedent. Instead, it is used to postpone, and thus give emphasis to, the subject of a sentence. If a sentence that begins with this expletive is wordy or awkward, replace *it* with the postponed subject.

> Trying to repair the car   useless
> It was no use trying to repair the car.

EXERCISE 4

Edit the following sentences to make all references clear.

1. A champion cyclist, a cancer survivor, and a humanitarian, it is no wonder that Lance Armstrong is one of the most highly celebrated athletes in the world.

2. Armstrong's mother encouraged his athleticism, which led to his becoming a professional triathlete by age sixteen.

3. Though you might not believe it, Armstrong was only a senior in high school when he started training for the Olympic developmental team.

4. Not long afterward, because of intense pain, he sought medical attention, and they told him he had testicular cancer.

5. Armstrong underwent dramatic surgery and aggressive chemotherapy; this eventually helped him recover.

6. Armstrong started training five months after their diagnosis and went on to win major championships, including the Tour de France.

5e | Pronoun consistency

Whenever you write, you must establish your point of view (perspective). Your point of view will be evident in the pronouns you choose. *I* or *we* indicates a first-person point of view, which is appropriate for writing that includes personal views or experiences. If you decide to address the reader as *you*, you are adopting a second-person point of view. However, because a second-person point of view is rare in academic writing, avoid using *you* unless you need to address the reader. If you select the pronouns *he, she, it, one,* and *they*, you are writing with a third-person point of view. The third-person point of view is the most common point of view in academic writing.

Although you may find it necessary to use different points of view in a paper, especially if you are comparing or contrasting other people's views with your own, be careful not to confuse readers by shifting perspective unnecessarily.

To an observer, a sleeping person appears passive, unresponsive,

and essentially isolated from the rest of the world and its barrage

of stimuli. While it is true that ~~you are~~ someone asleep is unaware of most surrounding

noises ~~when you are asleep,~~ ~~our~~ that person's brain is far from inactive. In fact,

the brain can be as active during sleep as it is ~~when you are awake~~ in a waking state.

When ~~our brains are~~ it is asleep, the rate and type of electrical activity

change.

EXERCISE 5

Revise the following paragraph so that there are no unnecessary shifts in point of view.

[1]Many car owners used to complain about deceptive fuel-economy ratings. [2]The issue was ignored until our gas prices started to rise dramatically. [3]Because of increased pressure from consumer organizations, the United States Environmental Protection Agency now takes into account factors such as quick acceleration, changing road grades, and the use of air conditioning, so the new ratings should reflect your real-world driving conditions. [4]Nonetheless, the ratings can never be exact because we all have different driving habits.

5f Use of first-person and second-person pronouns

Using *I* is appropriate when you are writing about personal experience. In academic and professional writing, the use of the first-person singular pronoun is also a clear way to distinguish your own views from those of others. However, if you frequently repeat *I feel* or *I think,* your readers may suspect that you do not understand much beyond your own experience.

We, the first-person plural pronoun, is trickier to use correctly. When you use it, make sure that your audience can tell which individuals are included in this plural reference. For example, if you are writing a paper for a college course, does *we* mean you and the instructor, you and your fellow students, or some other group (such as all Americans)? Because you may inadvertently use *we* in an early draft to refer to more than one group of people, as you edit, check to see that you have used this pronoun consistently.

If you address readers directly, you will undoubtedly use the second-person pronoun *you* (as we, the authors of this handbook, have done). There is some disagreement, though, over whether to permit the use of the indefinite *you* to mean "a person" or "people in general." If your instructor tells you to avoid using the indefinite *you*, recast your sentences. For example, use *one* instead of *you*.

Even in huge, anonymous cities, ~~you find~~ _{one finds} community spirit.

If the use of *one* is too formal, try changing the word order or using different words.

Community spirit is found even in huge, anonymous cities.

EXERCISE 6

Revise the following paragraph to eliminate the use of the first- and second-person pronouns.

[1]In my opinion, some animals should be as free as we are. [2]For example, I think orangutans, African elephants, and Atlantic bottlenose dolphins should roam freely rather than be held in captivity. [3]We should neither exhibit them in zoos nor use them for medical research. [4]If you study animals such as these you will see that, like us, they show emotions, self-awareness, and intention. [5]You might even find that some use language to communicate. [6]It is clear to me that they have the right to freedom.

6   Modifiers

Modifiers are words, phrases, or clauses that modify; that is, they qualify or limit the meaning of other words. When used effectively, modifiers enliven writing with details and enhance its coherence.

6a   Recognizing modifiers

You can distinguish an adjective from an adverb by determining what type of word is modified. **Adjectives** modify nouns and pronouns; **adverbs** modify verbs, adjectives, and other adverbs.

Adjectives	Adverbs
She looked **curious.** [modifies pronoun]	She looked at me **curiously.** [modifies verb]
productive meeting [modifies noun]	**highly** productive meeting [modifies adjective]
a **quick** lunch [modifies noun]	**very** quickly [modifies adverb]

In addition, consider the form of the modifier. Many adjectives end with one of these suffixes: *-able, -al, -ful, -ic, -ish, -less,* or *-y.*

accept**able** rent**al** event**ful** angel**ic** sheep**ish** effort**less** sleep**y**

Present participles (verb + -*ing*) and past participles (verb + -*ed*) can also be used as adjectives.

a **determining** factor   a **determined** effort

Be sure to include the -*ed* ending of a past participle.

Please see the ~~enclose~~ documents for more details.

enclosed

MULTILINGUAL WRITERS
USING PARTICIPLES AS ADJECTIVES

Present and past participles used as adjectives cannot be used interchangeably. To indicate an emotion, use a present participle. In the phrase *the exciting tennis match,* the tennis match is the cause of the excitement. Use the past participle to signal the experience of an emotion. In the phrase *the excited crowd,* the crowd is experiencing the excitement.

The easiest type of adverb to identify is the adverb of manner. It is formed by adding -*ly* to an adjective.

careful**ly**   unpleasant**ly**   silent**ly**

Although you may not hear the -*ly* ending when you speak, be sure to include it when you write.

They bought only ~~local~~ grown vegetables.

locally

However, not all words ending in -*ly* are adverbs. Certain adjectives related to nouns also end in -*ly* (*friend, friendly; hour, hourly*). In addition, not all adverbs end in -*ly*. Adverbs that indicate time or place (*today, tomorrow, here,* and *there*) do not have the -*ly* ending. Neither does the negator *not*.

A few words—for example, *fast* and *well*—can function as either adjectives or adverbs.

They like **fast** cars. [adjective]

They ran **fast** enough to catch the bus. [adverb]

(1) Modifiers of linking verbs and action verbs

An adjective used after a sensory linking verb (*look, smell, taste, sound,* or *feel*) modifies the subject of the sentence. A common error is to use an adverb after this type of verb.

I felt _{bad} ~~badly~~ about missing the rally. [The adjective *bad* modifies *I*.]

However, when *look, smell, taste, sound,* or *feel* is used as an action verb, it can be modified by an adverb.

She looked **angrily** at the referee. [The adverb *angrily* modifies *looked*.]

BUT She looked **angry.** [The adjective *angry* modifies *she*.]

Good is an adjective and so is not used with action verbs.

The whole team played _{well} ~~good~~.

EXERCISE 1

In the following sentences, use appropriate adjectives and adverbs.

1. My brother said he was real nervous.

2. He did not think he could drive good enough to pass the driver's test.

3. He looked calmly, though, as he got into the tester's car.

4. As I knew he would, my brother passed his test easy.

(2) Nouns as modifiers

Adjectives and adverbs are the most common modifiers, but nouns can also be modifiers (***movie*** *critic*, ***reference*** *manual*). A string of noun modifiers can be cumbersome. The following example shows how a sentence with too many noun modifiers can be revised.

The ~~Friday afternoon~~ Student Affairs Committee meeting has been postponed. *scheduled for Friday afternoon*

MULTILINGUAL WRITERS

NOUN MODIFIERS

In noun combinations, the first noun is the modifier. Different orders produce different meanings.

> A *company phone* is a phone that belongs to a company.

> A *phone company* is a company that sells phones or provides phone service.

---

(3) Phrases and clauses as modifiers

Participial phrases, prepositional phrases, and some infinitive phrases are modifiers.

Growing in popularity every year, mountain bikes now dominate the market. [participial phrase]

Mountain bikes first became popular **in the 1980s.** [prepositional phrase]

Some people use mountain bikes **to commute to work.** [infinitive phrase]

Adjectival and adverbial clauses are both modifiers.

BMX bicycles have frames **that are relatively small.**
[adjectival clause]

Although mountain bikes are designed for off-road use,
many people use them on city streets. [adverbial clause]

6b Comparatives and superlatives

Many adjectives and adverbs change form to show degrees of
quality, quantity, time, distance, manner, and so on. The **positive
form** of an adjective or adverb is the word you would look for
in a dictionary: *hard, deserving.* The **comparative form,** which
either ends in *-er* or is preceded by *more* or *less,* compares two
elements: *I worked **harder** than I ever had before.* The **superlative
form,** which either ends in *-est* or is preceded by *most* or *least,*
compares three or more elements: *Jeff is the **hardest** worker I have
ever met.*

Positive	Comparative	Superlative
hard	harder	hardest
deserving	more/less deserving	most/least deserving

(1) Complete and logical comparisons
When using the comparative form of an adjective or an adverb,
be sure to indicate what two elements you are comparing.

A diesel engine is **heavier** than a gas engine.

Occasionally, the second element in a comparison is implied. In the sentence below, the reader can infer that the grade on the second paper was better than the grade on the first paper.

She wrote **two** papers; the instructor gave her a **better** grade on the second.

A comparison should also be logical. The following example illogically compares *population* and *Wabasha*.

The **population** of Winona is larger than **Wabasha**.

You can revise this type of faulty comparison in three ways:

- Repeat the word that refers to what is being compared.

  The **population** of Winona is larger than the **population** of Wabasha.

- Use a pronoun that corresponds to the first element in the comparison.

  The **population** of Winona is larger than **that** of Wabasha.

- Use possessive forms.

  Winona's population is larger than **Wabasha's**.

(2) Double comparatives or superlatives

Use either an ending or a preceding qualifier, not both, to form a comparative or superlative.

The first bridge is **more narrower** than the second.

The ~~most~~ **narrowest** bridge is in the northern part of the state.

Comparative and superlative forms of modifiers that have absolute meanings, such as *a more perfect society* and *the most unique campus,* are rarely used in academic writing.

EXERCISE 2

Provide the comparative or superlative form of each modifier.

1. Amphibians can be divided into three groups. Frogs and toads are in the (common) group.

2. Because they do not have to maintain a specific body temperature, amphibians eat (frequently) than mammals do.

3. Reptiles may look like amphibians, but their skin is (dry).

4. During the Devonian period, the (close) ancestors of amphibians were fish with fins that looked like legs.

6c   **Double negatives**

The term **double negative** refers to the use of two negative words to express a single negation. Revise any double negatives you find in your writing.

He did**n't** keep any ~~no~~ records. *(any)*

OR

He ~~didn't keep~~ **no** records. *(kept)*

Using *not* or *nothing* with *hardly, barely,* or *scarcely* creates a double negative.

I could**n't** **hardly** quit in the middle of the job.

OR

I could**n't** ~~hardly~~ quit in the middle of the job.

MULTILINGUAL WRITERS

NEGATION IN OTHER LANGUAGES

The use of two negative words in one sentence is common in languages such as Spanish:

*Yo **no** compré **nada**.* ["I didn't buy anything."]

If your native language allows this type of negation, be sure to revise any double negatives you find in your English essays.

6d   Placement of modifiers

Effective placement of modifiers will improve the clarity and coherence of your sentences. A **misplaced modifier** obscures the meaning of a sentence.

(1) Keeping related words together

Place the modifiers *almost, even, hardly, just,* and *only* before the words or word groups they modify. Altering placement can alter meaning.

The committee can **only** nominate two members for the position. [The committee cannot *appoint* the two members to the position.]

The committee can nominate **only** two members for the position. [The committee cannot nominate more than two members.]

Only the committee can nominate two members for the position. [No person or group other than the committee can nominate members.]

(2) Placing modifiers near the words they modify

Readers expect phrases and clauses to modify the nearest grammatical element. The revision of the following sentence clarifies that the prosecutor, not the witness, was skillful.

> *With great skill, the*
> ~~The~~ prosecutor cross-examined the witness ~~with great skill~~.

The following revision makes it clear that the phrase *crouched and ugly* describes the phantom, not the boy.

> *The*   *crouched and ugly*
> ~~Crouched and ugly, the~~ young boy gasped at the phantom moving across the stage.

(3) Revising squinting modifiers

A **squinting modifier** can be interpreted as modifying either what precedes it or what follows it. To avoid such lack of clarity, you can reposition the modifier, add punctuation, or revise the entire sentence.

> Even though Erikson lists some advantages **overall** his vision of a successful business is faulty.

Revisions

> Even though Erikson lists some **overall** advantages, his vision of a successful business is faulty. [modifier repositioned; punctuation added]

> Erikson lists some advantages**; however, overall,** his vision of a successful business is faulty. [sentence revised]

MULTILINGUAL WRITERS

ADVERBS OF FREQUENCY

Adverbs of frequency (such as *always, never, sometimes,* and *often*) appear before one-word verbs.

He **rarely** goes to horror movies.

However, these adverbs appear after a form of *be* when it is the main verb.

Novels written by Stephen King are **always** popular.

When a sentence contains more than one verb in a verb phrase, the adverb of frequency is placed after the first auxiliary verb.

My friends have **never** read *The Shining.*

EXERCISE 3

Improve the clarity of the following sentences by moving the modifiers.

1. Alfred Hitchcock was only identified with thrillers after making his third movie, *The Lodger.*

2. Hitchcock's most famous movies revolved around psychological improbabilities that are still discussed by movie critics today.

3. Although his movies are known for suspense sometimes moviegoers also remember Hitchcock's droll sense of humor.

4. Hitchcock just did not direct movie thrillers; he also produced two television series.

5. Originally a British citizen, Queen Elizabeth knighted Alfred Hitchcock in 1980.

6e   Dangling modifiers

Dangling modifiers are phrases or elliptical clauses (clauses without a subject) that lack an appropriate word to modify. To avoid including dangling modifiers in your essays, first look carefully at any sentence that begins with a phrase or an elliptical clause. If the phrase or clause suggests an action, be sure that what follows the modifier (the subject of the sentence) names the actor. If there is no actor performing the action indicated in the phrase, the modifier is dangling. To revise this type of dangling modifier, name an actor—either in the modifier or in the main clause.

Lying on the beach, time became irrelevant. [Time cannot lie on a beach.]

Revisions

While **we** were lying on the beach, time became irrelevant. [actor in the modifier]

Lying on the beach, **we** found that time became irrelevant. [actor in the main clause]

While eating lunch, the phone rang. [A phone cannot eat lunch.]

Revisions

While **we** were eating lunch, the phone rang. [actor in the modifier]

While eating lunch, **we** heard the phone ring. [actor in the main clause]

Although you will most frequently find a dangling modifier at the beginning of a sentence, you may sometimes find one at the end of a sentence.

Adequate lighting is important ~~when~~ studying. *for anyone*

[Lighting cannot study.]

EXERCISE 4

Revise any misplaced or dangling modifiers.

1. Climbing a mountain, fitness becomes all-important.

2. In determining an appropriate challenge, considering safety precautions is necessary.

3. Even when expecting sunny weather, rain gear should be packed.

4. Although adding extra weight, climbers should not leave home without a first-aid kit.

5. By taking pains at the beginning of a trip, agony can be averted at the end of a trip.

S

EFFECTIVE SENTENCES

7   Sentence Unity

Effective academic and professional writing is composed of sentences that are consistent, clear, and complete.

7a   Choosing and arranging details

Well-chosen details add interest and credibility to your writing. As you revise, you may occasionally notice a sentence that would be clearer and more believable with the addition of a phrase or two about time, location, or cause.

Missing important detail	An astrophysicist from the Harvard-Smithsonian Center has predicted a galactic storm.
With detail added	An astrophysicist from the Harvard-Smithsonian Center has predicted **that** a galactic storm **will occur within the next 10 million years.**

Without the additional information about time, most readers would wonder when the storm was supposed to occur. The added detail not only makes the sentence clearer but also helps readers accept the information.

When considering how much detail to include, be sure that every detail contributes to the central thought, as in the following excerpt.

A given mental task may involve a complicated web of circuits, which interact in varying degrees with others throughout the brain—not like the parts in a machine, but like the instruments in a symphony orchestra combining their tenor, volume, and resonance to create a particular musical effect.

—JAMES SHREEVE, *Beyond the Brain*

7b   Revising mixed metaphors

When you use language that evokes images, make sure that the images are meaningfully related. Unrelated images that appear in the same sentence are called **mixed metaphors.** The following sentence includes incompatible images.

As he climbed the corporate ladder, he ~~sank into a sea of~~ debt.
(incurred a large)

The combination of two images—climbing a ladder and sinking into a sea—could create a picture in the reader's mind of a man hanging onto a ladder as it disappears into the water. The easiest way to revise such a sentence is to replace the words evoking one of the conflicting images.

7c   Revising mixed constructions

A sentence that begins with one kind of grammatical structure and shifts to another is a **mixed construction.** To untangle a mixed construction, make sure that the sentence includes a conventional subject—a noun, a noun phrase, a gerund phrase, an infinitive phrase, or a noun clause. Prepositional phrases and adverbial clauses are not typical subjects.

Practicing
~~By practicing~~ a new language daily will help you become proficient. [A gerund phrase replaces a prepositional phrase.]

Her scholarship award

~~Although she won a scholarship~~ does not give her the right
to skip classes. [A noun phrase replaces an adverbial clause.]

If you find a sentence that has a mixed construction, you can
either revise the subject or leave the beginning of the sentence
as a modifier and add a new subject after it.

> By practicing a new language daily, **you** will become more
> proficient.

> Although she won a scholarship, **she** does not have the right
> to skip classes.

7d   Relating sentence parts

When drafting, writers sometimes compose sentences in which
the subject is said to be something or to do something that is
not logically possible. This breakdown in meaning is called
faulty predication. Similarly, mismatches between a verb and
its complement can obscure meaning.

(1) Mismatch between subject and verb
The joining of a subject and a verb must create a meaningful
idea.

Mismatch	The absence of detail screams out at the reader. [An *absence* cannot scream.]
Revision	The reader immediately notices the absence of detail.

(2) Illogical equation with *be*
When a form of the verb *be* joins two parts of a sentence (the
subject and the subject complement), these two parts should be
logically related.

Free speech

~~The importance of free speech~~ is essential to a democracy.
[*Importance* cannot be essential.]

(3) Mismatches in definitions

When you write a sentence that states a formal definition, the term being defined should be followed by a noun or a noun phrase, not an adverbial clause. Avoid using *is when* or *is where*.

Ecology is ~~when you~~ study the relationships among living organisms and between living organisms and their environment.
[*the* ... *of* inserted]

Exploitative competition is ~~where~~ two or more organisms vie for a limited resource such as food.
[*the contest between* ... *vying* inserted]

(4) Mismatch of *reason* with *is because*

You can see why *reason* and *is because* are a mismatch by looking at the meaning of *because*: "for the reason that." Saying "the reason is for the reason that" is redundant. Thus, revise any sentence containing the construction *the reason is . . . because*.

The ~~reason the~~ old train station was closed ~~is~~ because it had fallen into disrepair.

(5) Mismatch between verb and complement

A verb and its complement should fit together meaningfully.

Mismatch	Only a few students used the incorrect use of *there*. [To "use an incorrect use" is not logical.]
Revision	Only a few students used *there* incorrectly.

To make sure that a relative pronoun in the object position is connected logically to a verb, replace the pronoun with its antecedent. In the following sentence, *the inspiration* is the antecedent for *that*.

Mismatch	The inspiration that the author created touched young writers. [To "create the inspiration" is not logical.]
Revision	The author inspired young writers.

Verbs used to report the words of others are followed by specific types of complements. A few common verbs and their typical complements are listed below.

VERBS FOR ATTRIBUTION AND THEIR COMPLEMENTS

Verb + *that* noun clause

agree	claim	report	suggest
argue	demonstrate	state	think

Example: The researcher **reported** that the weather patterns had changed.

Verb + noun phrase + *that* noun clause

convince	remind	tell

Example: He **told** the reporters that he was planning to resign.

Verb + *wh-* noun clause

demonstrate	discuss	report	suggest
describe	explain	state	wonder

Example: She **described** what had happened.

EXERCISE 1

Revise the following sentences so that each verb is followed by a conventional complement.

1. The committee chair discussed that funding requests had specific requirements.

2. He convinced that mass transit was affordable.

3. The two groups agreed how the problem could be solved.

4. Brown and Edwards described that improvements had been made to the old building.

5. They wondered that such a catastrophe could happen.

7e Including necessary words

When we speak or write quickly, we often omit small words. As you revise, be sure to include all necessary articles, prepositions, verbs, and conjunctions.

The ceremony took place in ^an^ auditorium.

We discussed a couple ^of^ issues at the meeting.

When a sentence has a **compound verb** (two verbs linked by a conjunction), you may need to supply a different preposition for each verb to make your meaning clear.

He neither **believes** ^in^ nor **approves of** exercise.

All verbs, both auxiliary and main, should be included to make sentences complete.

She ^*has* seen the movie three times.

Voter turnout has never ^*been* and will never be 100 percent.

When a sentence consists of two short clauses and the verb in both clauses is the same, the verb in the second clause can be omitted.

The wind **was** fierce and the thunder [was] deafening.

Include the word *that* before a clause when it makes the sentence easier to read. Without the added *that* in the following sentence, a reader may stumble over *discovered the fossil* before understanding that *the fossil* is linked to *provided*.

The paleontologists discovered ^*that* the fossil provided a link between the dinosaur and the modern bird.

That should always be retained when a sentence has two parallel clauses.

The graph indicated **that the population had increased** but **that the number of homeowners had not.**

7f   Completing comparisons

A comparison has two parts: someone or something is compared to someone or something else. As you revise your writing, make sure that your audience knows who or what is being compared. To revise incomplete comparisons, add necessary words, phrases, or clauses.

His first novel was better ^*than the one just published*.

After you are sure that your comparisons are complete, check to see that they are also logical.

Her test scores are higher than ~those of~ the other students.

In the original sentence, *scores* were being compared to *students*. You could also rewrite that sentence as follows:

Her test scores are higher than the other students'.

Because *test scores* have already been mentioned, it is clear that *students'* (with an apostrophe) is short for *students' test scores*.

7g Completing intensifiers

In speech, the intensifiers *so, such,* and *too* are used to mean "very," "unusually," or "extremely."

That movie was **so** funny.

In academic and professional writing, however, the intensifiers *so, such,* and *too* require a completing phrase or clause.

That movie was **so** funny **that I watched it twice.**

Julian has **such** a hearty laugh **that it makes everyone else laugh with him.**

The problem is just **too** complex **to solve in one day.**

EXERCISE 2

Revise the following sentences to make them clear and complete.

1. Ralph McQuarrie sketched designs for R2D2 and Darth Vader, including his mask. Ian McCaig wanted to create something scarier for *The Phantom Menace*.

2. He drew generic male face with metal teeth and long red ribbons of hair falling in front of it.

3. He designed a face that looked as though it been flayed.

4. The evil visage of Darth Maul was so horrible. To balance the effect, McCaig added elegant black feathers.

8 Subordination and Coordination

Understanding subordination and coordination can help you indicate connections between ideas as well as add variety to your sentences.

8a Using subordination effectively

Subordinate means "being of lower rank." A subordinate grammatical structure cannot stand alone; it is dependent on the main (independent) clause. The most common subordinate structure is the dependent clause, which usually begins with a subordinating conjunction or a relative pronoun.

(1) Subordinating conjunctions

A **subordinating conjunction** specifies the relationship between a dependent clause and an independent clause. For example, it might signal a causal relationship.

The painters finished early **because they work well together.**

Here are a few of the most frequently used subordinating conjunctions:

Cause	*because*
Concession	*although, even though*
Condition	*if, unless*
Effect	*so that*
Sequence	*before, after*
Time	*when*

By using subordinating conjunctions, you can combine short sentences and indicate how they are related.

_{After the}
⌃The crew leader picked us up early on Friday. _{, we} ⌃We̶ ate breakfast together at a local diner.

(2) Relative pronouns

A **relative pronoun** (*who, whom, which, that,* or *whose*) introduces a dependent clause that modifies the pronoun's antecedent.

The temple has a <u>portico</u> **that faces west.**

By using an **adjectival (relative) clause**—that is, a dependent clause introduced by a relative pronoun—you can embed details into a sentence without sacrificing conciseness.

_{, which has sold well in the United States}
Japanese automakers have produced a hybrid car⌃.

CAUTION

A relative clause beginning with *which* sometimes refers to an entire independent clause rather than modifying a specific word or phrase. Because this type of reference can be vague, you should avoid it if possible.

_{As}   _{he should have}
⌃He̶ ̶is̶ a graduate of a top university, ⌃which should provide him with many opportunities.

8b   Using coordination effectively

Coordinate means "being of equal rank." Coordinate grammatical elements have the same form. For example, they may be two words that are both adjectives, two phrases that are both prepositional, or two clauses that are both independent.

a **stunning** and **satisfying** conclusion [adjectives]

in the attic or **in the basement** [prepositional phrases]

The company was losing money, yet **the employees suspected nothing.** [independent clauses]

To indicate the relationship between coordinate words, phrases, or clauses, choose an appropriate coordinating conjunction.

Addition	*and*
Alternative	*or, not*
Cause	*for*
Contrast	*but, yet*
Result	*so*

By using coordination, you can avoid unnecessary repetition.

The hike to the top of Angels Landing has countless switchbacks. ~~It also has~~ ^{and} long drop-offs.

MULTILINGUAL WRITERS

CHOOSING CONJUNCTIONS

In English, use either a coordinating conjunction or a subordinating conjunction (but not both) to signal a connection between clauses.

Because he had a headache, ~~so~~ he went to the health center.

~~Because~~ ^{He} had a headache, **so** he went to the health center.

EXERCISE 1

Using subordination and coordination, revise the sentences in the following paragraph so that they emphasize the ideas you think are important.

[1]The Lummi tribe lives in the Northwest. [2]The Lummis have a belief about sorrow and loss. [3]They believe that grief is a burden. [4]According to their culture, this burden should not be carried alone. [5]After the terrorist attack on the World Trade Center, the Lummis wanted to help shoulder the burden of grief felt by others. [6]Some of the Lummis carve totem poles. [7]These carvers crafted a healing totem pole. [8]They gave this pole to the citizens of New York. [9]Many of the citizens of New York had family members who were killed in the terrorist attacks. [10]The Lummis do not believe that the pole itself heals. [11]Rather, they believe that healing comes from the prayers and songs said over it. [12]For them, healing is not the responsibility of a single person. [13]They believe that it is the responsibility of the community.

8c	**Avoiding faulty or excessive subordination and coordination**

(1) Choosing precise conjunctions

Effective subordination requires choosing subordinating conjunctions carefully. In the following sentence, the use of *as* is distracting because it can mean either "because" or "while."

> *Because*
> ^~~As~~ time was running out, I randomly filled in the remaining
> circles on the exam sheet.

Your choice of coordinating conjunction should also convey your meaning precisely. For example, to indicate a cause-and-effect relationship, *so* is more precise than *and*.

> *so*
> The rain continued to fall, ^~~and~~ the concert was canceled.

(2) Excessive subordination and coordination

As you revise your writing, make sure that you have not over-used subordination or coordination. In the following ineffective sentence, two dependent clauses compete for the reader's focus. The revision is clearer because it eliminates one of the dependent clauses.

Ineffective

Although researchers used to believe that ancient Egyptians were the first to domesticate cats, they now think that cats may have provided company for humans 5,000 years earlier **because** the intact skeleton of a cat has been discovered in a Neolithic village on Cyprus.

Revised

Although researchers used to believe that ancient Egyptians were the first to domesticate cats, they now think that cats may have provided company for humans 5,000 years earlier. They base their revised estimate on the discovery of an intact cat skeleton in a Neolithic village on Cyprus.

Overuse of coordination results in a rambling sentence in need of revision.

Ineffective

The lake was surrounded by forest, and it was large and clean, so it looked refreshing.

Revised

Surrounded by forest, the large, clean lake looked refreshing.

EXERCISE 2

Revise the following sentences to eliminate faulty or excessive coordination and subordination.

1. Duct tape was invented for the U.S. military during World War II to keep the moisture out of ammunition cases because it was strong and waterproof.

2. Duct tape was originally called "duck tape" as it was waterproof and ducks are like that too and because it was made of cotton duck, which is a durable, tightly woven material.

3. When the war was over, house builders used duck tape to connect duct work together, and the builders started to refer to duck tape as "duct tape" and eventually the color of the tape changed from the green that was used during the war to silver, which matched the ducts.

9 Parallelism

Parallelism is the use of grammatically equivalent structures to clarify meaning and to emphasize ideas.

9a Recognizing parallel elements

Two or more elements are considered parallel when they have similar grammatical forms—for example, when they are all nouns or all prepositional phrases. Parallel elements are frequently joined by a coordinating conjunction (*and, but, or, yet, so, nor,* or *for*). In the examples that follow, the elements in boldface have the same grammatical form.

Words

The dean is both **determined** and **dedicated.**

Phrases

Her goals include **publicizing student and faculty research, increasing the funding for that research,** and **providing adequate research facilities.**

Clauses

He said **that we would conduct a similar project** but **that we would likely get different results.**

Sentences

When I interviewed for the job, I tried not to sweat.
When I got the job, I managed not to shout.

9b Repeating words and grammatical forms

(1) The repetition of words
By repeating a preposition, the infinitive marker *to,* or the introductory word of a clause, you can create parallel structures that will help you convey your meaning clearly, succinctly, and emphatically.

Preposition

My embarrassment stemmed not **from** the money lost but **from** the notoriety gained.

Infinitive marker *to*

She wanted her audience **to remember** the protest song and **to understand** its origin.

Introductory word of a clause

The team vowed **that** they would support each other, **that** they would play their best, and **that** they would win the tournament.

(2) The repetition of form
Sometimes parallel structures are similar in form even though no words are repeated. The following example includes the *-ing* form (present participle) of three different verbs.

People all around me are **buying, remodeling,** or **selling** their houses.

As you edit a draft, look for sentences that include two or three structures joined by *and, but,* or *or.* Make sure the structures are parallel.

Whether **mortgage rates rise** or ~~the~~ **building codes ~~are changed~~,** the real estate market should remain strong this spring.

Each part of the dependent clause in the revised sentence includes a two-word subject and a one-word predicate.

9c Linking two or more sentences

Repeating a pattern emphasizes the relationship of ideas. The following two sentences come from the conclusion of "Letter from Birmingham Jail."

> **If I have said anything** in this letter <u>that overstates the truth and indicates an unreasonable impatience,</u> **I beg you to forgive me.** **If I have said anything** <u>that understates the truth and indicates my having a patience</u> that allows me to settle for anything less than brotherhood, **I beg God to forgive me.**
>
> —MARTIN LUTHER KING, JR.

Almost every structure in the second sentence is parallel to a structure in the first. To create this parallelism, King repeats words and uses similar grammatical forms.

THINKING RHETORICALLY

PARALLELISM

Parallel elements make your writing easy to read. But consider breaking from the parallel pattern on occasion to emphasize a point. For example, to describe a friend, you could start with two adjectives and then switch to a noun phrase.

> My friend Alison is **kind, modest,** and **the smartest mathematician in the state.**

9d   Using correlative conjunctions

Correlative conjunctions (or **correlatives**) are pairs of words that link other words, phrases, or clauses.

both . . . and

either . . . or

neither . . . nor

not only . . . but also

whether . . . or

Notice how the words or phrases following each conjunction in the pair are parallel.

He will major in **either** <u>biology</u> **or** <u>chemistry</u>.

Whether <u>at home</u> **or** <u>at school</u>, he is always busy.

Be especially careful when using *not only . . . but also*.

His team practices not only

_∧~~Not only practicing~~ at 6 a.m. during the week, but ~~his team~~ also ~~scrimmages~~ on Sunday afternoons.

OR

does his team practice   it

Not only _∧~~practicing~~ at 6 a.m. during the week, but _∧~~his team~~ also scrimmages on Sunday afternoons.

EXERCISE 1

Make the structures in each sentence parallel. In some sentences, you may have to use different wording.

1. Helen was praised by the vice president, and her assistant admired her.

2. When she hired new employees for her department, she looked for applicants who were intelligent, able to stay focused, and able to speak clearly.

3. At meetings, she was always prepared, participating actively yet politely, and generated innovative responses to department concerns.

4. In her annual report, she wrote that her most important achievements were attracting new clients and revenues were higher.

5. When asked about her leadership style, she said that she preferred collaborating with others rather than to work alone in her office.

10 Emphasis

In any piece of writing, some of your ideas will be more important than others. You can direct the reader's attention to these ideas by emphasizing them.

10a Placing words for emphasis

Words at the beginning or the end of a sentence receive emphasis. Notice how the revision of the following sentence adds emphasis to the beginning to balance the emphasis at the end.

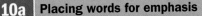

~~In today's society, most good~~ jobs require a college education.

(Good ... today)

You can also emphasize an important idea by placing it after a colon or a dash.

> At a later time [rocks and clay] may again become what they once were: dust.   —**LESLIE MARMON SILKO,** "Interior and Exterior Landscapes"

> By 1857, miners had extracted 760 tons of gold from these hills—and left behind more than ten times as much mercury, as well as devastated forests, slopes and streams.
> —**REBECCA SOLNIT,** *Storming the Gates of Paradise: Landscapes for Politics*

10b Using cumulative and periodic sentences

In a **cumulative sentence,** the main idea (the independent clause) comes first; less important ideas or supplementary details follow.

The day was hot for June, a pale sun burning in a cloudless sky, wilting the last of the irises, the rhododendron blossoms drooping.　—ADAM HASLETT, "Devotion"

In a **periodic sentence,** however, the main idea comes last, just before the period.

In a day when movies seem more and more predictable, when novels tend to be plotless, baggy monsters or minimalist exercises in interior emotion, **it's no surprise that sports has come to occupy an increasingly prominent place in the communal imagination.**　—MICHIKO KAKUTANI, "Making Art of Sport"

Both of these types of sentences can be effective. Because cumulative sentences are more common, however, the infrequently encountered periodic sentence tends to provide emphasis.

10c　Ordering ideas from least to most important

By arranging your ideas in **climactic order**—from least important to most important—you build up suspense. In the following example, the writer emphasizes a doctor's desire to help the disadvantaged and then implies that this desire has been realized through work with young Haitian doctors.

While he was in medical school, the soon-to-be doctor discovered his calling: to diagnose infectious diseases, to find ways of curing people with these diseases, and **to bring the lifesaving knowledge of modern medicine to the disadvantaged.** Most recently, he has been working with a small group of young doctors in Haiti.

10d　Repeating important words

Although effective writers avoid unnecessary repetition, they also understand that deliberate repetition emphasizes key words or ideas.

We **forget** all too soon the things we thought we could never **forget**. We **forget** the loves and betrayals alike, **forget** what we whispered and what we screamed, **forget** who we are.

—JOAN DIDION, "On Keeping a Notebook"

10e | Inverting word order

Most sentences begin with a subject and end with a predicate. When you move words out of their normal order, you draw attention to them.

At the back of the crowded room sat **a newspaper reporter.** [COMPARE: **A newspaper reporter** sat **at the back of the crowded room.**]

Notice the inverted word order in the second sentence of the following passage.

[1]The Library Committee met with the City Council on several occasions to persuade them to fund the building of a library annex. [2]So successful were their efforts that a new wing will be added by next year. [3]This wing will contain archival materials that were previously stored in the basement.

The modifier *so successful* appears at the beginning of the sentence, rather than in its normal position, after the verb: Their efforts were *so successful* that . . . . The inverted word order emphasizes the committee's accomplishment.

MULTILINGUAL WRITERS

INVERTING WORD ORDER

English sentences are inverted in various ways. Sometimes the main verb in the form of a participle is placed at the beginning of the sentence. The subject and the auxiliary verb(s) are then inverted.

part   *aux*   *s*

Carved into the bench **were someone's initials.**
[COMPARE: Someone's initials were carved into the bench.]

An adjective may also begin a sentence. In this type of sentence, the subject and the linking verb are inverted.

adj   *link v*   *s*

Crucial to our success **was the dedication of our employees.**
[COMPARE: The dedication of our employees was crucial to our success.]

10f   Using an occasional short sentence

In a paragraph of mostly long sentences, try using a short sentence for emphasis. To optimize the effect, lead up to the short sentence with an especially long sentence.

After organizing the kitchen, buying the groceries, slicing the vegetables, mowing the lawn, weeding the garden, hanging the decorations, and setting up the grill, I was ready to have a good time when my guests arrived. **Then the phone rang.**

EXERCISE 1

Add emphasis to each of the following sentences by using the strategy indicated. You may have to add some words and/or delete others.

1. (climactic order) In the 1960 Olympics, Wilma Rudolph tied the world record in the 100-meter race, she tied the record in the 400-meter relay, she won the hearts of fans from around the world, and she broke the record in the 200-meter race.

2. (periodic sentence) Some sports reporters described Rudolph as a gazelle because of her beautiful stride.

3. (inversion) Rudolph's Olympic achievement is impressive, but her victory over a crippling disease is even more spectacular.

4. (final short sentence) Rudolph was born prematurely, weighing only four and one-half pounds. As a child, she suffered from double pneumonia, scarlet fever, and then polio.

5. (cumulative sentence) She received help from her family. Her brothers and sister massaged her legs. Her mother drove her to a hospital for therapy.

11 Variety

To make your writing lively and distinctive, include a variety of sentence types and lengths.

11a Revising sentence length and form

To avoid the choppiness of a series of short sentences, combine some of the sentences into longer sentences. You can combine sentences by using coordinating conjunctions (such as *and, but,* and *or*), subordinating conjunctions (such as *because, although,* and *when*), or relative pronouns (such as *who, that,* and *which*).

Short	Minneapolis is one of the Twin Cities. St. Paul is the other. They differ in many ways.
Combined	Minneapolis **and** St. Paul are called the Twin Cities, **but** they differ in many ways. [coordinating conjunctions]
Short	Legislation on space tourism has not been passed. Plans for a commercial rocket service are going forward anyway.
Combined	**Although** legislation on space tourism has not been passed, plans for a commercial rocket service are going forward anyway. [subordinating conjunction]

| Short | Today, lawmakers discussed some new legislation. This legislation would promote the safety of rocket passengers. |
| Combined | Today, lawmakers discussed some new legislation **that** would promote the safety of rocket passengers. [relative pronoun] |

THINKING RHETORICALLY

SHORT SENTENCES

Occasionally, a series of brief sentences produces an intended effect. The short sentences in the following passage capture the quick actions taking place as an accident is about to occur.

"There's a truck in your lane!" my friend yelled. I swerved toward the shoulder. "Watch out!" she screamed. I hit the brakes. The wheels locked. The back of the car swerved to the right.

EXERCISE 1

Convert each set of short sentences into a single longer sentence.

1. It was the bottom of the ninth inning. The score was tied. The bases were loaded. There were two outs.

2. A young player stepped up to the plate. This was his first season. He had hit a home run yesterday. He had struck out his last time at bat.

3. He knew the next pitch could decide the game. He took a practice swing. The pitcher looked him over.

4. The pitch came in high. The batter swung low. He missed this first pitch. He also missed the second pitch.

5. He had two strikes against him. The young player hit the next ball. It soared over the right-field fence.

11b Varying sentence openings

Most writers begin more than half of their sentences with a subject. Although this pattern is common, relying on it too heavily can make writing sound dull. Experiment with the following alternatives for beginning your sentences.

(1) Beginning with an adverb

Immediately, the dentist stopped drilling and asked me how I was doing. [adverb]

(2) Beginning with a phrase

Reflecting on the election, we understood clearly how the incumbent defeated the challenger. [participial phrase]

A town of historic interest, Santa Fe also has many art galleries. [appositive phrase]

(3) Beginning with a transitional word or phrase

In each of the following examples, the transitional word or phrase shows the relationship between the ideas in the pair of sentences.

Many restaurants close within a few years of opening. **But** others, which offer good food at reasonable prices, become well established.

Independently owned restaurants struggle to get started for a number of reasons. **First of all,** they have to compete against successful restaurant chains.

(4) Beginning with a word that usually comes after the verb

I was an abysmal football player. **Soccer,** though, I could play well. [direct object]

Vital to any success I had were my mother's early lessons. [predicate adjective]

EXERCISE 2

Rewrite each sentence so that it does not begin with a subject.

1. John Spilsbury was an engraver and mapmaker from London who made the first jigsaw puzzle in about 1760.

2. He pasted a map onto a piece of wood and used a fine-bladed saw to cut around the borders of the countries.

3. The jigsaw puzzle was first an educational toy and has been a mainstay in households all over the world ever since its invention.

4. The original puzzles were quite expensive because the wooden pieces were cut by hand.

5. Most puzzles are made of cardboard today.

11c | Using questions, exclamations, and commands

You can vary the sentences in a paragraph by introducing an occasional question, exclamation, or command.

(1) Raising a question or two for variety

> If people could realize that immigrant children are better off, and less scarred, by holding on to their first languages as they learn a second one, then perhaps Americans could accept a more drastic change. What if every English-speaking toddler were to start learning a foreign language at an early age, maybe in kindergarten? What if these children were to learn Spanish, for instance, the language already spoken by millions of American citizens, but also by so many neighbors to the South?
>
> —ARIEL DORFMAN, "If Only We All Spoke Two Languages"

You can either answer the question or let readers answer it for themselves, in which case it is called a **rhetorical question.**

(2) Adding an exclamatory sentence for variety

But at other moments, the classroom is so lifeless or painful or confused—and I so powerless to do anything about it—that my claim to be a teacher seems a transparent sham. Then the enemy is everywhere: in those students from some alien planet, in the subject I thought I knew, and in the personal pathology that keeps me earning my living this way. What a fool I was to imagine that I had mastered this occult art—harder to divine than tea leaves and impossible for mortals to do even passably well!

—**PARKER PALMER**, *The Courage to Teach*

(3) Including a command for variety

Now I stare and stare at people shamelessly. Stare. It's the way to educate your eye. —**WALKER EVANS**, *Unclassified*

In this case, a one-word command, "Stare," provides variety.

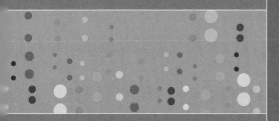

L

EFFECTIVE LANGUAGE

12 Good Usage

Using the right words at the right time can make the difference between having your ideas taken seriously and seeing them brushed aside. Keeping your audience and purpose in mind will help you use the right word at the right time.

12a Clear style

Although different styles are appropriate for different situations, you should strive to make your writing easy to read. To achieve a clear style, choose words that your audience understands and that are appropriate for the occasion.

Ornate	The majority believes that achievement derives primarily from the diligent pursuit of allocated tasks.
Clear	Most people believe that success results from hard work.

If you want readers to take your writing seriously, you must show them respect by not using obscure words when common words will do and by not using more words than necessary.

EXERCISE 1

Revise the following sentences for an audience that prefers a clear, straightforward style.

1. Expert delineation of character in a job interview is a goal that is not always possible to achieve.

2. In an employment situation, social pleasantries may contribute to the successful functioning of job tasks, but such interactions

should not distract attention from the need to complete all
assignments in a timely manner.

3. Commitment to an ongoing and carefully programmed schedule
of physical self-management can be a significant resource for
stress reduction in the workplace.

12b Appropriate word choice

Unless you are writing for a specialized audience and have
good reason to believe that this audience will welcome slang,
colloquial expressions, or jargon, the following advice can help
you determine which words to use and which to avoid. A good
dictionary will also help you. Words labeled *dialect, slang, colloquial, nonstandard,* or *unconventional* are generally inappropriate for college and professional writing. If a word has no
label, you can safely assume that it can be used in writing for
school or work.

(1) Slang
The term **slang** covers a wide range of words or expressions
that are considered casual or fashionable by people in a particular age group, locality, or profession. Although such words
are often used in private conversation or in writing intended to
mimic conversation, they are usually out of place in academic
or professional writing.

(2) Conversational (or colloquial) words
Words labeled *colloquial* in a dictionary are fine for casual conversation and for written dialogues or personal essays on a light
topic. Such words are sometimes used for special effect in academic writing, but you should usually replace them with more
appropriate words. For example, conversational words such as
dumb and *kid around* could be replaced by *illogical* and *tease*.

(3) Regionalisms

Regionalisms—such as *tank* for "pond" and *sweeper* for "vacuum cleaner"—can make writing lively and distinctive, but they are often considered too informal for academic and professional writing.

(4) Technical words or jargon

When writing for a diverse audience, an effective writer will not refer to the need for bifocals as *presbyopia*. However, technical language is appropriate when the audience can understand it (as when one physician writes to another) or when the audience would benefit by learning the terms in question.

12c Inclusive language

By choosing words that are inclusive rather than exclusive, you invite readers into your writing. Prejudiced or derogatory language has no place in academic or professional writing; using it undermines your authority and credibility.

(1) Nonsexist language

Effective writers show equal respect for men and women. For example, they avoid using *man* to refer to people in general because they understand that the word excludes women.

Achievements [OR Human achievements]
~~**Man's** achievements~~ in science are impressive.

Use the following tips to ensure that your writing is respectful.

TIPS FOR AVOIDING SEXIST LANGUAGE

When reviewing drafts, revise the following types of sexist language.

- **Generic *he*:** A doctor should listen to *his* patients.

  A doctor should listen to **his or her** patients. [use of the appropriate form of *he or she*]

  Doctors should listen to **their** patients. [use of plural forms]

  By listening to patients, **doctors obtain important diagnostic information.** [elimination of *his* by revising the sentence]

- **Terms such as *man* and *mankind* or those with *-ess* or *-man* endings:** Labor laws benefit the common *man*. *Mankind* benefits from philanthropy. The *stewardess* brought me some orange juice.

  Labor laws benefit **working people.** [replacement of the stereotypical term with a gender-neutral term]

  Everyone benefits from philanthropy. [use of an indefinite pronoun]

  The **flight attendant** brought me some orange juice. [use of a gender-neutral term]

- **Stereotypical gender roles:** I was told that the university offers free tuition to faculty *wives*. The minister pronounced them *man* and *wife*.

  I was told that the university offers free tuition to faculty **spouses.** [replacement of the stereotypical term with a gender-neutral term]

  The minister pronounced them **husband** and wife. [use of a term equivalent to *wife*]

- **Inconsistent use of titles:** *Mr. Holmes* and his *wife,* Mary, took a long trip to China.

  Mr. and Mrs. [or Ms.] Holmes took a long trip to China. [consistent use of titles]

  OR **Peter and Mary Holmes** took a long trip to China. [removal of titles]

  OR **Peter Holmes** and **Mary Wolfe** took a long trip to China. [use of full names]

(Continued on page 124)

(Continued from page 123)

■ **Unstated gender assumption:** Have your *mother make your costume* for the school pageant.

Have your **parents provide you with a costume** for the school pageant. [replacement of the stereotypical words with gender-neutral ones]

EXERCISE 2

Revise the following sentences to eliminate sexist language.

1. The ladies met to discuss the company's operating budget.

2. Mothers should read to their small children.

3. Some fans admired the actress because of her movies; others praised her for her environmental activism.

4. For six years, he worked as a mailman in a small town.

(2) Nonracist language

Rarely is it necessary to identify anyone's race or ethnicity in academic or professional writing. However, you may need to use appropriate racial or ethnic terms if you are writing a demographic report, an argument against existing racial inequities, or a historical account of a particular event involving ethnic groups. Determining which terms a particular group prefers can be difficult because preferences sometimes vary within a group and change over time. One conventional way to refer to Americans of a specific descent is to include an adjective before the word *American: African American, Asian American, European American, Latin American, Mexican American, Native American.* These words are widely used; however, members of a particular group may identify themselves in more than one way. In addition to *African American* and *European American, Black* (or *black*) and *White* (or *white*) have long been used. People of Spanish-speaking descent may prefer *Chicano/Chicana,*

Hispanic, Latino/Latina, Puerto Rican, or other terms. Members of cultures that are indigenous to North America may prefer a specific name such as *Cherokee* or *Haida,* though some also accept *American Indian* or *Native People.*

(3) Writing about any difference respectfully
If a writing assignment requires you to distinguish people based on age, ability, geographical area, religion, or sexual orientation, show respect to the groups or individuals you discuss by using the terms they prefer.

(a) Referring to age
Although some people object to the term *senior citizen,* a better alternative has not emerged. When used respectfully, the term refers to a person who has reached the age of retirement (but may not have decided to retire) and is eligible for certain privileges granted by society. However, if you know your audience would object to this term, find out which alternative is preferred.

(b) Referring to disability or illness
A current recommendation for referring to disabilities and illnesses is "to put the person first." In this way, the focus is placed on the individual rather than on the limitation. Thus, *persons with disabilities* is preferred over *disabled persons.* You can find out whether such person-first expressions are preferred by noting whether they are used in the articles and books (or by the people) you consult.

(c) Referring to geographical areas
Certain geographical terms need to be used with special care. Though most frequently used to refer to people from the United States, the term *American* may also refer to people from Canada, Mexico, and Central or South America. If your audience may be confused by this term, use *people from the United States* or *U.S. citizens* instead.

The term *Arab* refers to people who speak Arabic. If you cannot use specific terms such as *Iraqi* or *Saudi Arabian,* be sure you know that a country's people speak Arabic and not another language. Iranians, for example, are not Arabs because they speak Farsi.

British, rather than *English,* is the preferred term for referring to people from the island of Great Britain or from the United Kingdom.

(d) Referring to religion

Reference to a person's religion should be made only if it is relevant. If you must mention religious affiliation, use only those terms considered respectful. Because religions have both conservative and liberal followers, be careful not to make generalizations about political stances.

(e) Referring to sexual orientation

If your purpose for writing makes it necessary to identify sexual orientations, choose terms used by the people you are discussing.

13 Precise Word Choice

By choosing the right word and putting it in the right place, you can communicate exactly what you mean and make your writing memorable to your intended audience.

13a Accurate and precise word choice

(1) Denotations and connotations

Denotations are definitions of words, such as those that appear in dictionaries. For example, the noun *beach* denotes a sandy or pebbly shore. Select words whose denotations convey your point exactly.

Yosemite National Park ~~is really great.~~ astounds even an indifferent tourist like me.

[Because *great* can mean "extremely large" as well as "outstanding" or "powerful," its use in this sentence is imprecise.]

Connotations are the associations evoked by a word. The context in which a word appears affects the associations it evokes. In a treatise on shoreline management, *beach* has scientific and geographic connotations; in a fashion magazine, this word is associated with bathing suits, sunglasses, and sunscreen. The challenge for writers is to choose the words that are most likely to spark the appropriate connotations in their readers' minds.

Mr. Kreuger's ~~relentlessness~~ persistence has earned praise from his supervisors.

[*Relentlessness* has negative connotations, which make it an unlikely quality for which to be praised.]

(2) Providing readers with helpful details

A **general word** is all-inclusive, indefinite, and sweeping in scope. A **specific word** is precise, definite, and limited in scope.

General	Specific	More Specific/Concrete
food	fast food	cheeseburger
place	city	Atlanta

An **abstract word** refers to a concept or idea, a quality or trait, or anything else that cannot be touched, heard, or seen. A **concrete word** signifies a particular object, a specific action, or anything that can be touched, heard, or seen.

Abstract	democracy, evil, strength, charity
Concrete	mosquito, hammer, plastic, fog

As you select words to fit your context, be as specific and concrete as you can. Ask yourself one or more of these questions about what you want to say: Exactly who? Exactly what? Exactly when? Exactly where? Exactly how? In the following example, notice what a difference concrete words can make in expressing an idea and how adding details can expand or develop it.

Vague	She has kept no reminders of performing in her youth.
Specific	She has kept no sequined costume, no photographs, no fliers or posters from that part of her youth. —LOUISE ERDRICH, "The Leap"

(3) Figurative language

Figurative language is the use of words in an imaginative rather than a literal sense. Similes and metaphors are the chief **figures of speech.** A **simile** is a comparison of dissimilar things that includes *like* or *as*. A **metaphor** is an implied comparison of dissimilar things, without *like* or *as*.

Simile

He was **like a piece of rare and delicate china which was always being saved from breaking and finally fell.**

—ALICE WALKER, "To Hell with Dying"

Metaphor

His **money was a sharp pair of scissors** that snipped rapidly through tangles of red tape. —HISAYE YAMAMOTO, *The Brown House*

Single words can be used metaphorically.

These roses must be **planted** in good soil. [literal]

Keep your life **planted** wherever you can put down the most roots. [metaphorical]

13b Clichés and euphemisms

When forced or overused, certain expressions lose their impact. For example, the expressions *bite the dust, breath of fresh air,* and *smooth as silk* were once striking and thus effective. Excessive use, though, has drained them of their original force and made them **clichés.** Newer expressions such as *put a spin on something* and *think outside the box* have also lost their vitality because of overuse. Nonetheless, clichés are so much a part of the language that nearly every writer uses them from time to time. But effective writers often give a fresh twist to an old saying.

I seek a narrative, a fiction, to order days like the one I spent several years ago, on a gray June day in Chicago, when I took a roller-coaster ride on the bell curve of my experience.

—GAYLE PEMBERTON, "The Zen of Bigger Thomas"

[Notice how much more effective this expression is than a reference to "being on an emotional roller coaster."]

Sometimes writers coin new expressions to substitute for words that have coarse or unpleasant connotations. These expressions, called **euphemisms,** occasionally become standardized. To avoid the word *dying,* for example, a writer might say that someone was *terminally ill.* However, although euphemisms sound more pleasant than the words they replace, they sometimes obscure facts. Euphemisms such as *revenue enhancement* for *tax hike* and *pre-owned* for *used* are considered insincere or deceitful.

EXERCISE 1

Replace the following overused expressions with carefully chosen words. Then use the replacements in sentences.

1. an axe to grind

2. hit the nail on the head

3. eat like a pig

4. business as usual

13c   Idioms and collocations

Idioms are fixed expressions whose meanings cannot be entirely determined by knowing the meanings of their parts—*bear in mind, fall in love, in a nutshell, stand a chance.* **Collocations** are combinations of words that frequently occur together. Unlike idioms, they have meanings that *can* be determined by knowing the meanings of their parts—*depend on, fond of, little while, right now.* Regardless of whether you are using an idiom or a collocation, if you make even a small inadvertent change to the expected wording, you may distract or confuse your readers.

She tried to keep a ~~small~~ low profile.

They had ~~an invested~~ a vested interest in the project.

As you edit your writing, keep an eye out for idioms or collocations that might not be worded correctly. Then check a general dictionary or the Glossary of Usage at the end of this book to ensure that your usage is appropriate. Writers sometimes have trouble with the following collocations, all of which contain prepositions.

CHOOSING THE RIGHT PREPOSITION

Instead of	Use
according **with**	according **to** the source
accused **for**	accused **of** the crime
based **off of**	based **on** the novel
in accordance **to**	in accordance **with** policy
independent **to**	independent **of** his family
happened **on**	happened **by** accident
superior **than**	superior **to** others

13d Clear definitions

When words have more than one meaning, establish which meaning you have in mind in a particular piece of writing. A definition can set the terms of the discussion.

In this paper, I use the word *communism* **in the Marxist sense of social organization based on the holding of all property in common.**

A **formal definition** first states the term to be defined, then puts it into a class, and finally differentiates it from other members of that class.

A *phosphene* [term] is **a luminous visual image** [class] that **results from applying pressure to the eyeball** [differentiation].

A short dictionary definition may adequately convey the meaning of a word unfamiliar to readers.

Here, *galvanic* means **"produced as if by electric shock."**

A synonym can easily clarify the meaning of a term.

Machismo, **confidence with an attitude,** can be a pose rather than a reality.

Examples also help readers understand the meaning of a word.

Many homophones **(such as *be* and *bee, in* and *inn,* or *see* and *sea*)** are not spelling problems.

14   Conciseness

To facilitate readers' understanding, effective writers convey their thoughts clearly and efficiently, choosing each word wisely.

14a   Eliminating wordiness and other redundancies

After writing a first draft, review your sentences to make sure that they contain only the words necessary to make your point.

(1) Redundancy

Restating a key point in different words can help readers understand it. But if you rephrase readily understood terms, your work will suffer from **redundancy**—repetition for no good reason.

Ballerinas auditioned ~~in the tryouts~~ for *The Nutcracker*.

MULTILINGUAL WRITERS

USING RELATIVE PRONOUNS

Review your sentences to make sure that no clause includes both a personal pronoun (*I, me, he, him, she, her, it,* etc.) and a relative pronoun (*who, that, which*) referring to the same antecedent.

The drug **that** we were testing ~~it~~ has not been approved by the Food and Drug Administration.

(2) Unnecessary words and wordy phrases

As you edit a draft, delete words that add no meaning to adjacent words and shorten wordy expressions.

> If
>
> ~~In the event that~~ taxes are raised, ~~expect complaints on the part of the voters.~~ voters will complain.

In addition, watch for vague words such as *area, aspect, factor, feature, kind, situation, thing,* and *type.* They may signal wordiness.

> Effective
>
> ~~In an employment situation, effective~~ communication is essential at work.

REPLACEMENTS FOR WORDY EXPRESSIONS

Instead of	Use
at this moment (point) in time	now, today
due to the fact that	because
for the purpose of	for
it is clear (obvious) that	clearly (obviously)
without a doubt	undoubtedly
in the final analysis	finally

USELESS WORDS IN COMMON PHRASES

yellow [in color]	connect [up together]
at 9:45 a.m. [in the morning]	[really and truly] fearless
[basic] essentials	circular [in shape]

(3) *There are* and *it is*

There or *it* may function as an **expletive**—a word that signals that the subject of the sentence will follow the verb, usually a form of *be*. Writers use expletives to emphasize words that would not be emphasized in the typical subject-verb order.

Three children were playing in the yard. [typical order]

There were three children playing in the yard. [use of expletive]

However, if you find that you have drafted several sentences that begin with expletives, revise a few of them.

Hundreds were
~~There were hundreds~~ of fans crowding onto the field.

Joining the crowd
It was frightening ~~to join the crowd~~.

(4) Relative pronouns

If a relative pronoun (*who, which, that*) is followed by a form of the verb *be* (*am, is, are, was,* or *were*), you can often omit the relative pronoun and sometimes the verb as well.

The change ~~that~~ the young senator proposed yesterday angered most legislators.

Bromo, ~~which is~~ Java's highest mountain, towers above its neighbors.

14b Using elliptical constructions

An **elliptical construction** is one that deliberately omits words that can be understood from the context.

Speed is the goal for some swimmers, endurance ~~is the goal~~ for others, and relaxation ~~is the goal~~ for still others.

Sometimes, as an aid to clarity, commas mark omissions in elliptical constructions.

> My family functioned like a baseball team: my mom was the coach; my brother, the pitcher; and my sister, the shortstop. [Use semicolons to separate items with internal commas.]

EXERCISE 1

Rewrite the sentences below to make them less wordy.

1. He put in an application for every job offered.
2. Prior to the time of the ceremony, he had not received an award.
3. The library is located in the vicinity of the post office.
4. The fans who were watching television made a lot of noise.
5. There was nobody home.
6. It is important to register early.

P

PUNCTUATION

15 The Comma

Pauses are often signaled by commas; however, they are not the most reliable guide for comma placement, because commas are often called for where speakers do not pause and pauses can occur where no comma is necessary. A better guide is an understanding of some basic principles of comma usage.

15a Before a coordinating conjunction linking independent clauses

Use a comma before a coordinating conjunction (*and, but, for, nor, or, so,* or *yet*) that links two independent clauses. An **independent clause** is a group of words that can stand as a sentence. It consists of a subject and predicate.

INDEPENDENT CLAUSE, **CONJUNCTION** INDEPENDENT CLAUSE.		
	and	
	but	
	for	
Subject + predicate,	**nor**	subject + predicate.
	or	
	so	
	yet	

The Iditarod Trail Sled Dog Race begins in March, **but** training starts much sooner.

When the independent clauses are short, the comma is often omitted before *and, but,* or *or.*

My friend races **but** I don't.

If a coordinating conjunction joins two parts of a compound predicate (which means there is only one subject), a comma is not normally used before the conjunction.

The race starts in Anchorage and ends in Nome.

EXERCISE 1

Insert commas where needed.

1. Dinosaurs lived for 165 million years and then became extinct.

2. No one knows why dinosaurs became extinct but several theories have been proposed.

3. According to some theorists a huge meteor hit the earth so the climate may have changed dramatically.

4. Another theory suggests that dinosaurs did not actually become extinct but simply evolved into lizards and birds.

5. Another theory suggests that dinosaurs just grew too big but not all of the dinosaurs were huge.

15b **After an introductory word or word group**

If the subject of the main part of your sentence (the independent clause) is preceded by a word or a group of words, place a comma after the word or word group.

Apparently, she believed the rest of the world was like her own small town. [word]

Despite a downturn in the national economy, the number of students enrolled in this university has increased. [phrase]

Although the safest automobile on the road is expensive, the protection it offers justifies the cost. [clause]

If you begin a sentence with a short introductory word group, you may omit the comma as long as the resulting sentence is not difficult to read.

In 2009 the enrollment at the university increased.
BUT
In 2009, 625 new students enrolled in courses. [A comma separates two numbers.]

Use a comma to set off interjections, **vocatives** (words used to address someone directly), or transitional words.

Oh, I forgot about the board meeting. [interjection]
Bob, I want you to know that your design impressed everyone on the board. [vocative]
Moreover, the design will increase efficiency in the office. [transitional word]

EXERCISE 2

Insert commas wherever necessary in the following paragraph. Explain why each comma is needed. Some sentences may not require editing.

[1]If you had to describe sound would you call it a wave? [2]Although sound cannot be seen people have described it this way for a long time. [3]Envisioning waves in the air the Greek philosopher Aristotle hypothesized that sound would not be able to pass through a vacuum because there would be no air to transmit it. [4]Aristotle's hypothesis was not tested until nearly two thousand years later. [5]In 1654 Otto von Guericke found that he could not hear a bell ringing inside the vacuum he had created.

15c **Separating elements in a series**

A comma appears after each item in a series except the last one.

Ethics are based on **moral, social,** or **cultural values.**

The company's code of ethics encourages **seeking criticism of work, correcting mistakes,** and **acknowledging the contributions of everyone.**

Several circumstances can lead to unethical behavior: **people are tempted by a desire to succeed, they are pressured by others into acting inappropriately,** or **they are simply trying to survive.**

THINKING RHETORICALLY

COMMAS AND CONJUNCTIONS IN A SERIES

How do the following sentences differ?

We discussed them all: life, liberty, **and** the pursuit of happiness.
We discussed them all: life **and** liberty **and** the pursuit of happiness.
We discussed them all: life, liberty, the pursuit of happiness.

The first sentence follows conventional guidelines; that is, a comma and a conjunction precede the last element in the series. Having two conjunctions and no commas, the second sentence slows down the pace of the reading, causing stress to be placed on each of the three elements in the series. In contrast, the third sentence, with commas but no conjunctions, speeds up the reading, as if to suggest that the rights listed do not need to be stressed because they are so familiar.

Two or more adjectives that precede the same noun are called **coordinate adjectives.** To test whether adjectives are coordinate, either interchange them or put *and* between them. If the altered version of the phrase is acceptable, the adjectives are coordinate and should be separated by a comma.

Crossing the **rushing, shallow** creek, I slipped off a rock and fell into the water.

[COMPARE: a rushing and shallow creek OR a shallow, rushing creek]

If the adjectives cannot be interchanged or joined by *and*, they should not be separated by a comma.

Sitting in the water, I saw an **old wooden** bridge.

[NOT a wooden old bridge OR an old and wooden bridge]

15d   With nonessential elements

Nonessential (nonrestrictive) elements provide supplemental information, that is, information a reader does not need in order to identify who or what is being discussed. Use commas to set off nonessential words or word groups.

The Hilltop Folk Festival, **planned for late July,** should attract many tourists.

In the preceding sentence, the phrase placed between commas, *planned for late July,* conveys nonessential information: the reader knows which festival will attract tourists without being told when it will be held. When a phrase follows a specific name, such as *The Hilltop Folk Festival,* it is usually nonessential. In the following sentence, the phrase *planned for late July* is necessary for the reader to be able to identify the festival as the one scheduled for late July, not for a different time.

The festival **planned for late July** should attract many tourists.

(1) Nonessential elements used as modifiers

Nonessential modifiers are often **adjectival (relative) clauses**—those clauses usually introduced by the relative pronoun *who, which,* or *that.* In the following sentence, a comma sets off the adjectival clause because the reader does not need the content of that clause in order to identify the mountain.

> We climbed Mt. McKinley, **which is over 15,000 feet high.**

Nonessential modifiers also include **participial phrases** (phrases introduced by a present or past participle).

> Mt. McKinley, **towering above us,** brought to mind our abandoned plan for climbing it. [participial phrase beginning with a present participle]
>
> My sister, **slowed by a knee injury,** rarely hikes anymore. [participial phrase beginning with a past participle]

An **adverbial clause** begins with a subordinating conjunction signaling cause (*because*), purpose (*so that*), or time (*when, after, before*). This type of clause is usually considered essential and thus is not set off by commas when it appears at the end of a sentence.

> Dinosaurs may have become extinct **because their habitat was destroyed.**

In contrast, an adverbial clause that provides nonessential information, such as an extra comment, should be set off from the main clause.

> Dinosaurs are extinct, **though they are alive in many people's imaginations.**

(2) Nonessential appositives

Appositives refer to the same person, place, object, idea, or event as a nearby noun or noun phrase but with different words. Nonessential appositives provide extra details about nouns or noun phrases and are set off by commas. In the following sentence, the title of the article is mentioned, so the reader does not need the information provided by the appositive in order to identify the article. The appositive is thus set off by commas.

"Living on the Line**,**" **Joanne Hart's most recent article,** describes the lives of factory workers in China.

In the next sentence, *Joanne Hart's article* is nonspecific, so an essential appositive containing the specific title of the article is integrated into the sentence. It is not set off by commas. Without the appositive, the reader would not know which of Hart's articles describes the lives of factory workers in China.

Joanne Hart's article "Living on the Line" describes the lives of factory workers in China.

(3) Absolute phrases

An **absolute phrase** (the combination of a noun and a modifying word or phrase) provides nonessential details and so should always be set off by a comma or commas.

The actor**,** **his hair wet and slicked back,** began his audition.

(4) Transitional expressions and other parenthetical elements

Commas customarily set off transitional words and phrases such as *for example, that is,* and *namely.*

An airline ticket**,** **for example,** can be delivered electronically.

Because they generally indicate little or no pause in reading, transitional words and phrases such as *also, too, at least,* and *thus* need not be set off by commas.

Traveling has **thus** become easier in recent years.

Use commas to set off other parenthetical elements, such as words or phrases that provide commentary you wish to stress.

Over the past year, my flights have**,** **miraculously,** been on time.

(5) Contrasted elements

Commas set off sentence elements in which words such as *never* and *unlike* express contrast.

A planet, **unlike** a star, reflects rather than generates light.

In sentences in which contrasted elements are introduced by *not only . . . but also,* place a comma before *but* if you want to emphasize what follows it. Otherwise, leave the comma out.

Planets **not only** vary in size, **but also** travel at different speeds. [Comma added for emphasis.]

EXERCISE 3

Set off nonessential clauses, phrases, and appositives with commas.

1. Maine Coons long-haired cats with bushy tails have adapted to a harsh climate.

2. These animals which are extremely gentle despite their large size often weigh twenty pounds.

3. Maine Coons unlike most cats will play fetch with their owners.

15e | **With geographical names and items in dates and addresses**

Use commas to make geographical names, dates, and addresses easy to read.

(1) City and state

Nashville, Tennessee, is the largest country-and-western music center in the United States.

(2) Day and date

Martha left for Peru on **Wednesday, February 12, 2009,** and returned on March 12.

(3) Addresses

In a sentence containing an address, the name of the person or organization, the street address, and the name of the town or city are all followed by commas, but the abbreviation for the state is not.

> I had to write to **Ms. Melanie Hobson, Senior Analyst, Hobson Computing, 2873 Central Avenue, Orange Park, FL 32065.**

15f   With direct quotations

Many sentences containing direct quotations also contain attributive tags such as *The author claims* or *According to the author*.

(1) Attributive tag at the beginning of a sentence

Place the comma directly after the attributive tag, before the quotation marks.

> According to Jacques Barzun, "It is a false analogy with science that makes one think latest is best."

(2) Attributive tag in the middle of a sentence

Place the first comma inside the quotation marks that precede the attibutive tag; place the second comma directly after the tag, before the next set of quotation marks.

> "It is a false analogy with science," claims Jacques Barzun, "that makes one think latest is best."

(3) Attributive tag at the end of a sentence

Place the comma inside the quotation marks before the attributive tag.

> "It is a false analogy with science that makes one think latest is best," claims Jacques Barzun.

15g Unnecessary or misplaced commas

(1) No comma between a subject and its verb or a verb and its object

Although speakers often pause before or after a verb, such a pause should not be indicated by a comma.

In this climate, rain at frequent intervals produces mosquitoes.

The forecaster said that rain was likely.

(2) No comma following a coordinating conjunction

Avoid using a comma after a coordinating conjunction (*and, but, for, nor, or, so,* or *yet*).

We worked very hard on her campaign for state representative, but the incumbent was too strong to defeat in the northern districts.

(3) No comma separating elements in a compound predicate

In general, avoid using a comma between two elements of a compound predicate (a predicate in which both verbs agree with the same subject).

I **read** the comments carefully and then **started** my revision.

(4) No comma setting off essential words, phrases, or clauses

In the following sentences, the elements in boldface are essential and so should not be set off by commas.

Zoe was born **in Chicago during the Great Depression.**

Everyone **who has a mortgage** is required to have fire insurance.

Someone **wearing an orange wig** greeted us at the door.

(5) No comma preceding the first item of a series or following the last

Make sure that you place commas only between elements in a series, not before or after them.

She was known for her photographs, sketches, and engravings.

The exhibit included her most exuberant, exciting, and expensive photographs.

16 The Semicolon and the Colon

Although semicolons and colons both link independent clauses, they signal different grammatical relationships.

16a The semicolon

The semicolon most frequently connects two independent clauses when the second clause supports or contrasts with the first, but it can be used for other purposes as well.

(1) Connecting independent clauses

A semicolon placed between two independent clauses indicates that they are closely related. The second of the two clauses generally supports or contrasts with the first.

> For many cooks, basil is a key ingredient; it appears in recipes worldwide. [support]
>
> Sweet basil is used in many Mediterranean dishes; Thai basil is used in Asian and East Indian recipes. [contrast]

Sometimes, a transitional expression such as *for example* or *however* accompanies a semicolon and further establishes the relationship between the ideas.

> Basil is omnipresent in the cuisine of some countries; **for example,** Italians use basil in salads, soups, and many vegetable dishes.
>
> The culinary uses of basil are well known; **however,** this herb also has medicinal uses.

A comma is usually inserted after a transitional word, though it can be omitted if doing so will not lead to a misreading.

(2) Separating elements that contain commas

In a series of phrases or clauses that contain commas, semicolons indicate where each phrase or clause ends and the next begins.

> To survive, mountain lions need a large area in which to range; a steady supply of deer, skunks, raccoons, foxes, and opossums; and the opportunity to find a mate, establish a den, and raise a litter.

Semicolons do not set off phrases or dependent clauses unless they contain commas. Use commas for these purposes.

> We consulted Alinka Kibukian; the local horticulturalist.

> Our trees survived; even though we live in a harsh climate.

EXERCISE 1

Revise the following sentences, using semicolons to separate independent clauses or elements that contain internal commas.

1. Soccer is a game played by two opposing teams on a rectangular field, each team tries to knock a ball, roughly twenty-eight inches in circumference, through the opponent's goal.

2. The game is called *soccer* only in Canada and the United States, elsewhere it is known as *football*.

3. Generally, a team consists of eleven players: defenders (or fullbacks), who defend the goal by trying to win control of the ball, midfielders (or halfbacks), who play both defense and offense, attackers (or forwards), whose primary responsibility is scoring goals; and a goalkeeper (or goalie), who guards the goal.

4. In amateur matches, players can be substituted frequently, however, in professional matches, the number of substitutions is limited.

16b The colon

A colon calls attention to what follows. It also separates numbers in parts of scriptural references and titles from subtitles.

(1) Directing attention to an explanation, a summary, or a quotation

When a colon appears between two independent clauses, it signals that the second clause will explain or expand on the first.

> No one expected the game to end as it did: after seven extra innings, the favored team collapsed.

A colon is also used after an independent clause to introduce a direct quotation.

> Marcel Proust explained the importance of mindfulness: "The true journey of discovery consists not in seeking new landscapes but in having fresh eyes."

CAUTION

The rules for using an uppercase or a lowercase letter to begin the first word of an independent clause that follows a colon vary across style manuals.

MLA The first letter should be lowercase unless (1) it begins a word that is normally capitalized, (2) the independent clause is a quotation, or (3) the clause expresses a rule or principle.

APA The first letter should be uppercase.

CMS The first letter should be lowercase unless (1) it begins a word that is normally capitalized, (2) the independent clause is a quotation, or (3) two or more related sentences follow the colon.

(2) Signaling that a list follows

Writers frequently use colons to introduce lists. Note that an independent clause precedes the list.

> Three students received internships: Asa, Vanna, and Jack.

Avoid placing a colon between a verb and its complement or after the words *including* and *such as*.

> The winners were: Asa, Vanna, and Jack.
>
> Many vegetarians do not eat dairy products such as: butter and cheese.

(3) Separating a title and a subtitle

Use a colon between a work's title and its subtitle.

> *Collapse: How Societies Choose to Fail or Succeed*

(4) Citing scriptural references

Colons are often used between numbers in scriptural references.

> Psalms 3:5   Gen. 1:1

However, MLA requires the use of periods instead of colons.

> Psalms 3.5   Gen. 1.1

(5) Specialized uses in business correspondence

A colon follows the salutation of a business letter and any notations.

> Dear Dr. Horner: Dear Maxine: Enc:

A colon introduces the headings in a memo.

> To: From: Subject: Date:

EXERCISE 2

Insert colons where they are needed in the following sentences.

1. Before we discuss marketing, let's outline the behavior of consumers consumer behavior is the process individuals go through as they select, buy, or use products or services to satisfy their needs and desires.

2. The process consists of six stages recognizing a need or desire, finding information, evaluating options, deciding to purchase, purchasing, and assessing purchases.

3. When evaluating alternatives, a house hunter might use some of the following price, location, size, age, style, and landscaping design.

17 The Apostrophe

Apostrophes serve a number of purposes. For example, you can use them to show that someone owns something *(my neighbor's television),* that someone has a specific relationship with someone else *(my neighbor's children),* or that someone has produced or created something *(my neighbor's recipe).* Apostrophes are also used in contractions *(can't, don't)* and in certain plural forms *(x's and y's).*

17a   Indicating ownership and other relationships

An apostrophe, often followed by an *s*, signals the possessive case of nouns. Possessive nouns are used to express a variety of meanings.

Ownership	**Fumi's** computer, the **photographer's** camera
Origin	**Einstein's** ideas, the **student's** decision
Human relationships	**Linda's** sister, the **employee's** supervisor
Possession of physical or psychological traits	**Mona Lisa's** smile, the **team's** spirit
Association between abstractions and attributes	**democracy's** success, **tyranny's** influence

Identification of documents	**driver's** license, **bachelor's** degree
Identification of things or days named after people	**St. John's** Cathedral, **Valentine's** Day
Specification of amounts	a **day's** wages, an **hour's** delay

(1) Singular nouns, indefinite pronouns, abbreviations, and acronyms

Add an apostrophe and an *s* to indicate the possessive case of singular nouns, indefinite pronouns, abbreviations, and acronyms.

the dean's office [noun]

Yeats's poems [noun]

anyone's computer [indefinite pronoun]

the NFL's reputation [abbreviation]

OPEC's price increase [acronym]

Walter Bryan Jr.'s letter

When a singular proper noun ends in *s*, you will have to consult the style guide for the discipline in which you are writing. The *MLA Handbook for Writers of Research Papers* recommends always using *'s*, as in *Illinois's legislature* and *Dickens's novels.* CMS allows exceptions to this rule. An apostrophe without an *s* may be acceptable in the following circumstances: (1) when a name ends in a syllable pronounced "eez" *(Sophocles' poetry)*, (2) when a singular common noun ends in *s (physics' contribution)*, and (3) when the name of a place or an organization ends in *s* but refers to a single entity *(United States' foreign aid).*

Possessive pronouns *(my, mine, our, ours, your, yours, his, her, hers, its, their, theirs,* and *whose)* are not written with apostrophes.

The committee concluded **its** discussion.

CAUTION

Be careful not to confuse possessive pronouns with contractions. Whenever you write a contraction, you should be able to substitute the complete words for it without changing the meaning.

Possessive pronoun	Contraction
Its motor is small.	**It's** [It is] a small motor.
Whose turn is it?	**Who's** [Who is] representing us?

(2) Plural nouns ending in s

Add only an apostrophe to indicate the possessive case of plural nouns that end in *s*.

the boys' game   the babies' toys   the Joneses' house

Plural nouns that do not end in *s* need both an apostrophe and an *s*.

men's lives   women's health   children's projects

CAUTION

An apostrophe is not needed to make a noun plural. To make most nouns plural, add *s* or *es*. Add an apostrophe only to signal ownership, origin, and other similar relationships.

The ~~protesters'~~ protesters met in front of the conference center.

The protesters' meeting was on Wednesday.

To form the plural of a family name, use *s* or *es*, not an apostrophe.

The ~~Johnson's~~ Johnsons participated in the study.

[COMPARE: The Johnsons' participation in the study was crucial.]

(3) To show collaboration or joint ownership

An apostrophe and an *s* follow the second of two singular nouns.
Just an apostrophe follows the second of two plural nouns that
already ends in *s*.

the carpenter and the **plumber's** decision [They made the
decision collaboratively.]

the Becks and the **Lopezes'** cabin [They own one cabin jointly.]

(4) To show separate ownership or individual contributions

Each plural noun is followed by an apostrophe; each singular
noun is followed by *'s*.

the **Becks'** and the **Lopezes'** cars [Each family owns a car.]

the **carpenter's** and the **plumber's** proposals [They each
made a proposal.]

(5) Compound nouns

An apostrophe and an *s* follow the last word of a compound
noun.

my brother-in-**law's** friends, the attorney **general's** statements
[singular]

my brothers-in-**law's** friends, the attorneys **general's** statements
[plural]

To avoid awkward constructions such as the last two, consider
using a prepositional phrase beginning with *of* instead: *the
statements of the attorneys general.*

(6) Nouns preceding gerunds

Depending on its number, a noun that precedes a gerund takes
either an apostrophe and an *s* or just an apostrophe.

Lucy**'s having** to be there seemed unnecessary. [singular noun
preceding gerund]

The family appreciated the lawyers' **handling** of the matter.
[plural noun preceding gerund]

Sometimes you may find it difficult to distinguish between a gerund and a participle. A good way to tell the difference is to note whether the emphasis is on an action or on a person. In a sentence containing a gerund, the emphasis is on the action; in a sentence containing a participle, the emphasis is on the person.

Our successful completion of the project depends on **Terry's providing** the illustrations. [gerund]

I remember my **brother telling** me the same joke last year. [participle]

(7) Names of products and geographical locations
Follow an organization's preference for its name or the name of a product; follow local conventions for a geographical location.

Consumers Union	Actors' Equity	Taster's Choice
Devil's Island	Devils Tower	Devil Mountain

17b   Marking omissions of letters or numbers

Apostrophes mark omissions in contractions, numbers, and words mimicking speech.

they're [they are]   class of '09 [class of 2009]
y'all [you all]   singin' [singing]

17c   Forming certain plurals

These plurals are generally formed by adding *s* only:

1990s   fours and fives   YWCAs   two *and*s   the three Rs

Lowercase letters and abbreviations that include a combination of uppercase and lowercase letters are made plural by adding both an apostrophe and an *s*.

   x's and *y*'s   PhD's

The MLA differs from this style in recommending the use of apostrophes for the plurals of uppercase letters (*A*'s and *B*'s) as well as lowercase letters.

EXERCISE 1

Insert apostrophes where needed in the following sentences.

1. Whose responsibility is it to see whether its working?
2. Hansons book was published in the early 1920s.
3. NPRs fund drive begins this weekend.
4. Few students enrolled during the academic year 06–07.
5. There cant be more *x*s than there are *y*s in the equation.

18 Quotation Marks

Quotation marks indicate that the words between them were first written or spoken by someone else or that they are being used in an unconventional way.

18a Direct quotations

Double quotation marks set off direct quotations, including those in dialogue. Single quotation marks enclose a quotation within a quotation.

(1) Direct quotations

Double quotation marks enclose only quotations, not any expression such as *she said* or *he replied.* When a sentence ends with quoted material, place the period inside the quotation marks.

> "I believe that we learn by practice," writes Martha Graham. "Whether it means to learn to dance by practicing dancing or to learn to live by practicing living, the principles are the same."

When using direct quotations, reproduce all quoted material exactly as it appears in the original. Quotation marks are not used with indirect quotations or paraphrases (restatements of what someone else has said or written).

> Martha Graham believes that practice is necessary for learning, regardless of what we are trying to learn.

(2) Quotations within quotations

If the quotation you are using includes another direct quotation, use single quotation marks for the embedded quotation.

> According to Anita Erickson, "when the narrator says, 'I have the right to my own opinion,' he means that he has the right to his own delusion" (22).

However, if the embedded quotation appears in a block quotation, use double quotation marks. (Note that double quotation marks are not used to mark the beginning and end of a block quotation.)

> Anita Erickson claims that the narrator uses the word *opinion* deceptively.

> Later in the chapter, when the narrator says, "I have the right to my own opinion," he means that he has the right to his own delusion. Although it is tempting to believe that the narrator is making decisions based on a rational belief system, his behavior suggests that he is more interested in deception. (22)

(3) Dialogue

When creating a dialogue, enclose in quotation marks what each person says. Use a separate paragraph for each speaker, beginning a new paragraph whenever the speaker changes.

> Farmer looked up, smiling, and in a chirpy-sounding voice he said, "But that feeling has the disadvantage of being . . ." He paused a beat. "Wrong."
>
> "Well," I retorted, "it depends on how you look at it."
>
> —TRACY KIDDER, *Mountains Beyond Mountains*

When quoting more than one paragraph by a single speaker, put quotation marks at the beginning of each paragraph. However, place closing quotation marks only at the end of the last paragraph.

(4) Thoughts resembling speech
Quotation marks set off thoughts that resemble speech.

"His silence on this topic has surprised everyone," I noted to myself as I surveyed the faces of the other committee members.

Thoughts are usually marked by such phrases as *I thought, he felt,* and *she believed.*

(5) Short excerpts of poetry included within a sentence
When quoting fewer than four lines of poetry, enclose them in quotation marks; use a slash to indicate a line division.

After watching a whale swim playfully, the speaker in "Visitation" asks, "What did you think, that joy / was some slight thing?"

18b   Titles of short works

Quotation marks enclose the title of a short work, such as a story, an essay, a poem, or a song. The title of a larger work, such as a book, magazine, newspaper, or play, should be italicized.

Short stories	"The Lottery"	"The Fall of the House of Usher"
Essays	"Walden"	"Play-by-Play"
Articles	"Small World"	"Arabia's Empty Quarter"
Book chapters	"Rain"	"Cutting a Dash"
Short poems	"Orion"	"Mending Wall"
Songs	"Lazy River"	"The Star-Spangled Banner"
TV episodes	"Show Down!"	"The Last Time"

Use single quotation marks for a title within a longer title that is enclosed in double quotation marks.

"Irony in 'The Sick Rose'" [article about a poem]

CAUTION

Avoid using quotation marks around words that may not be appropriate for your audience or purpose. Instead, take the time to choose suitable words. The revised sentence in the following pair is more effective than the first.

Ineffective   He is too much of a "wimp" to be a good leader.

Revised   He is too indecisive to be a good leader.

18c With other punctuation marks

To decide whether to place some other punctuation mark inside or outside quotation marks, note whether the punctuation mark is part of the quotation or part of the surrounding context.

(1) With commas and periods

Quoted material is usually accompanied by an attributive tag such as *she said* or *he replied*. When your sentence starts with such an expression, place a comma after it to separate the tag from the quotation. Place a period inside closing quotation marks.

She replied, "There's more than one way to slice a pie."

If your sentence starts with the quotation instead, place the comma inside the closing quotation marks.

"There's more than one way to slice a pie," she replied.

When quoting material from a source, provide the relevant page number(s). If you are following MLA guidelines, note the page number(s) in parentheses after the final quotation marks. Place the period that ends the sentence after the final parenthesis, unless the quotation is a block quotation.

> According to Diane Ackerman, "Love is a demanding sport involving all the muscle groups, including the brain" (86).

CAUTION

Do not put a comma after *that* when it precedes a quotation.

> Diane Ackerman claims that⌀ "[l]ove is a demanding sport involving all the muscle groups, including the brain" (86).

---

(2) With semicolons and colons
Place semicolons and colons outside quotation marks.

> His favorite song was "Cyprus Avenue"; mine was "Astral Weeks."

> Because it is repeated, one line stands out in "The Conductor": "We are never as beautiful as now."

(3) With question marks, exclamation points, and dashes
If the direct quotation includes a question mark, an exclamation point, or a dash, place that punctuation *inside* the closing quotation marks.

> Jeremy asked, "What is truth?"

> Gordon shouted, "Congratulations!"

> Laura said, "Let me tell—" just as Dan walked into the room.

Use just one question mark inside the quotation marks when a question you write ends with a quoted question.

> Why does the protagonist ask, "Where are we headed?"

If the punctuation is not part of the quoted material, place it *outside* the closing quotation marks.

Who wrote "The Figure a Sentence Makes"?

You have to read "Awareness and Freedom"!

EXERCISE 1

Revise sentences in which quotation marks are used incorrectly and insert quotation marks where they are needed. Do not alter sentences that are written correctly. (The numbers in parentheses are page numbers, placed according to MLA guidelines.)

1. Have you read Nicholas Negroponte's essay Creating a Culture of Ideas?

2. Negroponte states, Innovation is inefficient (2).

3. However, he also believes that "without innovation we are doomed—by boredom and monotony—to decline" (2).

4. Negroponte suggests that new ideas are fostered by 'providing a good educational system, encouraging different viewpoints, and fostering collaboration' (3).

5. According to the author, "More than ever before, in the new "new economy," research and innovation will need to be housed in those places where there are parallel agendas and multiple means of support" (3).

19 The Period and Other Punctuation Marks

To indicate the end of a sentence, you can use one of three punctuation marks: the period, the question mark, or the exclamation point. Within sentences, you can use dashes, parentheses, square brackets, ellipsis points, and slashes.

Both CMS and MLA guidelines recommend using only one space after a period, a question mark, or an exclamation point, although the MLA style manual allows two spaces as long as they are used consistently. APA guidelines recommend two spaces after end punctuation marks.

19a The period

(1) A period at the end of a sentence
Use a period at the end of a sentence.

> Many adults in the United States are overfed yet undernourished.

In addition, place a period at the end of an instruction or recommendation.

> Eat plenty of fruits and vegetables.

(2) Periods after some abbreviations

> Dr. Jr. a.m. p.m. vs. etc. et al.

Only one period follows an abbreviation that ends a sentence.

> The tour begins at 1:00 p.m.

19b The question mark

Place a question mark after a direct question.

How does the new atomic clock work? Who invented this clock?

Use a period, instead of a question mark, after an indirect question—that is, a question embedded in a statement.

I asked whether the atomic clock could be used in cell phones.
[COMPARE: Can the atomic clock be used in cell phones?]

MULTILINGUAL WRITERS
INDIRECT QUESTIONS

In English, the subject and verb in indirect questions are not inverted as they would be in the related direct question.

We do not know when ~~will~~ the meeting will end.
[COMPARE: When will the meeting end?]

Place a question mark after each question in a series of related questions, even when they are not full sentences.

Will the new atomic clock be used in cell phones? Word processors? Car navigation systems?

19c The exclamation point

An exclamation point often marks the end of a sentence, but its primary purpose is rhetorical—to create emphasis.

Whoa! What a game!

Use the exclamation point sparingly so that you do not diminish its value. If you do not intend to signal strong emotion, place a comma after an interjection and a period at the end of the sentence.

Well, no one seriously expected this victory.

19d The dash

A dash (or em dash) marks a break in thought, sets off a nonessential element for emphasis or clarity, or follows an introductory list or series. To use your keyboard to create a dash, type two hyphens with no spaces between, before, or after them. Most word-processing programs can be set to convert these hyphens automatically to an em dash.

(1) Marking a break in the normal flow of a sentence
Use a dash to indicate a shift in thought or tone.

I was awed by the almost superhuman effort Stonehenge represents—but who wouldn't be?

(2) Setting off a nonessential element
Use a dash or a pair of dashes to set off extra comments or details.

Dr. Kruger's specialty is mycology—the study of fungi.

The trail we took into the Grand Canyon—steep, narrow, winding, and lacking guardrails—made me wonder whether we could call a helicopter to fly us out.

(3) Following an introductory list or series
If you decide to place a list or series at the beginning of a sentence in order to emphasize it, the main part of the sentence (after the dash) should sum up the meaning of the list or series.

Eager, determined to succeed, and scared to death—all of these describe how I felt on the first day at work.

THINKING RHETORICALLY

COMMAS, DASHES, AND COLONS

Although a comma, a dash, or a colon may be followed by an explanation, an example, or an illustration, is the rhetorical impact the same?

> He never failed to mention what was most important to him, the bottom line.
> He never failed to mention what was most important to him—the bottom line.
> He never failed to mention what was most important to him: the bottom line.

The comma, one of the most common punctuation marks, barely draws attention to what follows it. The dash, in contrast, signals a longer pause and so places more emphasis on the information that follows. The colon is more direct and formal than either of the other two punctuation marks.

19e   Parentheses

Use parentheses to set off information that is not closely related to the main point of a sentence or paragraph but that provides an interesting detail, an explanation, or an illustration.

> We might ask why affairs of state are classified as important and their discussants intelligent, while discussion of family and human interaction (what we disparagingly call "gossip") is dismissed as idle chatter.   —ROBIN LAKOFF, *Language and Woman's Place*

In addition, place parentheses around an acronym or an abbreviation when introducing it after its full form.

The Search for Extraterrestrial Intelligence (SETI) uses the Very Large Array (VLA) outside Sicorro, New Mexico, to scan the sky.

If you use numbers or letters in a list within a sentence, set them off by placing them within parentheses.

Your application should include (1) a current résumé, (2) a statement of purpose, and (3) two letters of recommendation.

THINKING RHETORICALLY

DASHES AND PARENTHESES

Dashes and parentheses are both used to set off part of a sentence, but they differ in the amount of emphasis they signal. Whereas dashes call attention to the material that is set off, parentheses usually deemphasize such material.

Her grandfather——born during the Great Depression——was appointed to the Securities and Exchange Commission.

Her grandfather (born in 1930) was appointed to the Securities and Exchange Commission.

19f   Square brackets

Square brackets set off additions or alterations used to clarify direct quotations. In the following example, the bracketed noun specifies what is meant by the pronoun *They*.

"They [hyperlinks] are what turn the Web from a library of pages into a web" (Weinberger 170).

Square brackets also indicate that a letter in a quotation has been changed from uppercase to lowercase, or vice versa.

David Weinberger claims that "[e]ven our notion of self as a
continuous body moving through a continuous map of space
and time is beginning to seem wrong on the Web" (10).

To avoid the awkwardness of using brackets in this way, you
may be able to quote only part of a sentence so that no change
in capitalization is needed.

David Weinberger claims that "our notion of self as a
continuous body moving through a continuous map of space
and time is beginning to seem wrong on the Web" (10).

Within parentheses, square brackets are used to avoid the
confusion of having two sets of parentheses.

People frequently provide personal information online. (See,
for example, David Weinberger's *Small Pieces Loosely Joined*
[Cambridge: Perseus, 2002].)

Angle brackets (< >) are used to enclose any Web address
included in an MLA works-cited list so that the period at
the end of an entry is not confused with the dot(s) in the
URL: <http://www.mla.org>.

19g Ellipsis points

Ellipsis points indicate an omission from a quoted passage or a
reflective pause or hesitation.

(1) Marking an omission from a quoted passage
The following examples illustrate how to use ellipsis points in
quotations from a passage by Patricia Gadsby.

Original
Cacao doesn't flower, as most plants do, at the tips of its outer
and uppermost branches. Instead, its sweet white buds hang from
the trunk and along a few fat branches, popping out of patches of

bark called cushions, which form where leaves drop off. They're tiny, these flowers. Yet once pollinated by midges, no-see-ums that flit in the leafy detritus below, they'll make pulp-filled pods almost the size of rugby balls.

—PATRICIA GADSBY, "Endangered Chocolate"

Whenever you omit anything from material you are quoting, replace the omitted material with ellipsis points—three equally spaced periods.

Patricia Gadsby notes that cacao flowers "once pollinated by midges . . . make pulp-filled pods almost the size of rugby balls."

Do not use ellipsis points to indicate that you have deleted words from the beginning of a quotation.

According to Patricia Gadsby, cacao flowers will become "pulp-filled pods almost the size of rugby balls."

To indicate omitted words from the end of a sentence, put a space between the last word and the set of three spaced ellipsis points. Then add the end punctuation mark (a period, a question mark, or an exclamation point). If the quoted material is followed by a parenthetical source or page reference, the end punctuation comes after the second parenthesis.

Claiming that cacao flowers differ from those of most plants, Patricia Gadsby describes how "the sweet white buds hang from the trunk and along a few fat branches . . . ."
OR ". . . branches . . ." (2).

To signal the omission of a sentence or more (even a paragraph or more), place an end punctuation mark (usually a period) before the ellipsis points.

Patricia Gadsby describes the flowering of the cacao plant: "its sweet white buds hang from the trunk and along a few fat branches, popping out of patches of bark called cushions, which form where leaves drop off. . . . Yet once pollinated by midges, no-see-ums that flit in the leafy detritus below, they'll make pulp-filled pods almost the size of rugby balls."

To signal the omission of a full line or more in quoted poetry, use spaced periods covering the length of either the line above it or the omitted line.

The yellow fog that rubs its back upon the window-panes,

. . . .

Curled once about the house, and fell asleep.
—**T. S. ELIOT, "The Love Song of J. Alfred Prufrock"**

(2) Indicating an unfinished sentence or marking a pause
Use ellipsis points to indicate that you are intentionally leaving a sentence incomplete or to signal a reflective pause.

Read aloud the passage that begins "The yellow fog . . ."

Keith saw four menacing youths coming toward him . . . and ran.

19h The slash

A slash between words, as in *and/or* and *he/she,* indicates that either word is applicable in the given context. There are no spaces before and after a slash used in this way. Because extensive use of the slash can make writing choppy, use it judiciously and sparingly. (If you are following APA or MLA guidelines, avoid using *he/she, him/her,* and so on.)

A slash is also used to mark line divisions in quoted poetry. A slash used in this way is preceded and followed by a space.

Wallace Stevens refers to the listener who, "nothing himself, beholds / Nothing that is not there and the nothing that is."

EXERCISE 1

Add appropriate dashes, parentheses, square brackets, and slashes to the following sentences.

1. Researchers in an exciting field Artificial Intelligence AI are working on devices to assist the elderly.

2. One such device is Pearl a robotic nurse that helps around the house.

3. Another application is cooking software that checks for missing and or incorrect ingredients.

4. The actual cost of such devices expensive now but more affordable later is yet to be determined.

M

MECHANICS

20 Spelling, the Spell Checker, and Hyphenation

Proofreading for spelling mistakes is essential as you near the end of the writing process. Your teachers, employers, or supervisors will expect you to submit polished work.

TIPS FOR USING A SPELL CHECKER

The spell checker is a wonderful invention, though you must use it with care.

- If a spell checker regularly flags a word that is not in its dictionary but is spelled correctly, add that word to its dictionary by clicking on the Add button. From that point on, the spell checker will accept the word you added.
- Reject any offers the spell checker makes to correct all instances of a particular error.
- Use a dictionary to evaluate the alternative spellings the spell checker provides, because some of them may be erroneous.

20a Spelling and pronunciation

Many words in English are not spelled the way they are pronounced, so pronunciation is not a reliable guide to correct spelling. Here are a few words typically misspelled because they include unpronounced letters:

condem*n*   foreign   lab*o*ratory   mus*c*le   solem*n*

Here are a few more that include letters that are often not heard in rapid speech.

can*d*idate   diff*e*rent   gover*n*ment   sep*a*rate

You can teach yourself the correct spellings of words by pronouncing them to yourself the way they are spelled, that is, by pronouncing each letter mentally so that you "hear" even silent letters.

CAUTION

The words *and, have,* and *than* are often not stressed in speech and are thus misspelled.

They would rather ᵒᶠ written two papers ₜₕₑₙ taken midterm ₐₙ final exams.
ʰᵃᵛᵉ · ᵗʰᵃⁿ · ᵃⁿᵈ

20b Words that sound alike

Words that sound alike but are spelled differently are frequently confused. Many of these words are listed with explanations in this handbook's Glossary of Usage. Also troublesome are two-word sequences that can be written as compound words or as separate words.

Everyday life was grueling.   She attended class **every day.**

They do not fight **anymore.**   They could not find **any more** evidence.

Other examples are *awhile/a while, everyone/every one, maybe/may be,* and *sometime/some time.*

Singular nouns ending in *-nce* and plural nouns ending in *-nts* are easily confused.

Assistance is available.   I have two **assistants.**

His **patience** wore thin.   Some **patients** waited for hours.

Be sure to write contractions but not possessive pronouns with an apostrophe.

Contractions   it's, you're, there's, who's

Possessives   its, your, theirs, whose

20c Prefixes and suffixes

When a prefix is added to a base word (often called the **root**), the spelling of the base word is unaffected.

necessary, **un**necessary   moral, **im**moral

However, adding a suffix to the end of a base word often changes the spelling.

(1) Dropping or retaining a final *e*

- If a suffix begins with a vowel, the final *e* of the base word is dropped: bride, brid**al;** come, com**ing.** However, to keep the /s/ sound of *ce* or the /j/ sound of *ge*, retain the final *e* before *-able* or *-ous:* notice**able,** courag**eous.**
- If a suffix begins with a consonant, the final *e* of the base word is retained: entire, entire**ly;** rude, rude**ness.** Some exceptions are *argument, ninth, truly,* and *wholly.*

(2) Doubling a final consonant

- If a consonant ends a one-syllable word with a single vowel or ends a stressed syllable with a single vowel, double the final consonant: stop, sto**pped;** omit, omi**tted.**
- If there are two vowels before the consonant, the consonant is not doubled: remain, remain**ed,** remain**ing.**
- If the final syllable is not stressed, the consonant is not doubled: edit, edit**ed,** edit**ing;** picket, picket**ed,** picket**ing.**

(3) Changing or retaining a final *y*

- Change a final *y* following a consonant to *i* when adding a suffix (except *-ing*): lazy, laz**ily;** defy, def**ied,** BUT defy**ing.**

- Retain the final *y* when it follows a vowel: gray, gray**ish**; stay, stay**s**, stay**ed**; obey, obey**s**, obey**ed**.
- Some verb forms are irregular and thus can cause difficulties. For a list of irregular verbs, see pages 35–36.

(4) Retaining a final *l*

The letter *l* at the end of a word is retained when *ly* is added.

cool, coo**lly** formal, forma**lly** real, rea**lly** usual, usua**lly**

EXERCISE 1

Add the specified suffix to the words that follow it.

Example

-ly: late, casual, psychological
    lately casually psychologically

1. *-ment*: manage, commit, require, argue

2. *-ous*: continue, joy, acrimony, libel

3. *-ed*: race, tip, permit, carry, pray

---

(5) Forming plurals

- Add *es* to most nouns ending in *s, z, ch, sh,* or *x*: box, box**es**.
- If a noun ends in a consonant and *y*, change the *y* to *i* and add *es*: company, compan**ies**; ninety, ninet**ies**.
- If a noun ends in a consonant and *o*, add *es*: hero, hero**es**. Note that sometimes just *s* is added (photo, photo**s**) and other times either *s* or *es* can be added (motto**s**, motto**es**).
- Certain nouns have irregular plural forms: woman, wom**en**; child, child**ren**; foot, f**eet**.
- Add *s* to most proper nouns: the Kennedy**s.** Add *es* to most proper nouns ending in *s, z, ch, sh,* or *x*: the Jones**es**.

Words borrowed from Latin or Greek generally form their plurals as they did in the original language.

Singular

| criterion | alumnus, alumna | analysis | datum | species |

Plural

| criteria | alumni, alumnae | analyses | data | species |

Sometimes two different forms are acceptable: the plural form of *syllabus is either syllabuses or syllabi.*

EXERCISE 2

Provide the plural forms for the following words.

1. virus   2. phenomenon   3. copy   4. delay   5. portfolio

20d   Confusion of *ei* and *ie*

An old rhyme will help you remember the order of letters in most words containing *e* and *i:*

Put *i* before *e*
Except after *c*
Or when sounded like *a*
As in *neighbor* and *weigh.*

Words with *i* before *e:* bel**ie**ve, ch**ie**f, pr**ie**st, y**ie**ld

Words with *e* before *i,* after *c:* conc**ei**t, perc**ei**ve, rec**ei**ve

Words with *ei* sounding like *a* in *cake:* **ei**ght, r**ei**n, th**ei**r, h**ei**r

Words that are exceptions to the rules in the rhyme include *either, neither, species, foreign,* and *weird.*

20e Hyphens

Hyphens link two or more words functioning as a single word and separate word parts to clarify meaning. They also have many conventional uses in numbers, fractions, and measurements.

(1) Linking two or more words

If two or more words serve as a single adjective before a noun, they should be hyphenated. If the words follow the noun, they are not hyphenated.

You submitted an **up-to-date** report.

The report was **up to date.**

When the second word in a hyphenated expression is omitted, the first word is still followed by a hyphen.

They discussed both **private-** and **public-sector** partnerships.

A hyphen is not used after adverbs ending in *ly* (*poorly planned event*).

(2) Other uses of the hyphens

A hyphen is also used after certain prefixes and in certain numbers.

Between repeated letters	anti-intellectual
To clarify meaning	re-sign (NOT resign) the petition
After *self-* or *ex-*	self-esteem, ex-wife
In numbers twenty-one through ninety-nine	one hundred thirty-two
In fractions	three-fourths, one-half

When you form a compound modifier that includes a number and a unit of measurement, place a hyphen between them: *two-year-old boy.*

EXERCISE 3

Convert the following word groups into hyphenated compounds.

Example

a movie lasting two hours   *a two-hour movie*

1. a man who is fifty years old

2. a street that runs only one way

3. history from the twenty-first century

4. a paper that is well written

21 Capitals

Capital letters draw attention to significant details—for example, the beginnings of sentences or the names of particular people, places, and products.

21a Proper names

Proper nouns are specific names. They are capitalized, even when they are used as modifiers (*Mexico, Mexican government*). Words such as *college, company, park,* and *street* are capitalized only if they are part of a name (*a university* but *Oregon State University*).

The following names and titles should be capitalized: personal names, including titles; names of deities, religions, religious followers, and sacred works; names of awards, products, and companies; names of countries, ethnic or cultural groups, and languages; names of bridges, buildings, monuments, and geographical features or regions; names of universities and specific courses; names of days of the week, months, and holidays (but not seasons); names of historical documents, periods, and events; names of political parties and government agencies; and military terms.

Capitalized	Not capitalized
Noam Chomsky, Chomskyan	a linguist, a theoretical perspective
Uncle Rory	my uncle
President Lincoln	the president

Capitalized	Not capitalized
God (a name)	a god
Bible, Koran, Talmud	sacred works
Academy Award	an award
Nike, Nike Free	a company, a running shoe
Japan, Japanese	a country, a language
Empire State Building	a building
Grand Canyon	a canyon
the West	a western state
Howard University	a university
Biology 101	a biology course
Fourth of July	a holiday
May	a month in spring
Bill of Rights	a historical document
Renaissance	the sixteenth century
Great Depression	a recession
Democratic Party	democratic process
Internal Revenue Service	a government agency
Gulf War	a war
U.S. Army	an army

21b Titles and subtitles

The first and last words in titles and subtitles are capitalized, as are major words—that is, all words other than articles (*a, an,* and *the*), coordinating conjunctions (*and, but, for, nor, or, so,* and *yet*), prepositions (such as *in, on,* and *of*), and the infinitive marker *to.*

Dictation: A Quartet

"To Be a Student or Not to Be a Student"

"Stop-and-Go Signals"

The American Psychological Association (APA) differs from the Modern Language Association (MLA) in recommending capitalizing any word in a title, including a preposition, that has four or more letters.

Southwestern Pottery from Anasazi to Zuni [MLA]

Southwestern Pottery From Anasazi to Zuni [APA]

21c Beginning a sentence

Of course a sentence begins with a capital letter, but there are certain types of sentences that deserve special note.

(1) A quoted sentence

Capitalize only the first word in a quoted sentence, even if you interrupt the sentence with commentary.

When asked to name the books she found most influential, Nadine Gordimer responded, "In general, the works that mean most to one—change one's thinking and therefore maybe one's life—are those read in youth."

"Oddly," states Ved Mehta, "like my earliest memories, the books that made the greatest impression on me were the ones I encountered as a small child."

MLA recommends that you use a bracketed lowercase letter when integrating someone else's sentence into a sentence of your own.

Nadine Gordimer believes that "[i]n general, the works that mean most to one—change one's thinking and therefore maybe one's life—are those read in youth" (102).

(2) A freestanding parenthetical sentence

Capitalize the first word of a freestanding sentence inside parentheses.

> Lance Armstrong won the Tour de France a record-breaking seven times. (**P**revious record holders include Jacques Anquetil, Bernard Hinault, Eddy Merckx, and Miguel Indurain.)

If the sentence inside the parentheses occurs within a sentence of your own, the first word should not be capitalized.

> Lance Armstrong won the Tour de France a record-breaking seven times (**p**reviously, he shared the record with four other cyclists).

(3) An independent clause following a colon

According to the *Chicago Manual of Style* (CMS), if only one independent clause (a clause with a subject and a predicate) follows a colon, the first word should be lowercased. However, if two or more independent clauses follow the colon, the first word of each clause is capitalized.

> The ear thermometer is used quite frequently now: **t**his type of thermometer records a temperature more accurately than a glass thermometer.

> Two new thermometers are replacing the old thermometers filled with mercury: **T**he digital thermometer uses a heat sensor to determine body temperature. **T**he ear thermometer is actually an infrared thermometer that detects the temperature of the eardrum.

The APA manual recommends capitalizing the first word of *any* independent clause following a colon. The MLA manual advises capitalizing the first word only when what follows is a rule or principle.

> Think of fever as a symptom, not as an illness: **I**t is the body's response to infection. [APA]

He has two basic rules for healthy living: **E**at sensibly and exercise strenuously at least three times a week. [APA and MLA]

(4) An abbreviated question
The first words of all abbreviated questions are capitalized when the intent is to draw attention to the questions.

How do we distinguish the legal codes for families? For individuals? For genetic research?

21d Computer keys, menu items, and icon names

When referring to specific computer keys, menu items, and icon names, capitalize the first letter of each.

To find the thesaurus, press Shift and the function key F7.

Instead of choosing Copy from the Edit menu, you can press Ctrl+C.

EXERCISE 1

Edit the capitalization errors in the following paragraph. Be prepared to explain any changes that you make.

[1]Diana taurasi (Her teammates call her dee) plays basketball for the Phoenix mercury. [2]She has all the skills she needs to be a Star Player: She can pass and shoot, as well as rebound, block, and steal. [3]In april of 2004, taurasi played on the u.s. national team against japan, and, in the Summer of 2004, she made her olympic debut in Athens.

22 Italics

Italics indicate that a word or a group of words is being used in a special way, for example, to indicate titles or foreign words.

22a Titles of works published or produced separately

Italics indicate the title of a work published or produced as a whole rather than as part of a larger work. A newspaper, for example, is a separate work, but an editorial in a newspaper is not; thus, the title of the newspaper is italicized, and the title of the editorial is enclosed in quotation marks.

The titles of the following kinds of separate works are italicized:

Books	*The Hours*	*Unaccustomed Earth*
Magazines	*Wired*	*National Geographic*
Newspapers	*USA Today*	*Wall Street Journal*
Plays, films, videotapes	*Death of a Salesman*	*Akeelah and the Bee*
Television and radio shows	*American Idol*	*A Prairie Home Companion*
Recordings	*Kind of Blue*	*Great Verdi Overtures*
Works of art	*American Gothic*	*David*
Long poems	*Paradise Lost*	*The Divine Comedy*
Pamphlets	*Saving Energy*	*Tips for Gardeners*
Comic strips	*Peanuts*	*Doonesbury*

According to the MLA, titles of Web sites are also italicized. When an italicized title includes the title of a separate work within it, the embedded title is not italicized.

Modern Interpretations of Paradise Lost

Neither italics nor quotation marks are necessary for titles of major historical documents or religious texts.

The Bill of Rights contains the first ten amendments to the U.S. Constitution.

The Bible, a sacred text just as the Koran or the Torah is, begins with the Book of Genesis.

According to MLA and CMS guidelines, an initial *the* in a newspaper or periodical title is not italicized.

The story was published in the *New York Times.*

22b Other uses of italics

Use italics for foreign words; genus and species names; legal cases; names of ships, submarines, aircraft, and spacecraft; words, letters, or figures referred to as such; and emphasized words.

Foreign word	*fútbol*
Genus and species	*Homo sapiens*
Legal case	*Miranda v. Arizona*
Name of ship or submarine	USS *Enterprise* USS *Hawkbill*
Name of aircraft or spacecraft	*Enola Gay* *Atlantis*
Reference to word	The word *love* is hard to define.
Reference to letter or figure	The number *2* and the letter *Z* often look similar.
Emphasized word	These *are* the right files.

22c   Words not italicized

Italics are not used for a reference to a legal case by an unofficial name.

All the major networks covered the O. J. Simpson trial.

But do italicize the shortened name of a well-known legal case.

The Supreme Court decision in *Brown* forced racial integration of schools.

Italics are also not used for the names of trains, the models of vehicles, and the trade names of aircraft.

Orient Express   Ford Mustang   Boeing 747

EXERCISE 1

Identify words that require italics in the following sentences.

1. Information about museum collections and exhibits can be found in art books, museum Web sites, and special sections of magazines and newspapers such as Smithsonian Magazine and the New York Times.

2. The title page of William Blake's Songs of Innocence is included in Masterpieces of the Metropolitan Museum of Art.

3. This book includes a photograph of a beautiful script used in the Koran; the script is known as the maghribi, or Western, style.

4. In 1998, the Songwriters Hall of Fame honored John Williams, who has written music for such movies as Jaws, Star Wars, and E.T.

5. The Smithsonian Institution's National Air and Space Museum houses an impressive collection of aircraft and spacecraft, including Spirit of St. Louis and Gemini 4.

23 Abbreviations, Acronyms, and Numbers

An **abbreviation** is a shortened version of a word or phrase: *assn.* (association), *dept.* (department), *et al.* (*et alii,* or "and others"). An **acronym** is formed by combining the initial letters and/or syllables of a series of words: *AIDS* (**a**cquired **i**mmune **d**eficiency **s**yndrome), *sonar* (**so**und **na**vigation **r**anging).

23a Abbreviations with names

Certain abbreviations are used before and/or after a person's name.

Ms. Gretel Lopez	**Mrs.** Marcus
Kim Beck, **MD**	Lee Evans, **PhD**
Dr. Redshaw	Samuel Levy **Jr.**
Mark Ngo **Sr.**	

A comma may be used to set off *Jr.* or *Sr.* However, these abbreviations are increasingly considered part of the names they follow.

Civil or military titles should not be abbreviated.

Senator Larry Johnson	Captain James
Professor Sue Li	Ambassador Aluarez

23b Addresses in correspondence

The names of states and words such as *Street, Road,* and *Company* are written out when they appear in a letter, including in the address at the top of the page. However, they are abbreviated when used in the address on an envelope.

> Derson Manufacturing Co.
> 200 Madison St.
> Watertown, MN 55388

When addressing correspondence within the United States, use the two-letter state abbreviations established by the U.S. Postal Service.

23c Acceptable abbreviations in academic and professional writing

Some abbreviations have become so familiar that they are considered acceptable substitutes for full words.

(1) Abbreviations for special purposes

Words such as *volume, chapter,* and *page* are abbreviated (*vol., ch.,* and *p.*) in bibliographies and in citations of research sources, but they are written out within sentences.

(2) Abbreviations for time periods and zones

> 82 BC [OR BCE] for before Christ [OR before the common era]
>
> AD 95 [OR 95 CE] for *anno Domini,* "in the year of our Lord" [OR the common era]

7:40 a.m. for *ante meridiem*, before noon
4:52 EST for Eastern Standard Time

(3) The abbreviation for the United States (U.S. or US) as an adjective

the U.S. Navy, the US economy
[COMPARE: They moved to the United States in 1990.]

The abbreviation *U.S.* or *US* should be used only as an adjective. When using *United States* as a noun, spell it out. MLA lists *US* as the preferred abbreviated form, but APA uses *U.S.*

(4) Some abbreviations for Latin expressions

Certain abbreviations for Latin expressions are common in academic writing.

cf. [compare]	et al. [and others]	i.e. [that is]
e.g. [for example]	etc. [and so forth]	vs. OR v. [versus]

23d   Acronyms

Introduce an acronym by placing it in parentheses after the group of words it stands for.

The Federal Emergency Management Administration (FEMA) was criticized by many after Hurricane Katrina.

MULTILINGUAL WRITERS

USING ARTICLES WITH ABBREVIATIONS, ACRONYMS, OR NUMBERS

When you use an abbreviation, an acronym, or a number, you sometimes need an indefinite article. Choose *a* or *an* based on the pronunciation of the initial sound of the abbreviation, acronym, or number: use *a* before a consonant sound and *an* before a vowel sound.

an IBM computer [*IBM* begins with a vowel sound.]

a NASA engineer [*NASA* begins with a consonant sound.]

a 1964 Mustang [*1964* begins with a consonant sound.]

23e   General uses of numbers

Depending on their uses, numbers are treated in different ways. MLA recommends spelling out numbers that are expressed in one or two words (*nine, ninety-one, nine hundred, nine million*). A numeral is used for any other number (*9½, 9.9, 999*), unless it begins a sentence.

The register recorded 164 names.

APA advises spelling out only numbers below ten. Both MLA and APA recommend using words rather than numerals at the beginning of a sentence.

One hundred sixty-four names were recorded in the register.

When numbers or amounts refer to the same entities throughout a passage, use numerals when any of the numbers would be more than two words long if spelled out.

Only 5 of the 134 delegates attended the final meeting. The remaining 129 delegates will be informed by e-mail.

23f   Special uses of numbers

Numerals can be used for the following:

Times of day	9:30 p.m.
Dates	September 11, 2001 OR 11 September 2001 OR 9/11
Decades	1999 to 2003 OR 1999–2003
Addresses	25 Arrow Drive, Apartment 1
Identification of proper nouns	Edward III Highway 61
Parts of books and plays	chapter 1, page 15 act 2, scene 1 OR Act II, Scene I
Decimals	a 2.5 average
Percents	12 percent

When monetary amounts are mentioned frequently, they can be expressed with numerals and symbols: $20.00, 99¢ or $0.99.

MULTILINGUAL WRITERS

COMMAS AND PERIODS WITH NUMERALS

In American usage, a decimal point (period) indicates a number or part of a number that is smaller than one, and a comma divides large numbers into units of three digits.

7.65 (seven and sixty-five   10,000
one-hundredths)   (ten thousand)

In some other cultures, these usages of the decimal point and the comma are reversed.

7,65 (seven and sixty-five   10.000
one-hundredths)   (ten thousand)

EXERCISE 1

Edit the following sentences to correct the usage of abbreviations and numbers.

1. A Natl. Historic Landmark, Hoover Dam is located about 30 miles s.e. of Las. Vegas, Nev.

2. The dam is named after Herbert Hoover, the 31st pres. of the U.S.

3. It is administered by the U.S. Dept. of the Interior.

4. Built by the fed. gov. between nineteen thirty-three and 1935, this dam is still considered one of the greatest achievements in the history of civ. engineering.

5. Spanning the Colorado River, Hoover Dam created Lake Mead—a reservoir covering 247 sq. miles.

W

WRITING

24 Writing and Reading Rhetorically

Rhetoric, the purposeful use of language, pervades your daily life. Whether you are reading textbooks or e-mails, writing assignments for class or text messaging your friends, composing with words or visuals, you are actively engaging the main elements of the **rhetorical situation** (see fig. 24.1).

Figure 24.1. The rhetorical situation.

24a Understanding the rhetorical situation

The rhetorical situation—the set of circumstances under which one writes or reads a text—is composed of six elements: exigence, writer, audience, message, purpose, and context. In a rhetorical situation, a **writer** (or reader) identifies an **exigence**, a reason to write (or read) something. Whether you want to solve a problem (the landlord has not provided enough parking spaces) or learn something new (how to upload photos to Snapfish), you use words to do so. You might compose a **message** (a visual and/or verbal text) in order to fulfill your purpose: persuading the landlord to open up two blocked parking spaces. Or you might read instructions from Snapfish that explain exactly how to upload pictures. First, though you might **preview** the Snapfish Web site, skimming over all the information to locate the specific content you need ("Need help uploading your photos?"). Then you will read it carefully, and even reread it until you understand how to perform the task.

In cases like these, you are writing or reading for a specific **purpose,** that of addressing and maybe even resolving the exigence. To fulfill the purpose, the message must reach an **audience** (such as the landlord or yourself) that can help address or resolve the problem. Every audience—no matter how willing or reluctant to help—reads, hears, or sees a message within a specific **context.** The landlord may be blocking those parking spaces for some reason or may have forgotten they exist. You might be trying to upload your photographs to a computer with out-of-date software, too narrow a bandwidth, or insufficient memory, or you might be unaware of the helpful instructions Snapfish provides.

In other words, every context for communication (writing or reading) includes resources (positive influences) and constraints (obstacles) that influence the rhetorical situation. Such resources and constraints include the history of what has been said about the problem, how well the writer communicates with the intended audience, how receptive the audience is, and the writer's reputation in relation to the audience.

In your role as an academic reader, you will follow the same steps as when finding and reading instructions from Snapfish. You will start by previewing or skimming the entire text. You'll examine the title of the text or the individual chapter titles to see whether the text is likely to contain the information you are searching for. Then, if possible, you will read the inside back cover or the author bio to learn about the author's reputation and credentials. What does the preface tell you about the author or text? An index or a bibliography can help you determine the breadth and depth of research that went into the text itself.

As you preview a text, you work to get a sense of what the author is trying to say. What is the author's purpose? Who is the audience? In order to determine these components of any rhetorical situation you enter, you need to stay alert for the author's major points. Often, transitional words—that is, words indicating purpose, result, summary, causation, repetition, exemplification, or intensification—alert you to important points.

24b   Addressing exigence with a specific purpose

The purposeful use of words can help resolve a particular problem or exigence. Once you have determined the exigence for writing or reading, you are in a position to gauge all the elements of the text—from choice of words to organizational pattern—in terms of overall purpose and intended audience. Knowing the reason for an author's written work will help orient you to what you might expect from reading (and rereading) the entire text. The simple question on the Snapfish site—"Need help uploading your photos?"—serves to orient your reading; the words and images themselves fulfill the purpose of instructing you, someone who needs help. In your academic reading, you may determine that an author is writing to explain a point or a process (for instance, how bridge safety is ensured or how Gettysburg National Battlefield Park became a national memorial).

Successful writers always work to clarify their purpose in terms of who makes up their intended audience and how they want to influence the thinking, understanding, or behavior of that audience. Thus, depending on the writer's overall purpose, the message may be classified as **expressive**, emphasizing the writer's feelings about and reaction to a person or an event. The Declaration of Independence is a powerful example of expressive writing. A message may also be **expository,** focusing more on objects, events, or ideas than on the writer's feelings about them. An example is a description or an analysis of typical American Fourth of July celebrations. Messages may also be classified as **argumentative**, or intended to influence the audience's attitudes or actions. Frederick Douglass's 1852 speech, "What to the Slave Is the Fourth of July?" exemplifies an argumentative text.

Whatever their purpose, writers can develop a message using one or more of the following methods, which are familiar to you from your own reading and writing: narration, description, cause-and-effect analysis, comparison and contrast, and so on. Whether writing or reading rhetorically, you need to assess the overall rhetorical purpose of the message in order to evaluate whether that message is aligned with that purpose. For instance, if you are writing in response to a specific assignment, talk with your instructor or examine the assignment sheet to review which elements of the rhetorical situation (purpose, context, and audience) have already been established for you. If you are reading rhetorically, take time to underline, highlight, or add comments or questions to the passages that suggest the writer's purpose, context, intended audience, and response to a problem. After all, reading rhetorically means reading actively. Writing rhetorically means writing with purposeful awareness.

24c   Considering audience

A clear understanding of the audience—its values, concerns, and knowledge—helps a writer tailor a message in terms of length, quality and quantity of details, word choice, and inclusion of effective examples. Of course, the audience is anyone who reads a text, but the rhetorical, or intended, audience consists of those people whom the writer considers capable of being influenced by the words or who are capable of bringing about change. If you're reading rhetorically, you may become a member of the writer's rhetorical audience.

Writers usually consider three kinds of audiences. A **specialized audience** has a demonstrated interest or expertise in the subject and can help resolve the exigence. Only someone who has an interest in downloading photos will read the information on the Snapfish Web site. A **diverse audience** consists of readers with differing levels of expertise and varying interest in the subject. When you're in a doctor's waiting room, reading whatever is available (*People, Newsweek, GQ*), you are part of a diverse audience. **Multiple audiences** are composed of a primary target audience of readers and a secondary audience who has access to and may read the text. E-mails are usually sent to a primary audience and often circulated to a secondary audience, whom the writer of the message may not have taken into consideration.

As a writer, you need to think clearly about who exactly will be reading (or who might end up reading) what you write and ask yourself whether your language choices and examples are appropriate for that audience, especially if it is an unintended audience. As a reader, you want to weigh the opinions the author holds and determine the message the author is trying to impart. In other words, how well supported are those opinions? How reliable or believable does the author seem? You also want to determine how the author is addressing you as a member of the audience. How does the author's choice of words, tone, examples, and organization connect—or not— with your values and your opinions?

24d Writing and reading a message within a context

Context includes the time and place in which a message is read or written, the writer and the audience of that message, and the medium of delivery—it is the entire set of the circumstances under which writer and reader communicate. Social, political, religious, and other cultural factors all influence the context by helping or hindering successful communication. After all, your background and beliefs often shape the attitude you take whether you are writing or reading, just as the medium (print, online, or visual) in which you are writing or reading influences how you produce or interpret the message. Writing material for a Web page, for instance, requires you to think differently about organization, design, and style than does writing a traditional academic essay or a letter to your landlord. Reading a novel in book format or an article online requires you to adjust your expectations: reading a stable print text is a markedly different experience from reading an online text, which may be enhanced by visual, video, and audio elements.

Writers who consider the context—as well as their own attitude toward the subject—are more likely to communicate the ideas to the audience effectively. Readers who consider the context in which the writer has produced a message are more likely to read actively by responding to, questioning, and agreeing or disagreeing with the text. Writing and reading rhetorically are imperative to clear communication and understanding—and to your success in college.

25 Planning and Drafting Essays

Writing is a process. Effective writers know they cannot do everything at once, so they generate, organize, develop, and clarify their ideas as well as polish their prose during a series of sometimes separate—but often overlapping—steps.

25a Stages of the writing process

Prewriting is the initial stage of the writing process. Consider what is expected of you in terms of your intended audience, context, and overall purpose. Then jump-start your thinking by talking with others working on the same assignment, keeping a journal, freewriting, or questioning.

Drafting involves writing down as much as you can without worrying about being perfect or staying on topic. The more ideas you get down on paper, the more options you will have as you begin to clarify your thesis and purpose for writing. Progress is your goal at this stage, not perfection.

Revising offers you the opportunity to focus your purpose for writing, establish a clear thesis statement, and organize your ideas toward those ends. During revision, you can start stabilizing the overall structure of your essay, the structure of the individual paragraphs, and your introduction and conclusion. Revising means producing another draft for further revision and editing.

Editing focuses on surface features: punctuation, spelling, word choice, grammar, sentence structure, and all the rest of the details of Standardized English.

25b   Focusing a topic into a clearly stated thesis

To bring your topic into focus, consider your interests, purpose, the needs of your audience, and the time and space available. Once you have focused your subject into a topic, you have come a long way toward developing the main idea you want to convey as well as your purpose for writing (to explain, teach, analyze, argue, or compare). Your subject, purpose, supporting information, and focus all come together in a controlling idea, or **thesis statement,** an explicit declaration (usually in one sentence) of the main idea.

An explicitly formulated thesis statement helps keep your writing on target, unifies your writing, and guides your readers through the content that follows.

CHECKLIST for Assessing a Topic

- Are you interested in the topic?
- Is the topic appropriate for your audience?
- Can you interest the audience in your topic?
- What is your purpose in writing about this topic?
- Can you do justice to the topic in the time and space available to you? Or should you narrow it down or expand it?
- Do you know enough about the topic to write a paper of the required length? If not, how will you get additional information?
- Are you willing to learn more about the topic?

TIPS FOR DEVELOPING A THESIS STATEMENT

- Decide which feature of the topic interests you most.
- Write down your point of view or assertion about that feature.
- Mark the passages in your rough draft that support your position.
- Draft a thesis statement, and consider whether it is too broad or too narrow to be developed sufficiently.
- After your initial drafts, ask yourself whether the scope of your thesis should be adjusted to reflect the direction your essay has taken.
- If you are still unhappy with your thesis, start again with the first tip and be even more specific.

25c Creating an outline

Many writers need a working plan to direct their ideas and keep their writing on course. Others rely on outlines.

When Richard Petraglia was assigned to assess the reasons for studying a foreign language, he drafted the following tentative outline:

TENTATIVE THESIS STATEMENT: Studying a foreign language is the best way to learn about English.

    I. Many Americans don't think they need to learn another language.

        A. English is the language of global communication.

        B. English speakers always have an advantage in intercultural communication.

   II. English-only speakers miss out on benefits of learning another language.

        A. Learning another language is not just about being able to talk to people in different countries.

B. Studying another language increases a student's knowledge of another culture and so promotes tolerance and understanding.

C. Knowing the language enriches a student's stay in a foreign country.

III. Students who take a foreign language do better on standardized tests.

A. Students can compare grammars to better remember the rules of their own language.

B. Studying a foreign language opens up a student's mind to different ways of speaking and expressing ideas.

C. Studying a foreign language helps students acquire better reading skills.

25d Drafting well-developed paragraphs

You compose a draft by developing the information that will constitute the paragraphs of your essay.

(1) Using details

The following well-developed paragraph uses details to bring an idea to life:

I stood in front of the mirror and looked at myself and laughed. My hair was one of those odd, amazing, unbelievable, stop-you-in-your-tracks creations—not unlike a zebra's stripes, an armadillo's ears, or the feet of the electric-bluefooted boobie—that the Universe makes for no reason other than to express its own limitless imagination. I realized I had never been given the opportunity to appreciate hair for its true self. That it did, in fact, have one. I remembered years of enduring hairdressers—from my mother onward—doing missionary work on my hair. They dominated, suppressed, controlled. Now, more or less free, it stood this way and that. I would call up my friends around the country to report on its antics. It never thought of lying down. Flatness, the missionary position, did not interest it. It grew. Being short, cropped off near the root, another missionary "solution," did not interest it either. It sought more and more space, more light, more of itself. It loved to be washed; but that was it.

—ALICE WALKER, "Oppressed Hair Puts a Ceiling on the Brain"

(2) Providing examples

Like details, examples contribute to paragraph development by making specific what otherwise might seem general and hard to grasp. The author of the following paragraph uses both methods:

It began with coveting our neighbor's chickens. Lily would volunteer to collect the eggs, and then she offered to move in with them. Not the neighbors, the chickens. She said if she could have some of her own, she would be the happiest girl on earth. What parent could resist this bait? Our lifestyle could accommodate a laying flock; my husband and I had kept poultry before, so we knew it was a project we could manage, and a responsibility Lily could handle largely by herself. I understood how much that meant to her when I heard her tell her grandmother, "They're going to be just *my* chickens, grandma. Not even one of them will be my sister's." To be five years old and have some other life form entirely under your control—not counting goldfish or parents—is a majestic state of affairs.   —BARBARA KINGSOLVER, "Lily's Chickens"

26 Revising and Editing Essays

Revising entails rethinking what you have already written in terms of your overall purpose: how successfully you have addressed your audience, how clearly you have stated your thesis, how effectively you have arranged your information, and how thoroughly you have developed your assertions. When you are **editing,** you are polishing your writing: you choose words more precisely, shape prose more distinctly, and structure sentences more effectively. When you are **proofreading,** you focus even more sharply to eliminate surface errors in grammar, punctuation, and mechanics.

26a Revising for unity and coherence

When revising the body of an essay, writers are likely to discover ways to make each paragraph more **unified** by relating every sentence within the paragraph to the single main idea of the topic sentence. After weeding out unrelated sentences, writers concentrate on **coherence,** ordering the sentences so that ideas progress logically and smoothly from one sentence to the next. A successful paragraph is well developed, unified, and coherent.

(1) Stating the main idea
Much like the thesis statement of an essay, a **topic sentence,** such as the one in italics in the following paragraph, states the main idea of a paragraph and comments on that main idea.

I think we are innately suspicious of . . . rapid cognition. We live in a world that assumes that the quality of a decision is directly related to the time and effort that went into making it. When doctors are faced with a difficult diagnosis, they order more tests, and when we are uncertain about what we hear, we ask for a second opinion. And what do we tell our children? Haste makes waste. Look before you leap. Stop and *think.* Don't judge a book by its cover. We believe that we are always better off gathering as much information as possible and spending as much time as possible in deliberation. We really only trust conscious decision making. But there are moments, particularly in times of stress, when haste does not make waste, when our snap judgments and first impressions can offer a much better means of making sense of the world. —**MALCOLM GLADWELL,** *Blink*

You can also end a paragraph with a topic sentence:

The first time I visited Texas, I wore a beige polyester-blend lab coat with reinforced slits for pocket access and mechanical-pencil storage. I was attending a local booksellers' convention, having just co-written a pseudo-scientific book . . . , and my publicist suggested that the doctor getup would attract attention. It did. Everyone thought I was the janitor. *Lesson No. 1: When in Texas, do not dress down.* —**PATRICIA MARX,** "**Dressin' Texan**"

(2) Unifying each paragraph

Paragraphs are **unified** when every sentence relates to the main idea. The following tips may help you improve paragraph unity.

TIPS FOR IMPROVING PARAGRAPH UNITY

Identify	Identify the topic sentence for each paragraph.
Relate	Read each sentence in a paragraph and decide if and how it relates to the topic sentence.
Eliminate	Any sentence that violates the unity of a paragraph should be cut (or saved for use elsewhere).

Clarify	Any sentence that "almost" relates to the topic sentence should be revised until it does relate. You may need to clarify details or add information or a transitional word or phrase to make the relationship clear.
Rewrite	If more than one idea is conveyed in a single paragraph, either split the paragraph in two or rewrite the topic sentence so that it establishes a relationship between both ideas.

(3) Establishing coherence

Some paragraphs are unified but not coherent. In a unified paragraph, every sentence relates to the main idea of the paragraph. In a **coherent** paragraph, the relationship among the ideas is clear, and the progression from one sentence to the next is easy for readers to follow, as in the following paragraph.

> When we moved into our new apartment, we found that the kitchen was in horrible shape. The previous tenant had left behind lots of junk that we had to get rid of, from dented canisters and broken can openers to dirty dish towels and towel rack parts. The inside of the refrigerator was covered with black mold, and it smelled as if something had been rotting in there for years. The stove was as dirty as the refrigerator. So we set to work. All the drawers and cabinets had to be washed. I put new paper down on all the shelves, and my roommate took care of lining the drawers. We had to scrub the walls with a brush and plenty of Lysol to get rid of the grease.

To achieve coherence and unity in your paragraphs, make conscious decisions about how to order the information. Use **chronological order** (particularly useful in narration) to arrange ideas according to the order in which things happened. With **spatial order** (effective in description), you orient the reader's focus from right to left, near to far, top to bottom, and so on. With **emphatic order** (useful in expository and persuasive writing), information is arranged in order of importance, usually from least to most important, which helps readers understand logical relationships. And, sometimes, information is presented in **logical order,** from specific to general or from general to specific, as in the following paragraph.

> It was not the only disappointment my mother felt in me. In the years that followed, I failed her so many times, each time asserting my own will, my right to fall short of expectations. I didn't get straight As. I didn't become class president. I didn't get into Stanford. I dropped out of college. —**AMY TAN, "Two Kinds"**

26b Editing and proofreading

If you are satisfied with the revised structure of your essay and the content of your paragraphs, you can edit individual sentences for clarity, effectiveness, and variety and then proofread the entire draft for correctness.

CHECKLIST for Editing

Sentences

- What is the unifying idea of each sentence?
- Are the sentences varied in length?
- How many of your sentences use subordination? Coordination? If you overuse any one sentence structure, revise for variation.
- Which sentences should have parallel structure?
- Do any sentences contain misplaced modifiers?
- Does each verb agree with its subject? Does every pronoun agree with its antecedent?

Diction

- Have you unintentionally repeated any words?
- Are any of your word choices vague or too general?
- Is the vocabulary you have chosen appropriate for your audience, purpose, and context?
- Have you defined any technical or unfamiliar words for your audience?

CHECKLIST for Proofreading

Spelling

- Have you double-checked the words you frequently misspell and any the spell checker may have missed (for example, misspellings that still form words, such as *form* for *from*)?

- If you used a spell checker, did it overlook homophones (such as *there/their, who's/whose,* and *it's/its*)?

- Have you double-checked the spelling of all foreign words and all proper names?

Punctuation and Capitalization

- Does each sentence have appropriate closing punctuation, and have you used only one space after each end punctuation mark?

- Is all punctuation within sentences—commas, semicolons, apostrophes, hyphens, and dashes—used appropriately and placed correctly?

- Are direct quotations carefully and correctly punctuated? Where have you placed end punctuation with a quotation? Are quotations capitalized properly?

- Are all proper names, people's titles, and titles of published works correctly capitalized?

- Are titles of works identified with quotation marks, underlining, or italics?

26c   Sample final draft

The essay that Richard Petraglia ultimately submitted to his teacher follows.

Richard Petraglia

Professor Glenn

English 15

20 October 2008

Why Take a Foreign Language?

Native English speakers have an advantage when it comes to intercultural communication: English is the language of business, diplomacy, and global communication in general. It is therefore tempting to think that English speakers don't need to learn a foreign language. But they do—and for reasons other than being able to communicate with people in foreign countries. Students who study a foreign language in school often have better writing skills, reading comprehension, and scores on standardized tests.

One good reason for American students to study a foreign language is that learning a second or even third language helps them learn more about English. For me, learning about English has been the most rewarding part of studying foreign languages continuously since middle school. Students need to look beyond the idea that all they will learn in a foreign language class is how to speak someone else's language and realize that learning another language has the fortunate effect of teaching them more about their own.

For example, there is an ongoing debate about just how useful teaching grammar is in improving student writing. Because students intuitively know how to conjugate English verbs and generally make themselves understood, it can seem pointless and frustrating for them to be taught the minutiae of the language they already speak. But, as students learn how to express themselves in a foreign language, they also indirectly learn about their own language's structure. Therefore, learning German grammar improves writing in English because it improves the student's knowledge of grammatical structures.

By gaining a better understanding of their own language through studying the language of another country, students begin to understand the subtle changes of meaning that happen with changes of grammar. As they absorb the subtleties of grammar, students write and speak with more variety and precision and use their own language more effectively.

Statistics indicate that students who pursue several years of foreign languages in high school tend to score higher on standardized tests. One might conclude that more highly motivated students will be the ones who pursue an elective like Spanish or French all four years and that language study is just a characteristic of the more motivated students who will score higher on standardized tests anyway. But their success is at least partially due to the way studying a foreign language builds awareness of their own language. Studying a foreign language improves reading comprehension because students begin to think about how ideas are expressed through language. Once a student has this awareness, he or she can more easily grasp the ideas a writer is trying to convey.

Studying a foreign language also makes students better learners because it teaches them to learn in a combination of ways. First, students practice learning intuitively, using the knowledge of their native language to make educated guesses about the way the foreign language will work. In conjunction with this intuitive method, foreign language learning develops the students' ability to follow complex rules. Another language often expresses ideas in a different way than English does, using unfamiliar grammatical rules and structures. The students are therefore forced to rely on their knowledge of complex grammatical rules to express ideas in a foreign language. Because learning a foreign language teaches students to learn by a combination of both intuitive and rule-based methods, it makes them better learners in general. A student can carry this knowledge of being able to apply complex rules as well as the ability to learn intuitively to any other discipline.

27 Using Visuals

In today's visual culture, it is hard to find a report, an essay, or an article that does not include graphics or images. Tables, charts, graphs, and pictures are the most common visual elements used in text documents.

27a Using graphics

Many academic and professional documents that are primarily composed of text also include substantial visual displays, or **graphics,** to clarify written material. Different types of graphics—tables, charts, and graphs—serve different purposes, and some may serve multiple purposes in a given document.

(1) Tables

Tables use a row-and-column arrangement to organize data (numbers or words) spatially; they are especially useful for presenting great amounts of numerical information in a small space, enabling the reader to draw direct comparisons among pieces of data or even to locate specific items. When you design a table, be sure to label all of the columns and rows accurately and to provide both a title and a number for the table. The table number and title traditionally appear above the table body, as table 27.1 demonstrates, and any notes or source information should be placed below it.

(2) Charts and graphs

Charts and graphs display relationships among statistical data in visual form by using lines, bars, or other visual elements rather than just letters and numbers. **Pie charts** are especially useful

Table 27.1   MODIFIED MONTHLY TORNADO STATISTICS

Month	2007 Final	2006 Final	2005 Final	2004 Final	4-Year Average
Jan	21	47	33	3	26
Feb	52	12	10	9	21
Mar	171	150	62	50	108
Apr	165	245	132	125	167
May	250	139	123	509	255
Jun	128	120	316	268	208
Jul	69	71	138	124	101
Aug	73	80	123	179	114
Sep	51	84	133	295	141
Oct	87	76	18	79	65
Nov	7	42	150	150	87
Dec	19	40	26	26	28
Total	1093	1106	1264	1817	1321

Source: National Weather Service.

for showing the relationship of parts to a whole (see fig. 27.1), but they can only be used to display sets of data that add up to 100 percent (a whole).

Bar charts show correlations between two variables that do not change smoothly over time. For instance, a bar chart might illustrate the relative speeds of various computer processors or statistics about the composition of the U.S. military (see fig. 27.2).

27b   Using pictures

Pictures include photos, sketches, technical illustrations, paintings, icons, and other visual representations. Photographs are often used to reinforce textual descriptions or to show a reader

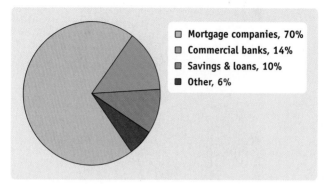

Figure 27.1. Pie chart showing issuers of mortgage-based securities.

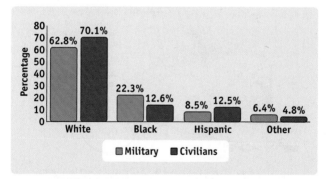

Figure 27.2. Bar chart illustrating the composition of the U.S. military.

exactly what something looks like. But photographs are not always the most informative type of picture. Compare the two images in fig. 27.3. Although the photograph is a more realistic image of the actual printer, the illustration more clearly shows the printer's important features: buttons, panels, and so forth. Line drawings enable the designer of a document, such as a user manual, to highlight specific elements of an object while deemphasizing or eliminating unnecessary information.

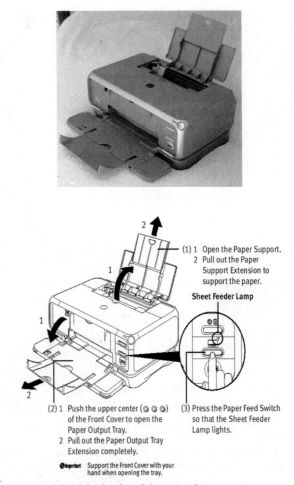

(1) 1 Open the Paper Support.
2 Pull out the Paper Support Extension to support the paper.

Sheet Feeder Lamp

(2) 1 Push the upper center (◎ ◎ ◎) of the Front Cover to open the Paper Output Tray.
2 Pull out the Paper Output Tray Extension completely.

Important Support the Front Cover with your hand when opening the tray.

(3) Press the Paper Feed Switch so that the Sheet Feeder Lamp lights.

Figure 27.3 A photo and a drawing of the same printer.

28 Writing Arguments

When you express a point of view and use logical reasoning to invite a specific audience to accept that point of view or adopt a course of action, you are writing an **argument.** Arguments serve three basic purposes: to analyze a complicated issue or question an established belief, to express or defend a point of view, and to invite or convince an audience to change a position or adopt a course of action.

28a Determining the purpose of your argument

What is your topic? What is at stake? What is likely to happen as a result of making this argument? Who is in a position to act or react in response to your argument?

When writing an argument, you need to establish the relationships among your topic, purpose, and audience.

- If there is little likelihood that you can convince members of your audience to change a strongly held opinion, you might achieve a great deal by inviting them to understand your position.
- If the members of your audience are not firmly committed to a position, you might be able to convince them to agree with the opinion you are expressing or defending.
- If the members of your audience agree with you in principle, you might invite them to undertake a specific action—such as voting for the candidate you are supporting.

No matter how you imagine those in your audience responding to your argument, you must establish **common**

ground with them, stating a goal toward which you both want to work or identifying a belief, assumption, or value that you both share.

28b Considering differing viewpoints

If everyone agreed on everything, there would be no need for argument, for taking a position. Therefore, a good deal of the writing you will do in school or at work will require you to take an arguable position on a topic.

Behind any effective argument is a question that can generate more than one reasonable answer. Answers differ because people approach questions with various backgrounds, experiences, and assumptions. As a consequence, they are often tempted to use reasoning that supports what they already believe. As a writer, employing such reasoning is a good place to start. But as you expand your argument, you will want to demonstrate not only that you are knowledgeable about your topic but also that you have given fair consideration to other views about it.

When you choose a topic for argumentation, you will want to take a stance that provides you an exigence (or reason) for writing. First, you focus on a topic, on the part of some general subject that you will address in your essay, and then you pose a question about it. As you craft your question, consider the following: (1) your own values and beliefs with respect to the question, (2) how your assumptions might differ from those of your intended audience, and (3) how you might establish common ground with members of your audience, while at the same time respecting any differences between your opinion and theirs. The question you raise will evolve into your **thesis,** an arguable statement. To determine whether a topic might be suitable, make a statement about the topic ("I believe strongly that . . . " or "My view is that . . . ") and then check to see if that statement can be argued.

28c Distinguishing between fact and opinion

When you develop your thesis statement into an argument, you use both facts and opinions. **Facts** are reliable pieces of information that can be verified through independent sources or procedures. **Opinions,** on the other hand, are assertions or inferences that may or may not be based on facts. Opinions that are widely accepted may seem to be factual when they are not. Facts are significant only when they are used responsibly to support a claim; otherwise, a thoughtful and well-informed opinion might have more impact.

28d Taking a position or making a claim

When making an argument, a writer takes a position (called the **claim**) on a particular topic, which clearly states what the writer wants the audience to do with the information being provided. The claim is the thesis of the argument.

Claims can be absolute or moderate, large or limited. Absolute claims assert that something is always true or false, completely good or bad; moderate claims make less sweeping assertions.

Absolute claim   College athletes are never good students.

Moderate claim   Most colleges have low graduation rates for their athletes.

The stronger the claim, the stronger the evidence needed to support it. Be sure to consider the quality and the significance of the evidence you use—not just its quantity.

Claims also vary in terms of how much they encompass. **Substantiation claims,** for instance, assert that something exists or is evident. Without making a value judgment, such a claim makes a point that can be supported by evidence.

The job market for those who just received a PhD in English is limited.

The post office is raising rates again.

Evaluation claims assert that something has a specific quality, is good or bad, effective or ineffective, attractive or unattractive, successful or unsuccessful.

The graduation rate for athletes at Penn State is very high compared with that at the other Big Ten universities.

The public transportation system in Washington DC is reliable and safe.

Finally, **policy claims** call for a specific action.

We must find the funds to hire better qualified high school teachers.

We need to build a light-rail system linking downtown with the airport and the western suburbs.

28e Providing evidence for an effective argument

Effective arguments are well developed and supported by intelligent and ethical evidence. They also take into consideration the reasons others might disagree.

(1) Establishing reasons for the claim

If you want readers to take your ideas seriously, you must communicate the reasons that have led to your position as well as the values and assumptions that underlie your thinking. When you are exploring your topic, make a list of the reasons that have led to your belief. For example, when Anna Seitz was working on her argumentative essay (presented at the end of this chapter), she listed the following reasons for her belief that universities should not allow individuals or corporations to buy naming rights to campus buildings:

1. By purchasing naming rights, donors gain influence over educational policy decisions, even though they are not qualified to make such decisions.

2. Significant donations can adversely affect overall university finances by replacing existing funding sources.

3. Donors who purchase naming rights are associated with the university, in spite of the fact that they or their corporations may subscribe to a different set of values.

Although it is possible to base an argument on one good reason (such as "The selling of naming rights distracts from the educational purposes of universities"), doing so can be risky. When you show that you have more than one reason for believing as you do, you increase the likelihood that your audience will find merit in your argument. Sometimes, however, one reason is more appropriate than several others you could advance. To develop an argument for which you have only one good reason, explore the bases underlying your reason: the values and assumptions that led you to take your stand.

Whether you have one reason or several, be sure to provide sufficient evidence from credible sources to support your claim: facts, statistics, examples, and testimony from personal experience or professional expertise.

This evidence must be accurate, representative, and sufficient. Accurate information should be verifiable by others. Recognize, however, that even if the information a writer provides is accurate, it may not be representative or sufficient if it was drawn from an exceptional case, a biased sample, or a one-time occurrence. Whatever form of evidence you use—facts, statistics, examples, or testimony—you need to make clear to your audience exactly *why* and *how* the evidence supports your claim.

(2) Responding to diverse views

Effective arguments consider and respond to other points of view, fairly and respectfully. The most common strategy for addressing opposing points of view is **refutation:** you introduce diverse views and then respectfully demonstrate why you disagree with or accept each of them. When you find yourself agreeing with a point that supports another side of the issue, you can benefit from offering a **concession,** which can demonstrate your fair-mindedness. If you admit that others are partially right, they are more likely to admit that you could be partially right as well.

28f	Using the rhetorical appeals to ground your argument

Effective arguments always incorporate a combination of three persuasive strategies: the **rhetorical appeals** of ethos, logos, and pathos. **Ethos** (an ethical appeal) establishes the speaker's or writer's credibility and trustworthiness. An ethical appeal demonstrates goodwill toward the audience, good sense or knowledge of the subject at hand, and good character. Establishing common ground with the audience is another feature of ethos. **Logos,** a logical appeal, demonstrates an effective use of reason and judicious use of evidence, whether that evidence consists of facts, statistics, comparisons, anecdotes, expert opinions, personal experiences, or observations. You employ logos in the process of supporting claims, drawing reasonable conclusions, and avoiding rhetorical fallacies. **Pathos** (an emotional appeal) involves using language that will engage (not manipulate) the feelings of the audience by establishing empathy and authentic understanding. The most effective arguments combine these three persuasive appeals responsibly and knowledgeably.

28g Arranging an effective argument

No single arrangement is right for every written argument. The decisions you make about arrangement should be based on several factors: your topic, your audience, and your purpose. You can develop a good plan by listing the major points you want to make, deciding what order to put them in, and determining where to include refutation or concession. You must also decide where to place your thesis statement or claim.

Your conclusion should move beyond what has already been stated to reinforce your rhetorical purpose: the course of action you want your audience to take, an invitation to further understanding, or the implications of your claim.

(1) The classical arrangement
One way to organize your argument is to use classical arrangement, which assumes that an audience is prepared to follow a well-reasoned argument.

(2) Placement of the refutation and concession
Classical arrangement places the refutation after the proof or confirmation of the argument, an arrangement that usually works well. Sometimes, however, that refutation can come too late to be effective. Therefore, when you are taking a controversial stand on an emotionally loaded subject, strive to establish common ground, state your position (offering one strong reason for it), and then acknowledge and respond to opposing viewpoints. Keep at least one other reason in reserve (often one that relies on pathos) so that you can present it after responding to opposing views, thereby ending with an emphasis on confirmation.

FEATURES OF THE CLASSICAL ARRANGEMENT

Introduction	Introduce your issue and capture the attention of your audience. Begin establishing your credibility (using ethos) and common ground.
Background information	Provide your audience with a history of the situation and state how things currently stand. Define any key terms. Draw the attention of your audience to those points that are especially important and explain why they are meaningful.
Proposition	Introduce the position you are taking: present the argument itself and provide the basic reasons for your belief. Frame your position as a thesis statement or a claim.
Proof or confirmation	Discuss the reasons that have led you to take your position. Each reason must be clear, relevant, and representative. Provide facts, expert testimony, and any other evidence that supports your claim.
Refutation	Recognize and disprove the arguments of people who hold a different position and with whom you continue to disagree.
Concession	Concede any point with which you agree or that has merit; show why this concession does not damage your own case.
Conclusion	Summarize your most important points and appeal to your audience's feelings, making a personal connection. Describe the consequences of your argument in a final attempt to encourage your audience to consider (if not commit to) a particular course of action.

28h   Sample argument

As you read the following essay by Anna Seitz, note her use of classical rhetorical appeals (ethos, logos, and pathos), her reasoning, and her arrangement. Also, identify the kinds of evidence she uses (facts, examples, testimony, or authority).

Anna Seitz

Professor Byerly

Library Science 313

30 November 2007

Naming Opportunities: Opportunities for Whom?

All over the nation, football stadiums, business schools, law

schools, dining halls, and even coaching positions have become

naming opportunities (also known as "naming rights" and "legacy

opportunities"). Since the first college deal in 1979—when

Syracuse University signed a deal with the Carrier Corporation

for lifetime naming rights to its sports stadium, the Carrier

Dome—naming has become a common practice with an alleged

two-fold payoff: universities raise money, and donors get their

names writ large. Universities use the money, from naming

opportunities to hire more faculty, raise salaries, support faculty

research, provide travel opportunities for students, and build

stadium suites and boxes for game watching. Reser Stadium

(Oregon State), The Donald Bren School of Law (University

of California–Irvine), or the Malloy Paterno Head Football

Coach Endowment (Penn State University)—all these naming

opportunities seem like a good solution for raising money,

especially at a time when state legislatures have cut back on

Introduction

Seitz 2

Introduction

university funding and when wealthy alumni are being besieged for donations from every college they have ever attended. Naming opportunities seem like a good solution for donors, too, because their donations will be broadly recognized. While naming opportunities may seem like a perfect solution for improving colleges and universities and simplifying funding, in reality they are not. In this paper, I argue against naming opportunities on college and university campuses because they create more problems than they solve.

Background
information

The naming of sports stadiums is a familiar occurrence; after all, universities commonly highlight the sponsors of their athletic programs. But naming opportunities in other spheres of academic life are unfamiliar to most people, even though such naming is an established practice. A quick search of the Web pages of university libraries reveals that many of them, especially those in the midst of major development campaigns, have created a price list just for naming opportunities. Entire buildings are available, of course. For example, a $5 million donation earns the right to name the music library at Northwestern University (Northwestern). But parts of buildings are also available these days. North Carolina State University will name an atlas stand according to the donor's wishes for only $7,500 or put a specific name on a lectern for $3,500 (North Carolina).

Seitz 3

Naming opportunities can clearly bring in a good deal of money. It has become commonplace for schools to offer naming opportunities on planned construction in exchange for 51 percent of the cost of the building! That's a big head start to a building project, and naming opportunities may be what allow some schools to provide their students with better facilities than their unnamed counterparts. In fact, donors are often recruited for the opportunity to pay for named faculty chairs, reading rooms, or major library or art collections—all of which enhance student life.

Background information

Clearly the more opportunities and resources any university can offer current and potential students and even alumni, the more that university enhances its own growth and that of its faculty. Library donors and recipients say that if it is possible for a library to pay for a new computer lab just by adding a sign with someone's name over the door, the advantages often seem to outweigh the disadvantages. Proponents of naming opportunities point out that small donors are often hailed as library supporters, even when big donors are maligned as corporate flag-wavers.

Few would argue that these donations necessarily detract from the educational mission of the institution. However, selling off parts of a university library, for example, does not always please people,

Seitz 4

especially those whose responsibility includes managing that donation.

The curator of rare books and manuscripts at a prominent state

Background information

university told me that one of the most frustrating parts of her job is

dealing with "strings-attached" gifts, which is what too many library

donations turn out to be (and why she wishes to remain anonymous).

Some major donors like to make surprise visits, during which they

monitor the prominence of their "legacy opportunity." Others like

to create rules which limit the use of their funds to the purchase of

certain collections or subjects; still others just need constant personal

maintenance, including lunches, coffees, and regular invitations to

events. But meddling in their donation after the fact is just a minor

inconvenience compared to some donors' actions.

Donors who fund an ongoing educational program and

Proposition

give money on a regular basis often expect to have regular input.

Because major donors want major prestige, they try to align

themselves with successful programs. Doing that can result in

damage to university budgets. First, high-profile programs can

become increasingly well funded, while less prominent, less

glamorous ones are ignored. Second, regularly available corporate

or private funds can erode existing funding sources. Simply put,

if a budgeted program becomes funded by donation, the next time

the program needs funding, the department or unit will likely

Seitz 5

be told that finding a donor is their only option. Essentially, once
donor-funded, always donor-funded.

Additionally, many academics feel that selling off naming
rights can create an image problem for a university. While buildings,
schools, endowed chairs, even football stadiums were once named for
past professors, university presidents, or others with strong ties to the
university, those same facilities are now named for virtually anyone
who can afford to donate, especially corporations. Regular input
from a corporation creates the appearance of a conflict of interest
in a university, which is exactly the reason such arrangements are so
often vehemently opposed by the university community. Boise State
University in Idaho received such negative press for negotiating a
deal with labor-unfriendly Taco Bell that it was finally pressured
to terminate the $4 million contract (Langrill 1).

Given these drawbacks, many universities are establishing
guidelines for the selection of appropriate donors for named gifts.
To that end, fundraising professional and managing director of
Changing Our World, Inc. Robert Hoak suggests that naming
opportunities should be mutually beneficial for the donor
(whether a corporation or an individual) and the organization
(university, for instance) and that these opportunities should
be viewed as the start of a long-term relationship between the

Proposition

Proof

Seitz 6

Proof

two, not the final gift. Additionally, he cautions that even if the donor seems the right fit for the organization, it is in the best interest of both parties to add an escape clause to the contract in order to protect either side from potential embarrassment or scandal. He provides the example of Seton Hall University, which regrettably had both an academic building and the library rotunda named for Tyco CEO Dennis Kozlowski. When Kozlowski was convicted of grand larceny, the university pulled the names (Hoak).

Refutation

Although many people prefer that naming be a recognition of an accomplished faculty member or administrator, most realize that recruiting named gift donors is good business. Whether it is "good education" is another question. Naming university property for major donors should not be merely a sales transaction. New College in Cambridge, Massachusetts, was just that—until local clergyman John Harvard died and left half his estate and his entire library to what would soon become Harvard College. Modern naming opportunities, however, do not necessarily recognize and remember individuals who had significant influence on university life; rather, they create obligations for the university to operate in such a way as to please living donors or their descendants. Pleasing wealthy donors should not replace educating students as a university's primary goal.

Seitz 7

Works Cited

Hoak, Robert. "Making the Most of Naming Opportunities."

onPhilanthropy. Changing Our World, 28 Mar. 2003. Web.

5 Nov. 2007.

Langrill, Chereen. "BSU Faculty Says 'No Quiero' to Taco Bell."

Idaho Statesman [Boise] 27 Oct. 2004: 1+. Print.

North Carolina State University Libraries. "NCSU Libraries East

Wing Renovation: Naming Opportunities." *NCSU Libraries*.

North Carolina State U, n.d. Web. 5 Nov. 2007. <http://www.

lib.ncsu.edu/renovation/namingOp/>.

Northwestern University Library. "Making a Gift: Naming

Opportunities." *Naming Opportunities: Library Development

Office*. Northwestern U, 2007. Web. 20 Nov. 2007.

✳ 29 Finding Sources in Print, Online, and in the Field

To conduct useful and authoritative research efficiently, you must develop skills in accessing information.

29a   Research and the rhetorical situation

To make the most of the time you spend doing research, determine your rhetorical situation early in the research process.

(1) Identifying an exigence to form a research question

The starting point for any research project is your exigence—the issue or problem that has prompted you to write; to locate, analyze, and substantiate information before you write; and to craft a challenging question that guides your research and focuses your working thesis.

TIPS FOR FINDING A CHALLENGING RESEARCH QUESTION

- What problem or issue from one of your classes would you like to address?
- What have you read or observed recently that piqued your curiosity?
- What local or campus problem would you like to explore?
- Is there anything (lifestyles, political views, global events) that you find unusual or intriguing and would like to investigate?

(2) Establishing a purpose
You also need to establish the rhetorical purpose of your research, which could be any of the following:

- *To inform an audience.* The researcher reports current thinking on a specific topic, including opposing views, without analyzing them or siding with a particular position.
- *To analyze and synthesize information and then offer possible solutions.* The researcher analyzes a topic and synthesizes the available information about it, looking for points of agreement and disagreement and for gaps in coverage. Sometimes the researcher offers possible ways to address any problems found.
- *To convince or issue an invitation to an audience.* The researcher states a position and backs it up with data, statistics, testimony, corroborating texts or events, or supporting arguments. The researcher's purpose is to persuade readers to take the same position.

(3) Using primary and secondary sources
Experienced researchers consult both primary and secondary sources. **Primary sources** for researching topics in the humanities are generally documents such as archived letters, records, and papers, as well as literary, autobiographical, and philosophical texts. In the social sciences, primary sources can be field observations, case histories, and survey data. In the

Primary sources, such as a report from an archeological dig, are useful for many research projects.

natural sciences, primary sources are generally empirical and include field observations, measurements, or discoveries and experimental results. **Secondary sources** are commentaries on primary sources.

29b Finding books

Three types of books are commonly used in the research process. **Scholarly books** are written by experts to advance knowledge of a certain subject. Most include original research and are reviewed by scholars in the same field as the author(s). **Trade books** may also be written by experts, scholars, journalists, or freelance writers. Authors of trade books write to inform a general audience of research that has been done by others. **Reference books** such as encyclopedias and dictionaries provide factual information in short articles or entries written and reviewed by experts in the field.

(1) Locating sources through an online catalog

The easiest way to find books related to your research question is to consult your library's online catalog, doing either keyword searches or subject searches. To perform a **keyword search,** choose a word or phrase that you think might be found in the title of a book or in notes in the catalog's records. By using a word or part of a word followed by asterisks, you can find all sources that include that root, even when suffixes have been added. For example, if you entered *environment***, you would find not only sources with *environment* in the title, subject headings, and content notes, but also sources with *environments, environmental,* or *environmentalist* in those locations.

You can also use a **Boolean search.** Combining words or phrases using *and, or, not,* or *near* will limit or widen a search. For example, you could try *Marion and Ohio, Buckeye or Ohio, Marion not Ohio,* or *Marysville near Marion.*

Once you find the online catalog record for a book you would like to use, write down its **call number,** which indicates where the book is shelved.

(2) Specialized reference books

A specialized encyclopedia or dictionary can provide background information related to the topic you are researching. To find such sources using an online search page, enter the type of reference book and one or two keywords identifying your topic.

USEFUL REFERENCE BOOKS

For a detailed list of reference books and a short description of each, consult *Guide to Reference Books* by Robert Balay and *American Reference Books Annual* (*ARBA*). A few widely used reference books are listed here.

Specialized Dictionaries and Encyclopedias

- *Dictionary of American History*
- *Dictionary of Art*
- *Encyclopedia of Bioethics*
- *Encyclopedia of Higher Education*
- *Encyclopedia of Psychology*

Collections of Biographies

- *American National Biography*
- *Dictionary of Scientific Biography*
- *Notable American Women*
- *Who's Who in America*

29c Finding articles

Articles can be found in various **periodicals** (publications that appear at regular intervals), which offer information that is often more recent than that found in books. **Scholarly journals** contain reports of original research written by experts for an academic audience. **Professional,** or **trade, magazines** feature articles written by staff writers or industry specialists. **Popular magazines** and **newspapers,** generally written by staff writers, carry a combination of news stories and essays.

The best strategy for finding print articles is to use your library's **electronic database,** which is a collection of articles indexed according to author, title, date, keywords, and other features. Similar to an online catalog, an electronic database allows you to search for sources by author, title, keyword, and so on.

College libraries subscribe to a wide variety of database services, but the following are the most common:

ERIC: Articles related to education

JSTOR: Articles from journals in the arts, humanities, ecology, and social sciences

PsycINFO: Articles related to psychology

InfoTrac: Articles on a wide variety of subjects from journals and magazines

Vendors such as EBSCO and Lexis Nexis offer a variety of databases.

TIPS FOR CONDUCTING A SEARCH FOR PERIODICAL LITERATURE

- Identify keywords that clearly represent the topic.
- Determine the databases you want to search.
- Refine your search strategy if the first search returns too many, too few, or (worse) irrelevant citations.
- Download and print the relevant articles.

Finding online sources

Most researchers start their online research by using **search engines,** electronic indexes of words and terms from Web pages. The following are the addresses for some commonly used search engines:

Ask	**www.ask.com**
Google	**www.google.com**
Bing	**www.bing.com**
Lycos	**www.lycos.com**
Yahoo	**www.yahoo.com**

Unlike search engines, **subject directories** are collections of Web sources arranged topically. The following are some useful subject directories for academic and professional research:

Academic Info	**www.academicinfo.net**
The Internet Public Library	**www.ipl.org/ref**
Librarians' Index to the Internet	**lii.org**
The WWW Virtual Library	**vlib.org**

(1) Keeping track of your sources on the Web
As you click from link to link, you can keep track of your location by looking at the Web address, or **URL (uniform resource locator),** at the top of the screen. Web addresses generally include the following information: server name, domain name, directory (and perhaps subdirectory) name, file name, and file type.

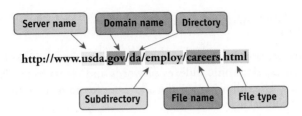

Because sites change and even disappear, some scholarly organizations require that bibliographic entries for Web sites include both the **access date** (the date on which the site was visited) and the **publication date** (the date when the site was published or last modified). When you print out material from the Web, the access date usually appears at the top or bottom of the printout. The publication date often appears on the site itself. Keeping a separate record of this information can help you when you need to verify information on a site or list it in a bibliography.

(2) Using U.S. Government Web sites

If you need information on particular federal laws, court cases, or population statistics, U.S. Government documents may be your best sources. You can find these documents by using online databases such as these:

FirstGov	**www.firstgov.gov**
U.S. Government Printing Office	**www.gpoaccess.gov**
U.S. Courts	**www.uscourts.gov**
FedWorld	**www.fedworld.gov**

(3) Using images

If your rhetorical situation calls for the use of images, the Internet offers you billions from which to choose. If an image you choose is copyrighted, you need to contact the author, artist, or designer for permission to use it. You do not need to obtain permission to use public domain images or those that are cleared for reuse. Collections of specific types of images are available at the following Web sites:

Advertisements

Ad*Access	**library.duke.edu/ digitalcollections/ adaccess**
Adflip	**www.adflip.com**
Advertising World	**advertising.utexas.edu/ world**

Art

The Artchive	**www.artchive.com**
The Web Gallery of Art	**www.wga.hu**

Clip art

The Icon Browser	**www.ibiblio.org/gio/ iconbrowser**
Webclipz	**www.webclipz.com**

Photography

The New York Public Library Picture Collection Online	**digital.nypl.org/mmpco**
Smithsonian Images	**smithsonianimages.com**

29e Field research

Interviews, discussions, and questionnaires are the most common methods of **field research** used to gather information in a natural setting.

(1) Interviewing an expert

After you have consulted some sources on your topic, you may still have questions that might best be answered by someone who has firsthand experience in the area you are researching: a teacher, government official, business owner, or another person with the relevant background.

To arrange an interview, introduce yourself, briefly describe your project, and then explain your reasons for requesting the interview. Try to accommodate the person you hope to interview by asking him or her to suggest an interview date. If you intend to tape your interview, ask for permission ahead of time.

Start preparing your list of questions before the day of the interview, using a blend of open (or broad) questions and focused (or narrow) questions that begin with *why, when, what, who, where,* or *how.* By doing so, you give your interviewee a chance to elaborate. Take notes or record the interview. After the interview, review and expand your notes or transcribe the relevant parts of the recording. Write extensively about the interview, asking yourself what you found most important, most surprising, and most puzzling.

(2) Participating in an online discussion group

Online discussion groups, or forums, allow you to read messages posted to all the members of a group interested in a specific topic and to post messages or questions yourself. You can find addresses of online discussion groups at **www.forumone .com** or **groups.google.com**.

(3) Using a questionnaire

Whereas an interview elicits information from one person whose name you know, a questionnaire provides information from a number of anonymous people. To be effective, a questionnaire should be short and focused. If the list of questions is too long, people may not be willing to take the time to answer them all. If the questions are not focused on your research topic, you will find it difficult to integrate the results into your paper.

EXAMPLES OF TYPES OF SURVEY QUESTIONS

Questions that require a simple yes-or-no answer:

Do you commute to work in a car? (Circle one.)

Yes   No

Multiple-choice questions:

How many people do you commute with? (Circle one.)

0   1   2   3   4

Questions with answers on a checklist:

How long does it take you to commute to work? (Check one.)

___ 0–30 minutes   ___ 60–90 minutes
___ 30–60 minutes   ___ 90–120 minutes

Questions with a ranking scale:

Other than a car, which of the following types of transportation do you rely on? (Rank the choices from 1 for most frequently used to 4 for least frequently used.)

___ bus   ___ shuttle van   ___ subway   ___ taxi

Open questions:

What feature of commuting do you find most irritating?

Begin your questionnaire with an introduction stating the purpose of the questionnaire, how the results will be used, and how many questions it contains or approximately how long it should take to complete. In the introduction, assure participants that their answers will remain confidential. Before you distribute your questionnaire, check with the institutional review board (IRB) on your campus to make certain that you have followed its guidelines.

It is a good idea to send out twice as many copies of the questionnaire as you would like returned because the proportion of responses is generally low. If you mail out a questionnaire, provide a self-addressed envelope and directions for returning it. Questionnaires can sometimes be distributed in college dormitories, in classes, or through listservs (if approved by school officials).

Once the questionnaires have been completed and returned, tally the results for all but the open questions. To find patterns in the responses to the open questions, first read through them all and try to create categories for the responses, which will help you tally the answers.

CHECKLIST for Creating a Questionnaire

- Does each question relate directly to the purpose of the survey?
- Are the questions easy to understand?
- Are they designed to elicit short, specific responses?
- Are they designed to collect concrete data that can be analyzed easily?
- Have respondents been given enough space to write their answers to open questions?
- Do you have access to the group you want to survey?
- Have you asked a few classmates to "test-drive" your questionnaire?

*30 Evaluating Print and Online Sources

As you find sources that seem to address your research question and support your working thesis, you have to evaluate them to determine whether the information they contain is credible, relevant, and timely.

30a Credibility of authors

Credible (or trustworthy) authors present facts accurately, support their opinions with compelling evidence, connect their ideas reasonably, and demonstrate respect for any opposing views. To evaluate the credibility of the authors of your sources, find out what their credentials are, consider what world view informs their ideas, and note how other readers respond to their work. Credentials include academic or professional training, publications, and experience. The author's credentials may be found on the jacket or in the preface of a book, in a note in an article, or on a page devoted to providing background on contributors.

CHECKLIST for Assessing an Author's Credentials

- Does the author's education or profession relate to the subject of the work?
- With what institutions, organizations, or companies has the author been affiliated?
- What awards has the author won?
- What other works has the author produced?
- Do other experts speak of the author as an authority?

An author's values and beliefs about the world constitute his or her **world view,** which underpins his or her research and publications. To determine what these values and beliefs are, consider the author's purpose and intended audience. As you read and use sources, keep in mind that they reflect the world views of the authors and often of the audience for whom they were written. By identifying these values and beliefs, you can responsibly represent and report the information in your sources.

CHECKLIST for Determining an Author's World View

- What is the author's educational and professional background?
- With what types of organizations do the author and publisher affiliate themselves?
- What is the editorial slant of the organization publishing the author's work? Where does it lie on the political spectrum from conservative to liberal?
- What, if any, signs of bias on the part of the author or the publisher can you detect?
- Is the information purported to be factual? Objective? Personal?
- Who advertises in the source?
- To what types of Web sites do any links lead?
- How can you use the source? As fact? Opinion? Example? Authoritative testimony? Material to be refuted?

You can learn even more about an author's background or other works by searching the Internet for information, using a general search engine such as Google or a specialized search engine such as the People search option offered by Lycos (**www .whowhere.com**).

Book reviews, both in print and online, often include information for determining whether an author is credible. Even a work by a credible author may get some negative responses, but dismiss from further consideration any writer whom more than one reviewer characterizes as ill-informed, careless with facts, biased, or dishonest in any way.

30b Credibility of publishers

When you are doing research, consider not only the credibility of authors but also the credibility of the media through which their work is made available to you. Some publishers hold authors accountable to higher standards than others do.

When evaluating books, you can usually assume that publishers associated with universities demand a high standard of scholarship. Books published by commercial (or trade) presses, in contrast, typically do not undergo the same type of review. Thus, to determine how a trade book has been received by others writing in the same area, you have to rely on book reviews.

An article published in a scholarly journal is generally considered more credible than one published in a popular magazine because it has been both written and reviewed by an expert. Authors of scholarly journal articles are expected to include both in-text citations and bibliographies so that other researchers can consult the sources used.

Articles that appear in popular magazines and newspapers may also be reliable but are usually written quickly and chosen for publication by someone on the periodical's staff—not by an expert in the field. Because magazines and newspapers often report research results that were initially published elsewhere, you should try to find the original source to ensure the accuracy of their reports.

When evaluating an article in a magazine or newspaper, also take into account the reputation of the publication itself, examining several issues in terms of the space devoted to various stories, the tone of the commentary on the editorial pages, and the extent to which staff members (as opposed to wire services) are responsible for stories.

30c   Online sources

If you are evaluating a periodical source that you obtained online, you can follow the guidelines for print-based sources. But if you are evaluating a Web site, you also need to consider the nature of the site and its sponsor. Although many sites are created by individuals working on their own, many others are sponsored by colleges or universities, professional or nonprofit organizations, and commercial enterprises. The type of sponsor is typically indicated in the site's address (URL) by a suffix that represents the domain. Colleges and universities are indicated by the suffix **.edu**, government departments and agencies by **.gov**, professional and nonprofit organizations by **.org**, network sites by **.net**, and businesses by **.com**. As you access the various types of sites to evaluate their content, remember that every site is shaped to achieve a specific purpose and to address a specific audience.

30d   Relevance and timeliness

A source is useful only when it is relevant to your research question and working thesis. As you conduct research, draft, and revise, you may reject some sources altogether and use only parts of others. Seldom will an entire book, article, or Web site be useful for a specific research project.

Useful sources are also timely. You should always seek up-to-date information. However, if you are writing about a specific era in the past, you should also consult sources written during that period.

CHECKLIST for Establishing Relevance and Timeliness

- Does the table of contents, index, or directory of the work include key words related to your research question?
- Does the abstract of a journal article contain information on your topic?
- If an abstract is not available, are any of the article's topic sentences relevant to your research question?
- Do the section heads of the source include words connected to your topic?
- On a Web site, are there hyperlinks that lead you to relevant information?
- Is the work recent enough to provide up-to-date information?
- If you need a source from another time period, is the work from the right period?

31 Using Sources Effectively and Responsibly

To use sources effectively, you need to remember that you are a *writer,* not just a compiler of data. To use sources responsibly, you acknowledge others' ideas and words as you incorporate them into your paper. But even when you use sources responsibly, your voice remains the most important voice in the paper.

31a The rhetorical situation and the research paper

Like any other paper, a research paper should respond to an exigence with a purpose appropriate for a particular audience and context. In a research paper, you discuss what others have discovered, creating a conversation in which you play an essential role: you orchestrate how your sources interact with one another and at the same time talk back to them. You also establish yourself as a credible author. By conducting research and citing sources, you demonstrate that you have

- educated yourself about your topic,
- drawn accurately on the work of others (including diverse points of view),
- understood what you have discovered,
- integrated research data into a paper that is clearly your own, and
- provided all the information readers will need to consult the sources you have used.

31b Organizing notes

Taking thorough and organized notes (on screen or on paper) is critical when you are preparing to write a research paper in which you attribute specific words and ideas to others while taking credit for your own ideas.

(1) Taking notes on photocopies and printouts

An easy way to take notes is to use photocopies of articles and excerpts from books or printouts of sources from the Web, marking quotable material while also jotting down your own ideas in the margins. This method reduces the risk of including inaccurate quotations in your paper, because you have eliminated the step of copying quotations exactly as they appear in the original source. Make sure to record the source on a photocopy if this information is not shown on the original page(s). Printouts from the Web almost always indicate the source and the date of access, but you should also note the date on which the site was posted or last updated.

(2) Organizing notes in computer files

You may find it efficient to use a computer for taking notes—recording them quickly and storing them safely. Then, later, you can easily copy and paste information into various files and ultimately into a draft of your paper. Given the ease of computer use, though, it is important to remember to identify which records are direct quotations, which are paraphrases, and which are your own thoughts. Always provide complete bibliographic information so that you will not have trouble finding the source later.

TIPS ON USING A COMPUTER TO ORGANIZE NOTES

- Create a separate master folder (or directory) for the paper.
- Create folders within the master folder for your bibliography, notes, and drafts.
- Keep all the notes for each source in a separate file.
- Use a distinctive font or a different color to distinguish your own thoughts from the ideas of others.
- Place direct quotations in quotation marks.
- When taking notes, record exactly where the information came from.
- When you discover new sources, add them to your working bibliography.
- Consider using the Annotation or Comment feature of your word-processing program to make notes on documents you have downloaded.

(3) Arranging notes on note cards

Taking notes on index cards can be useful if you are working in a library without a laptop or if you prefer handwritten notes that you can rearrange as your research proceeds. Each index card should show the author's name (and a short title if the bibliography contains more than one work by that author), the exact page number(s) from which the information is drawn, and a brief comment on how you intend to use the information or a reflection on what you think about it. By putting a heading of two or three key words at the top of each card, you can easily arrange your cards as you prepare to draft your paper.

TIPS FOR TAKING NOTES

- Identify the source, including page number(s), for every note.
- Put the full bibliographic citation on the first page of every photocopy.
- Copy verbatim any useful passage you think you may quote. Put quotation marks around quoted words. In computer files, you can also use different fonts or different colors to identify quoted text.
- When a source has stimulated your thinking, identify both the source and your own idea based on that source.

31c Working bibliography and annotated bibliography

A **working bibliography,** or preliminary bibliography, contains information (titles, authors' names, publication dates, and so on) about the materials you think you might use. Creating a working bibliography can help you evaluate the quality of your research.

It is a good idea to follow the bibliographical format you have been instructed to use in your paper right from the start, such as that of the Modern Language Association (MLA) or that of the American Psychological Association (APA). The examples given in the rest of this chapter follow the MLA's bibliographical and documentation style.

If you are asked to prepare an **annotated bibliography,** you should list all your sources alphabetically according to the last name of the author. Then, at the end of each entry, summarize the content of the source in one or two sentences.

Zimmer, Carl. *Soul Made Flesh: The Discovery of the Brain—and How It Changed the World*. New York: Free, 2004. Print. This book is a historical account of how knowledge of the brain developed and influenced ideas about the soul. It covers a span of time and place, beginning four thousand years ago in ancient Egypt and ending in Oxford, England, in the seventeenth century.

31d Integrating sources

You can integrate sources into your own writing in a number of ways: quoting exact words, paraphrasing sentences, and summarizing longer pieces of text or even entire texts. Remember to be careful to integrate the material—properly cited—into your own sentences and paragraphs.

(1) Introducing sources

When you borrow textual material, introduce it to readers by establishing the source, usually an author's name. You may also need to include additional information about the author, especially if the author is unfamiliar to your audience. For example, in a paper on medications given to children, the following statement becomes more credible if the audience is given the added information about Jerome Groopman's background.

According to Jerome Groopman, *professor of medicine at Harvard University,* "Pediatricians sometimes adopt extraordinary measures to insure that their patients are not harmed by treatments that have not been adequately studied in children" (33).

Phrases such as *According to Jerome Groopman* and *from the author's perspective* are called **attributive tags** because they attribute, or ascribe, information to a source. Most attributive tags consist of the name of an author (or a related noun or pronoun) and a verb in order to report what that author has said or written.

VERBS USED IN ATTRIBUTIVE TAGS

argue	conclude	find	point out
believe	disagree	imply	reject
claim	discuss	note	state
concede	explain	observe	suggest

If you decide to integrate graphics as source material, you must label them as figures and assign them arabic numbers. You can then refer to them within the text of your paper in a parenthetical

Figure 31.1. Western coral snake.

comment, as in this example: "The red and black bands of the Western coral snake are bordered by narrower bands of yellow or white (fig. 31.1)." You may also want to include a title or caption with the figure number.

(2) Using direct quotations

Include a direct quotation in a paper only if

- you want to retain the beauty or clarity of someone's words,
- you need to reveal how the reasoning in a specific passage is flawed or insightful, or
- you plan to discuss the implications of the quoted material.

Keep quotations as short as possible, and make them an integral part of your text.

Quote *accurately.* Any quotation of another person's words should be placed in quotation marks or, if longer than four lines, set off as an indented block. If you need to clarify a quotation by changing it in any way, place square brackets around the added or changed words.

"In this role, he [Robin Williams] successfully conveys a diverse range of emotion."

If you want to omit part of a quotation, replace the deleted words with ellipsis points.

"Overseas markets . . . are critical to the financial success of Hollywood films."

When modifying a quotation, never alter its essential meaning.

CHECKLIST for Using Direct Quotations

- Have you copied all the words and punctuation accurately?
- Have you attributed the quotation to a specific source?
- Have you used square brackets around anything you added to or changed in a direct quotation?
- Have you used ellipsis points to indicate anything you omitted?
- Have you used quotations sparingly? If not, consider paraphrasing or summarizing the information instead.

---

(3) Paraphrasing another person's ideas

A **paraphrase** is a restatement of someone else's ideas in approximately the same number of words. Paraphrasing allows you to demonstrate that you have understood what you have read; it also enables you to help your audience understand it. Paraphrase when you want to

- clarify difficult material by using simpler language,
- use another writer's idea but not his or her exact words,

- create a consistent tone for your paper as a whole, or
- interact with a point that your source has made.

Your paraphrase should be almost entirely in your *own* words and should accurately convey the content of the original passage.

(a) Using your own words and sentence structure

As you compare the source below with the paraphrases that follow, note the similarities and differences in both sentence structure and word choice.

Source

Zimmer, Carl. *Soul Made Flesh: The Discovery of the Brain—and How It Changed the World*. New York: Free, 2004. 7. Print.

> The maps that neuroscientists make today are like the early charts of the New World with grotesque coastlines and blank interiors. And what little we do know about how the brain works raises disturbing questions about the nature of our selves.

Inadequate paraphrase

The maps used by neuroscientists today resemble the rough maps of the New World. Because we know so little about how the brain works, we must ask questions about the nature of our selves (Zimmer 7).

If you simply change a few words in a passage, you have not adequately restated it. You may be committing plagiarism if the wording of your version follows the original too closely, even if you provide a page reference for the source.

Adequate paraphrase

Carl Zimmer compares today's maps of the brain to the rough maps made of the New World. He believes that the lack of knowledge about the workings of the brain makes us ask serious questions about our nature (7).

In the second paraphrase, both vocabulary and sentence structure differ from those in the original. This paraphrase also includes an attributive tag ("Carl Zimmer compares").

(b) Maintaining accuracy

Any paraphrase must accurately and ethically maintain the sense of the original. Compare the original statement below with the paraphrases.

Source

Hanlon, Michael. "Climate Apocalypse When?" *New Scientist*
17 Nov. 2007: 20. Print.

> Disastrous images of climate change are everywhere. An alarming graphic recently appeared in the UK media showing the British Isles reduced to a scattered archipelago by a 60-metre rise in sea level. Evocative scenes of melting glaciers, all-at-sea polar bears and forest fires are routinely attributed to global warming. And of course Al Gore has just won a Nobel prize for his doomsday flick *An Inconvenient Truth,* starring hurricane Katrina.
> . . . There is a big problem here, though it isn't with the science. The evidence that human activities are dramatically modifying the planet's climate is now overwhelming—even to a former paid-up sceptic like me. The consensus is established, the fear real and justified. The problem is that the effects of climate change mostly haven't happened yet, and for journalists and their editors that presents a dilemma. Talking about what the weather may be like in the 2100s, never mind the 3100s, doesn't sell.

Inaccurate or unethical paraphrase

Evocative scenes of melting glaciers, landless polar bears, and forest fires are attributed to global warming in Al Gore's *An Inconvenient Truth.* The trouble is that Gore cannot predict what will happen (Hanlon 20).

Accurate paraphrase

According to Michael Hanlon, the disastrous images of climate change that permeate the media are distorting our understanding of what is actually happening now globally and what might happen in the future (20).

Although both paraphrases include a reference to an author and a page number, the first focuses misleadingly on Al Gore, whereas the second paraphrase notes the much broader problem, which can be blamed on the media's focus on selling a story.

(4) Summarizing an idea

A **summary** reports a writer's main idea and the most important support given for it. Whereas the length of a paraphrase is usually close to that of the original material, a summary conveys the gist of the author's ideas, in fewer words. Summaries can include short quotations of key phrases or ideas, but you must always enclose another writer's exact words in quotation marks when you blend them with your own.

Source

Marshall, Joseph M., III. "Tasunke Witko (His Crazy Horse)." *Native Peoples* Jan.-Feb. 2007: 76-79. Print.

> The world knows him as Crazy Horse, which is not a precise translation of his name from Lakota to English. *Tasunke Witko* means "his crazy horse," or "his horse is crazy." This slight mistranslation of his name seems to reflect the fact that Crazy Horse the man is obscured by Crazy Horse the legendary warrior. He was both, but the fascination with the legendary warrior hides the reality of the man. And it was as the man, shaped by his family, community and culture—as well as the events in his life—that he became legend.

Summary

The Lakota warrior English speakers refer to as "Crazy Horse" was actually called "his crazy horse." That mistranslation may distort what Crazy Horse was like as a man.

This example reduces five sentences to two, retaining the key idea but eliminating the source author's analysis and speculation.

31e   Avoiding plagiarism

To use the work of other writers responsibly, you need to ensure that your audience can distinguish between those writers' ideas and your own contributions and that you give credit for all information you gather through research. It is not necessary to credit information that is **common knowledge,** which includes well-known facts. If you have been scrupulous about recording your own thoughts as you took notes, you should have little difficulty distinguishing between what you knew to begin with and what you learned through your research. If you take even part of someone else's work and present it as your own, you leave yourself open to charges of **plagiarism.** Plagiarism is illegal, and penalties range from failing a paper or course to being expelled from school. Never compromise your integrity or risk your future by submitting someone else's work as your own.

To review how to draw responsibly on the words and ideas of others, consider the following examples.

Source

McConnell, Patricia B. *The Other End of the Leash*. New York: Ballantine, 2002. 142. Print.

> Status in male chimpanzees is particularly interesting because it is based on the formation of coalitions, in which no single male can achieve and maintain power without a cadre of supporting males.

Paraphrase with documentation

Patricia B. McConnell, an authority on animal training, notes that by forming alliances with other male chimpanzees, a specific male can enjoy status and power (142).

This example includes not only the original author's name but also a parenthetical citation, which marks the end of the paraphrase and provides the page number where the source can be found. Paraphrases must include citations.

Quotation with documentation

Patricia B. McConnell, an authority on animal training, argues that male chimpanzees achieve status "based on the formation of coalitions, in which no single male can achieve and maintain power without a cadre of supporting males" (142).

Quotation marks show where the copied words begin and end; the number in parentheses indicates the exact page on which those words appear. Again, the author is identified in the sentence, although her name could have been omitted at the beginning of the sentence and noted within the parenthetical reference instead:

An authority on animal training argues that male chimpanzees achieve status "based on the formation of coalitions, in which no single male can achieve and maintain power without a cadre of supporting males" (McConnell 142).

CHECKLIST of Sources That Should Be Cited

- Writings, both published and unpublished
- Opinions and judgments that are not your own
- Statistics and other facts that are not widely known
- Images and graphics, such as works of art, drawings, charts, graphs, tables, photographs, maps, and advertisements
- Personal communications, such as interviews, letters, and e-mail messages
- Electronic communications, including television and radio broadcasts, motion pictures and videos, sound recordings, Web sites, and online discussion groups or forums

31f   Responding to sources

When incorporating sources, not only will you summarize, paraphrase, quote, and document them, you will respond to them as well. To prepare for interacting with your sources, make notes in the margins of whatever you are reading. Next to relevant passages, jot down your agreement, disagreement, questions, and so on.

As you read and work with published research, you will want to know whether facts are accurate or erroneous, whether logic is strong or weak, whether the information is well or poorly organized, and whether conclusions are valid or doubtful. You will also evaluate the strengths and weaknesses of sources in order to motivate your own line of research. Overall, consider responding to your sources by examining their timeliness, coverage, reliability, and reasoning.

(1) Considering the currency of sources

Using up-to-date sources is crucial when researching most topics. Even a source published in the same year that you are doing research may include data that are several years old and thus possibly irrelevant.

(2) Noting the thoroughness of research

Coverage refers to the comprehensiveness of research. The more comprehensive a study is, the more convincing are its findings. Similarly, the more examples an author provides, the more compelling are his or her conclusions.

(3) Checking the reliability of findings

Research, especially when derived from experiments or surveys, must be reliable. Experimental results are considered **reliable** if they can be reproduced by researchers using a similar methodology. Results that cannot be replicated in this way are not reliable because they are supported by only one experiment.

Reliability is also a requirement for reported data. Researchers are expected to report their findings accurately and honestly, not distorting them to support their own beliefs or claiming others' ideas as their own. To ensure the reliability of their work, researchers must also report all relevant information, not intentionally excluding any that weakens their conclusions.

(4) Examining the author's reasoning

When a source is logical, its reasoning is sound. Lapses in logic may be the result of using evidence that does not directly support a claim, appealing to the reader's emotions, or encouraging belief in false authority.

32   Writing about Literature

You have been interpreting and writing about literature—talking about plot, characters, and setting—ever since you wrote your first book report. When you write about literature in college, you will still discuss plot, characters, and setting. But you will also establish an exigence for writing, explore and focus your subject, formulate a purposeful thesis statement that is supported by reference to the literary work itself, address an audience, and arrange your thoughts in the most effective way. In short, when you write about literature, you respond to the rhetorical situation.

32a   Literature and its genres

Works of literature can be divided into categories, which are referred to as **genres.** A genre can be identified by its particular features and conventions. Some genres are timeless and universal (drama and poetry, for instance); others are context-specific and develop within particular cultures (the graphic novel, for instance, is a fairly recent cultural phenomenon). Even when genres overlap (for example, some poems are referred to as prose poems, and Shakespeare's plays are written in verse), the identifiable features of each genre are still evident.

Some of the most widely studied literary genres are fiction, drama, and poetry, though many forms of nonfiction (including personal essays and memoirs, literacy narratives, and manifestos) are being studied in college courses on literature. All imaginative literature can be characterized as fictional, but the term *fiction* is applied specifically to novels and short stories. Drama differs from all other imaginative literature in one specific way: it is meant to be performed. Poetry shares the components of both drama and fiction but is primarily characterized by extensive use of connotative language, imagery, allusions, figures of speech, symbols, sound, meter, and rhythm.

32b Rhetorical reading and literary interpretation

The most successful writing about literature starts with rhetorical (or active) reading. Therefore, as you read, examine your own reactions. Were you amused, moved, or confused? Which characters interested you? Were you able to follow the plot? Did the work remind you of any experience of your own or other works you have read? Did it introduce you to a different historical or geographical setting, or did you encounter a familiar setting and cast of characters? These first impressions can provide the seeds from which strong essays will grow.

(1) Your personal response to reading literature

When reflecting on your response to some element in a work of literature, consider how your reading might be shaped by the factors that define who you are. If you respond positively or negatively to a character, a plot twist, or the setting, you might ask yourself whether this response has anything to do with your psychological makeup, political beliefs, gender or sexual orientation, cultural or ethnic group, social class, religion, or geographic location. Thinking about what you bring to a work of literature helps you focus on an exigence for your writing and may suggest a theoretical approach to use as a basis for your interpretation.

(2) Developing your topic using evidence in the text

If you are choosing your own topic, your first step is to reflect on your personal response as you formulate a tentative thesis statement. Next, consider what specific evidence from the text will best explain and support your interpretation and thesis statement.

Most readers (including your instructor) will be interested in what *you* think, so you need to discover a way to demonstrate your originality by focusing on a topic you can develop adequately and then applying one or more rhetorical methods. You might explain why you consider a character heroic. Or you might explain how the repeated appearance of an object throughout a story serves as a reminder of a particular idea or theme.

(3) Researching what other readers have said about a literary work

You will undoubtedly anchor your essay in your own interpretation, but you enrich that interpretation with the sometimes conflicting responses of others, from literary experts to classmates. Although it is tempting to lean heavily on the interpretations of scholarly experts, you should use them in the same way you use other outsides sources: to enrich your own interpretation and support your own points. No matter what outside sources you tap, be sure to give credit to them by citing them.

To locate scholarly material on a specific writer, work, or literary theory, you can start by consulting your library's resources. Your library's catalog and certain reference books are the best starting points. For instance, *The MLA International Bibliography,* an index of books and articles about literature, is an essential resource for literary studies and is available in print and online. Works such as *Contemporary Authors, The Oxford Companion to English Literature,* and *The New Princeton Handbook of Poetic Terms* can be useful when you are beginning your research or when you have encountered terms you need to clarify.

(4) Types of literary interpretation

Writing about a literary work requires you to focus on the work itself and to demonstrate that you have read it carefully—a process known as **close reading.** Close reading allows you to offer an **interpretation,** an explanation of what you see in a work. When your interpretation explains the contribution of one feature of a literary work (such as the setting, main character, or theme) to the work's overall meaning, it is called an **analysis.**

Explication, usually used only with poetry, is an interpretation that attempts to explain every element in a literary work. When explicating William Wordsworth's "A Slumber Did My Spirit Seal," a writer might note that the *s* sound reinforces the hushed feeling of sleep and death in the poem. But it would also be necessary to consider the meanings of *slumber, spirit,* and *seal.*

An **evaluation** of a literary work gauges how successfully the author communicates meaning to readers. The most common types of evaluation are book, theater, and film reviews. Like any other interpretation, an evaluation is a type of argument in which a writer cites both positive and negative textual evidence to persuade readers to accept a clearly formulated thesis.

32c Vocabulary for discussing literature

Like all specialized fields, literature has its own vocabulary, which describes the various features of literary texts and the concepts of literary analysis. As you learn this vocabulary, you will learn more than just a list of terms: you will learn how to understand, interpret, and write about literature.

(1) Characters

The **characters** are the humans or humanlike personalities (aliens, robots, animals, and other creatures) who carry the plot forward; they usually include a main character, called a **protagonist,** who is in external conflict with another character or an

Understanding how a particular character moves the plot forward will help you interpret a work as a whole.

institution or in internal conflict with himself or herself. This conflict usually reveals the **theme,** or the central idea of the work.

Because you need to understand the characters in any work you read, it is important to pay close attention to their appearance, their language, and their actions. You also need to pay attention to what the narrator or other characters say about them and how the other characters treat and react to them.

(2) Imagery

The imagery in a piece of literature is conveyed by **descriptive language,** or words that describe a sensory experience. Notice the images in the following excerpt from a prose poem by Pinkie Gordon Lane that focuses on the death—and life—of a mother.

> My mother died walking along a dusty road on a Sunday morning in New Jersey. The road came up to meet her sinking body in one quick embrace. She spread out like an umbrella and dropped into oblivion before she hit the ground. In that one swift moment all light went out at the age of forty-nine. Her legacy: the blackened knees of the scrub-woman who ransomed her soul so that I might live, who bled like a tomato whenever she fought to survive, who laughed fully when amused—her laughter rising in one huge crescendo—and whose wings soared in dark despair . . . .
>
> —**PINKIE GORDON LANE,** "Prose Poem: Portrait"

The dusty road, the sinking body, the quick embrace—these images convey the loneliness and swiftness of death. The blackened knees, tomato-like bleeding, and rising laughter are, in contrast, images of a life's work, struggle, and joy.

(3) Narrator

The **narrator** of a literary work tells the story. The voice doing the telling can seem to be that of the author's **persona** (which is a fictional construction and not actually the author), a specific character (or one of several characters who are taking turns telling the story), or an all-knowing presence (referred to as an **omniscient narrator**) that transcends characters and author alike. Whatever the voice, the narrator's tone reveals his or her attitude toward events and characters and even, in some circumstances, toward readers.

(4) Plot

The plot is what happens in the story, the sequence of events (the narrative)—and more. The plot establishes how events are patterned or related in terms of conflict and resolution. Narrative answers "What comes next?" and plot answers "Why?" Consider this example:

Narrative
A woman is confined to a room with yellow wallpaper.

Plot
The physician husband of a highly imaginative woman moves her into a room with yellow wallpaper, where she is restricted to silence and idleness.

A plot usually begins with a conflict, an unstable situation that sets events in motion. In what is called the **exposition,** the author introduces the characters, setting, and background—the elements that not only constitute the unstable situation but

JULIET LANDAU · ARIC CUSHING · VERONICA CARTWRIGHT · RAYMOND J. BARRY · DALE DICKEY · MICHAEL MORIARTY

the Yellow Wallpaper

In "The Yellow Wallpaper," a doctor confines his wife to an upstairs bedroom in an attempt to restore her mental health by means of a rest cure.

also relate to the events that follow. The subsequent series of events leads to the **climax** (or **turning point).** What follows is **falling action** (or **dénouement**) that leads to a resolution of the conflict and a more stable situation, though not necessarily a happy ending.

(5) Setting

Setting involves place—not just the physical setting, but also the social setting (the morals, manners, and customs of the characters). Setting also involves time—not only historical time, but also the length of time covered by the narrative. Setting includes **atmosphere,** or the emotional response to the situation, often shared by the reader with the characters. Being aware of the features of the setting will help you better understand a story, whether it is written as fiction, drama, or poetry.

(6) Symbols

Frequently used by writers of literature, a **symbol** is usually a physical object that stands for something else, usually something abstract. For example, at the beginning of *A Streetcar Named Desire,* a play by Tennessee Williams, one of the main characters buys a paper lantern to cover a naked lightbulb. During the scenes that follow, she frequently talks about light, emphasizing her preference for soft lighting. Anyone seeing this play performed or reading it carefully would note that the paper lantern is a symbol. It is an object that is part of the setting and the plot, but it also stands for something more—a character's avoidance of harsh truths.

When you write about a particular symbol, first note where it appears in the literary work. To determine what the symbol might mean, consider why it appears in those places and to what effect. Once you have an idea about the meaning, trace the incidents in the literary work that reinforce that interpretation.

(7) Theme

The main idea of a literary work is its **theme.** To test whether an idea is central to the work in question, check to see if the idea is supported by the setting, plot, characters, and symbols. If so, it can be considered the work's theme. The most prominent literary themes arise out of external or internal conflict: character versus character, character versus herself or himself, character versus nature, or character versus society.

When you believe you have identified the theme of a literary work, state it as a sentence—and be precise. A theme conveys a specific idea; it should not be confused with a topic.

Topic	a physician's care of his ill wife
Vague theme	the subordination of nineteenth-century married women
Specific theme	"The Yellow Wallpaper" deals with a conflict between an imaginative woman and a society that insists that she abandon her artistic endeavors.

> ### CHECKLIST for Interpreting a Literary Work
>
> - From whose point of view is the story told?
> - Who is the protagonist? How is his or her character developed?
> - With whom or what is the protagonist in conflict?
> - How are the other characters depicted and distinguished through dialogue?
> - What symbols, imagery, or figures of speech does the author use? To what effect?
> - What is the theme of the work? How does the author use setting, plot, characters, and symbols to establish that theme?

32d Approaches to interpreting literature

An interpretation of a literary work can be shaped by your personal response to what you have read, by the views of other readers whom you wish to support or challenge, or by a specific type of literary theory.

Literary theory, the scholarly discussion of how the nature and function of literature can be determined, ranges from approaches that focus almost exclusively on the text itself (its language and structure) to approaches that show how the text relates to author, reader, language, society, culture, economics, or history. Familiarity with literary theory enriches your reading of literature as well as your understanding of the books and essays about literature that you will discover when you do research.

(1) Reader-response theory

According to **reader-response theory,** readers construct meaning as they read and interact with the elements within a text, with each reader bringing something different (intellectual values and life experiences) to the text with every reading.

Thus, meaning is not fixed *on* the page but rather depends on what each reader brings *to* the page. Furthermore, the same reader can have different responses to the same literary work when rereading it later: a father of teenagers, for example, might find Gwendolyn Brooks's "we real cool" more disturbing now than when he first read it in high school. Although a reader-response approach to literature encourages diverse interpretations, you cannot simply say, "Well, that's what this work means to me," or "That's my interpretation." You must demonstrate to your audience how the elements of the work support your interpretation.

(2) Feminist and gender-based literary theories

The significance of sex, gender, or sexual orientation within a particular social context is the interpretive focus of **feminist** and **gender-based literary theories.** These theories enable a reader to analyze the ways in which a work (through its characters, theme, or plot) promotes or challenges the prevailing intellectual or cultural assumptions of its day regarding issues related to gender and sexuality, such as patriarchy and compulsory heterosexuality. For instance, Edith Wharton's *The Age of Innocence* compares two upper-class nineteenth-century women with respect to the specific social pressures that shaped and constricted their lives and loves. A feminist critic might emphasize the oppression of these women and the repression of their sexuality. Using a gender-based approach, another critic might focus on issues of the two women's financial dependence on men.

(3) Text-based literary theory

Text-based literary theory demands concentration on the piece of literature itself, Nothing more than what is contained within the text itself—not information about the author's life, culture, or society—is needed to understand and appreciate the text's unchanging meaning. Readers may change, but the meaning of the text does not.

(4) Context-based literary theory

Context-based literary theory considers the historical period during which a work was written and the cultural and economic patterns that prevailed during that period. For example, recognizing that Willa Cather published *My Ántonia* during World War I can help account for the darker side of that novel about European immigrants' harsh life in the American West. Critics who use a context-based and class-based approach known as **cultural studies** consider how a literary work interacts with economic conditions, socioeconomic classes, and other cultural artifacts (such as songs or fashion) of the period in which it was written.

32e   Conventions for writing about literature

Writing about literature involves adhering to several conventions.

(1) Using first person

When writing an analysis of a piece of literature, you may use the first-person singular pronoun, *I*.

Although some critics believe Rudolfo Anáya's novel to be about witchcraft, I think it is about the power of belief.

By using *I*, you indicate that you are presenting your opinion about a work. When you propose or argue for a particular belief or interpretation or offer an opinion, you must support it with specific evidence from the text itself.

(2) Using present tense

Use the present tense when discussing a literary work or reporting how others have interpreted the work you are discussing.

In "A Good Man Is Hard to Find," the grandmother reaches out to touch her killer just before he pulls the trigger.

As Toni Morrison demonstrates in her analysis of the American literary tradition, black Americans continue to play a vital role.

(3) Documenting sources

When writing about a work, cite the version of the work you are discussing by using the MLA format for listing works cited or by acknowledging the first quotation from or reference to the work using a superscript number and then providing an explanatory note on a separate page at the end of your paper.

In-text citation

… as Toni Morrison states (127).[1]

OR

… tendency to misread texts by African American writers (Morrison 127).[1]

Note

   1. Toni Morrison, *Playing in the Dark: Whiteness and the Literary Imagination* (New York: Vintage, 1992). All subsequent references to this work will be identified with page numbers in parentheses within the text.

If you use this note form, you do not need to repeat the bibliographical information in a separate entry or include the author's name in subsequent parenthetical references to page numbers. Check with your instructor about the format he or she prefers.

   When you use a bibliography to provide publication data, you must indicate specific references whenever you quote a line or passage. According to MLA style, such bibliographic information should be placed in the text in parentheses directly after the quotation. A period, a semicolon, or a comma should follow the parentheses. Quotations from short stories and novels are identified by the author's name and page number:

"A man planning to spend money on me was an experience rare enough to feel odd" (Gordon 19).

Quotations from poems are referred to by line number:

"O Rose, thou are sick!" (Blake 1).

Quotations from Shakespeare's plays are identified using abbreviations of the titles; the following line is from act I, scene i, line 28 of Shakespeare's play *Much Ado about Nothing*:

"How much better it is to weep at joy than to joy at weeping" (*Ado* 1.1.28).

(4) Quoting poetry

When quoting from poems and verse plays, type quotations involving three or fewer lines in the text and insert a slash with a space on each side to separate the lines.

"Does the road wind uphill all the way? / Yes, to the very end" (Rossetti 1-2). Christina Rossetti opens her poem "Uphill" with this two-line question and answer.

Quotations of more than three lines should be indented one inch from the left-hand margin and double-spaced. Do not use slashes at the ends of lines and make sure to follow the original text for line breaks, special indenting, or spacing. For this type of block quotation, place your citation after the final punctuation mark.

(5) Referring to authors' names

Use the full name of the author of a work in your first reference and only the last name in all subsequent references. For instance, write "Charles Dickens" or "Willa Cather" the first time and use "Dickens" or "Cather" after that. Never refer to a female author differently than you do a male author.

32f Literary interpretation of a short story

In the following literary interpretation, English major Kristin Ford focuses on the political and personal implications of a woman's mental illness as portrayed in Charlotte Perkins Gilman's short story "The Yellow Wallpaper."

Ford 1

Kristin Ford

Professor Glenn

English 232

19 November 2010

The Role of Storytelling in Fighting

Nineteenth-Century Chauvinism

The writer provides a critical overview of the story, demonstrating her understanding of it.

Widely considered to be one of the most influential pieces of early feminist literature, "The Yellow Wallpaper," published in 1892 by Charlotte Perkins Gilman, illustrates nineteenth-century men's patronizing treatment of and abusive power over women, exploring the smudged line between sanity and insanity, men's alleged ability to distinguish between the two, and women's inability to pull themselves out of depression or any form of mental illness without seeming to further demonstrate their insanity. The protagonist of Gilman's story descends into madness, a mental state unnecessarily exacerbated, if not caused, by her husband's prescribed "rest cure," which entailed total inactivity and isolation. Such was her double bind: the stronger the constraints of the cure, the worse her mental illness. She had no way to resolve her problem.

The writer defines *double bind*, which is the operative term for her thesis.

During Gilman's time, women were understood largely in relation to the "Cult of True Womanhood," which prescribed

Ford 2

women's "proper" place in society, especially within the middle and upper classes. Piety, purity, submissiveness, and domesticity were not merely encouraged but demanded in order for a woman to avoid breaking this strict social code (Lavender). Such virtues meant that a "true woman" of that time was a wife, housewife, and mother—always yielding to the demands of her husband and her family. Any woman who went against these norms risked being cast out or labeled insane (Mellor 156). Men dominated medicine, and mental illness remained largely unexplored and thus misunderstood. Many doctors still feared it and thus ignorantly tried to pass off serious psychological disorders as cases of "nervousness" or "hysteria" or "fragile constitutions" (Tierny 1456). One of the most influential doctors at that time, Silas Weir Mitchell, made popular his "rest cure," which was thought to be especially effective for such disorders.

> The writer includes historical background for the story. She uses past tense to refer to these actions and beliefs.

These societal views are reflected in "The Yellow Wallpaper." The physician husband of the main character imposes the "rest cure" on her. She is forced to obey her husband and has no choice in her treatment. Furthermore, her husband does not listen when she tries to tell him more about her condition, her fears, and her aspirations. This feature of the story—men not listening to their wives—accurately reflects the

> The writer uses the literary present tense to describe the action in the story itself.

social climate of the late nineteenth century, when husbands
could impose their rules on their wives, with little (if any)
thought given to what the women knew, felt, or wanted.

Such a male-centered ideology fostered the development of
the "rest cure," initiated by Weir Mitchell in the late 1880s. He
describes his "Rest Treatment for Nervous Disorders" (Tierny
1456) as well as the temperament of women in his book *Fat and
Blood: and How to Make Them*:

The writer uses information from a physician's writings to support her interpretation and bolster her historical connection.

> The American woman is, to speak plainly, too often
> physically unfit for her duties as woman, and is perhaps
> of all civilized females the least qualified to undertake
> those weightier tasks which tax so heavily the nervous
> system of man. She is not fairly up to what nature asks
> from her as wife and mother. How will she sustain
> herself under the pressure of those yet more exacting
> duties which nowadays she is eager to share with the
> man? (13)

Because of this general belief about American women's fragility
(or weakness), Weir Mitchell often diagnosed patients as having
neurasthenia, a catch-all term for any nervous disorder that
affected mainly women. Many cases, like the one depicted in
"The Yellow Wallpaper," were what would now be considered

Ford 4

postpartum depression, a legitimate psychological disorder requiring medication and therapy.

Conversely, Weir Mitchell's theory was that neurasthenia was all in a woman's head. His rest treatment, prescribed only for women, involved complete rest, little mental stimulation, and overfeeding. A woman was not allowed to leave her bed for months at a time, and she was certainly never allowed to read or write (Weir Mitchell 39). This tendency to diagnose women as "hysterical," coupled with the era's chauvinism, made it easy for doctors like Weir Mitchell to simply, almost flippantly, dismiss the protesting pleas of mentally ill women.

Gilman herself was prescribed this treatment. In "Why I Wrote 'The Yellow Wallpaper,'" Gilman describes how she tried the "rest cure" for three months and "came so near the border of mental ruin that I could see over" (820). In the end, in order to save herself from insanity, Gilman had to ignore what society told her. She could not lead a domestic, sedentary life without falling into insanity. However, according to Weir Mitchell, such a life was considered sane for a woman, a prime indicator of her mental stability. The resulting conflict between Gilman's personal experience and Weir Mitchell's impersonal theory begs the question "What is true sanity?" For Gilman, the only way to cure

The writer presents relevant biographical information about the author of the story.

herself of her madness was the very thing she was told she could not do: write and engage in mental stimulation. This is the double bind that women of the day faced. What Gilman was prescribed to do caused her to fall further into mental illness, but doing what she needed to do to get over the illness was considered a symptom of insanity. This is the same double bind trapping Gilman's protagonist throughout the story.

The rest cure is a tool to suppress all mental activity in women (Tierny 1457). At the beginning of the story, the struggle is among competing factors: what the protagonist is told, what she knows is right, and what she feels she should do. She wants to listen to her husband, but she senses that her illness will not be cured by his proposed remedy. All the while her husband assures her that she only needs the "rest cure" and she will be the wife and mother she should be. Throughout "The Yellow Wallpaper," the wife repeatedly says that although she may be getting physically better, mentally she is not. Her husband repeatedly replies, "Never for one instant let that idea enter your mind! There is nothing so dangerous, so fascinating to a temperament like yours" (Gilman, "Yellow Wallpaper" 814). In addition, he often admonishes her to get well. Gilman juxtaposes what men believed at this time with the actual implications of this cure for the female mind. Although her husband remarks that she seems to be getting better and better, the woman slowly descends further into her madness, showing just how oblivious men, even renowned physicians, were to the struggles of women.

Gilman's goal in this story is to expose this "rest cure" for what it truly is and make clear the struggle women have in a society in which they are expected to be entirely domestic and submissive to men. Gilman makes a particular yet subtle argument when she demonstrates the "domesticated" woman's double bind: If she uses her imagination in an "unsuitable" way, she is exhibiting mental illness. The cure for that illness is constraint, a prohibition on imagination and activity, which only worsens her mental condition. Gilman experienced another double bind as a female author functioning within a realm of male control and expectations. Any woman who published, particularly if her stories dealt with mentally ill women, was revealing her own mental instability. Of course, if an author was not able to write and publish, she would feel even worse.

Gilman portrays the feminist challenge to society's standards through character development and the interactions between the physician husband and his wife. When developing the character of the husband, Gilman illustrates his dominance over his wife through much of their dialogue. The physician speaks to his wife much like an adult speaking to a child. Gilman juxtaposes the husband's view of the woman's improving health against what the reader actually sees happening: the woman creeps around the room becoming completely involved in the pattern of the wallpaper, clearly a sign that she is becoming increasingly ill. This disconnect between what the husband wants to believe and the reality of his wife's condition exemplifies the disconnect in their marital life. It demonstrates the lack of understanding men had toward women and the lack of concern with which they reacted to women's problems.

In "The Yellow Wallpaper," Gilman produced an insightful work using the symbolism of a room turned jail cell to express her views on the way women were treated in her society. Gilman masterfully crafted a story that describes a woman's descent into madness, using that descent as an allegory for the oppression of women of the late nineteenth century. Beyond its importance as a powerful piece of feminist literature, "The Yellow Wallpaper" made a profound impact on its society. After the publication of "Why I Wrote 'The Yellow Wallpaper,'" Weir Mitchell quietly changed his "rest cure." For a respected physician in the late nineteenth century to change his practice based on the

literary work of a woman is powerful testimony to the impact of

"The Yellow Wallpaper."

Ford 9

Works Cited

Gilman, Charlotte P. "Why I Wrote 'The Yellow Wallpaper.'" *The*
    Norton Anthology of American Literature. 7th ed. Vol. C.
    New York: Norton, 2007. Print.

---. "The Yellow Wallpaper." *The Norton Anthology of American*
    Literature. 7th ed. Vol. C. New York: Norton, 2007. Print.

Lavender, Catherine. "The Cult of Domesticity & True Womanhood."
    Women in New York City, 1890–1940. The College of Staten
    Island of CUNY, Fall 1998. Web. 21 Nov. 2008. <http://
    www.csi.cuny.edu/dept/history/lavender/386/
    truewoman.html>.

Mellor, Ann K. *Romanticism and Feminism.* Bloomington: Indiana
    UP, 1988. Print.

Tierny, Helen. *Women's Studies Encyclopedia.* Westport:
    Greenwood, 1997. Print.

Weir Mitchell, Silas. *Fat and Blood: and How to Make Them.*
    Philadelphia: Lippincott, 1882. Print.

(33) MLA Documentation

The Modern Language Association (MLA) provides guidelines for documenting research in literature, languages, linguistics, and composition studies. The *MLA Handbook for Writers of Research Papers* is published specifically for undergraduates.

33a MLA-style in-text citations

(1) Citing material from other sources

The citations you use within the text of a research paper refer your readers to the list of works cited at the end of the paper, tell them where to find the borrowed material in the original source, and indicate the boundaries between your ideas and those you have borrowed. In the following example, the parenthetical citation guides the reader to page 88 of the book by Pollan in the works-cited list.

In-text citation

Since the 1980s virtually all the sodas and most of the fruit drinks sold in the supermarkets have been sweetened with high-fructose corn syrup (HFCS)—after water, corn sweetener is their principal ingredient (Pollan 88).

Works-cited entry

Pollan, Michael. *The Omnivore's Dilemma: A Natural History of Four Meals.*
     New York: Penguin, 2006. Print.

The MLA suggests reserving numbered notes for supplementary comments—for example, when you wish to explain a point further but the subject matter is tangential to your topic. When numbered notes are used, superscript numbers are inserted in the appropriate places in the text, and the notes are gathered at the end of the paper on a separate page titled "Notes." Each note begins with an indent.

In-text note number

Most food found in American supermarkets is ultimately derived from corn.[1]

Notes entry

1. Nearly all farm animals—from cows and chickens to various kinds of farmed fish—are fed a diet of corn.

An in-text citation usually provides two pieces of information about borrowed material: (1) information that directs the reader to the relevant source on the works-cited list and (2) information that directs the reader to a specific page or section within that source. An author's last name and a page number generally suffice. To create an in-text citation, either place both the author's last name and the page number in parentheses or introduce the author's name in the sentence and supply just the page number in parentheses.

A "remarkably narrow biological foundation" supports the variety of America's supermarkets (Pollan 18).

Pollan explains the way corn products "feed" the familiar meats, beverages, and dairy products that we find on our supermarket shelves (18).

When referring to information from a range of pages, separate the first and last pages with a hyphen: (34-42). If the page numbers have the same hundreds or thousands digit, do not repeat it when listing the final page in the range: (234-42) or (1350-55) but (290-301) or (1395-1402). If you refer to an entire work or a work with only one page, no page numbers are necessary.

The following examples are representative of the types of in-text citations you might be expected to use.

1. Work by one author

Set on the frontier and focused on characters who use language sparingly, Westerns often reveal a "pattern of linguistic regression" (Rosowski 170).

OR

Susan J. Rosowski argues that Westerns often reveal a "pattern of linguistic regression" (170).

2. More than one work by the same author(s)

When your works-cited list includes more than one work by the same author(s), provide a shortened title in your in-text citation that identifies the relevant work. Use a comma to separate the name (or names) from the shortened title when both are in parentheses. For example, if you listed two works by Antonio Damasio on your works-cited page, then you would cite one of those within your text as follows:

According to one neurological hypothesis, "feelings are the expression of human flourishing or human distress" (Damasio, *Looking for Spinoza* 6).

OR

Antonio Damasio believes that "feelings are the expression of human flourishing or human distress" (*Looking for Spinoza* 6).

3. Work by two or three authors

Some environmentalists seek to protect wilderness areas from further development so that they can both preserve the past and learn from it (Katcher and Wilkins 174).

Use commas to separate the names of three authors: (Bellamy, O'Brien, and Nichols 59).

4. Work by more than three authors

Use either the first author's last name followed by the abbreviation *et al.* (from the Latin *et alii,* meaning "and others") or all the last names. (Do not italicize the abbreviated Latin phrase, which ends with a period.)

In one important study, women graduates complained more frequently about "excessive control than about lack of structure" (Belenky et al. 205).

OR

In one important study, women graduates complained more frequently about "excessive control than about lack of structure" (Belenky, Clinchy, Goldberger, and Tarule 205).

5. Works by different authors with the same last name

When your works-cited list includes works by different authors with the same last name, provide a first initial, along with the last name, in parenthetical citations, or use the author's first and last name in the text. For example, if your works-cited list included entries for works by both Richard Enos and Theresa Enos, you would cite the work of Theresa Enos as follows:

Pre-Aristotelian rhetoric still has an impact today (T. Enos 331-43).

OR

Theresa Enos mentions the considerable contemporary reliance on

pre-Aristotelian rhetoric (331-43).

If two authors have the same last name and first initial, spell out each author's first name in a parenthetical citation.

M L A

6. Work by a corporate author

A work has a corporate author when individual members of the group that created it are not identified. If the corporate author's name is long, you may use common abbreviations for parts of it—for example, *Assn.* for "Association" and *Natl.* for "National." Do not italicize the abbreviations.

Strawbale constructions are now popular across the nation (Natl. Ecobuilders

Group 2).

7. Two or more works in the same citation

When two sources provide similar information or when you combine information from two sources in the same sentence, cite both sources, separating them with a semicolon.

Agricultural scientists believe that crop productivity will be adversely affected

by solar dimming (Beck and Watts 90; Harris-Green 153-54).

8. Multivolume work

When you cite material from more than one volume of a multivolume work, include the volume number (followed by a colon and a space) before the page number.

Katherine Raine claims that "true poetry begins where human personality

ends" (2: 247).

You do not need to include the volume number in a parenthetical citation if your list of works cited includes only one volume of a multivolume work.

9. Anonymous work

The Tehuelche people left their handprints on the walls of a cave, now called

Cave of the Hands ("Hands of Time" 124).

Use the title of an anonymous work in place of an author's name. If the title is long, provide a shortened version. For example, the shortened title for "Chasing Down the Phrasal Verb in the Discourse of Adolescents" is "Chasing Down."

10. Indirect source

If you need to include material that one of your sources quoted from another work because you cannot obtain the original source, use the following format (*qtd.* is the abbreviation for "quoted").

The critic Susan Hardy Aikens has argued on behalf of what she calls

"canonical multiplicity" (qtd. in Mayers 677).

A reader turning to the list of works cited should find a bibliographic entry for Mayers, the source consulted, but not for Aikens.

11. Poetry, drama, and sacred texts

When you refer to poetry, drama, or sacred texts, you should give the numbers of lines, acts, and scenes or of chapters and verses, rather than page numbers. This practice enables readers to consult an edition other than the one you have used. Act, scene, and line numbers (all arabic numerals) are separated by periods with no space before or after them. The MLA suggests that biblical chapters and verses be treated similarly, although some writers prefer to use colons instead of periods in such citations. In all cases, the progression is from larger to smaller units.

The following example illustrates a citation referring to lines of poetry.

Emily Dickinson alludes to her dislike of public appearance in "I'm Nobody! Who Are You?" (5-8).

The following citation shows that the famous "To be, or not to be" soliloquy appears in act III, scene i, lines 56–89 of *Hamlet*.

In *Hamlet*, Shakespeare presents the most famous soliloquy in the history of the English theater: "To be, or not to be . . ." (3.1.56-89).

Citations of biblical material identify the book of the Bible, the chapter, and the pertinent verses. In the following example, the writer refers to the creation story in Genesis, which begins in chapter 1 with verse 1 and ends in chapter 2 with verse 22.

The Old Testament creation story, told with remarkable economy, culminates in the arrival of Eve (*New American Standard Bible*, Gen. 1.1-2.22).

Mention in your first citation which version of the Bible you are using; list only book, chapter, and verse in subsequent citations. Note that the names of biblical books are neither italicized nor enclosed in quotation marks.

The MLA provides standard abbreviations for the parts of the Bible, as well as for the works of Shakespeare and Chaucer and certain other literary works.

12. Constitution

When referring to the U.S. Constitution, use in-text citations only. You do not need to include a works-cited entry. The following are common abbreviations for in-text citations:

United States Constitution	US Const.
article	art.
section	sec.

The testimony of two witnesses is needed to convict someone of treason (US Const., art. 3, sec. 3).

13. Works with numbered paragraphs or sections

If paragraphs in an electronic source are numbered, cite the number(s) of the paragraph(s) after the abbreviation *par.* (for one paragraph) or *pars.* (for more than one). If a section number is provided, cite that number after the abbreviation *sec.* (or *secs.* for more than one).

Alston describes three types of rubrics for evaluating customer service (pars. 2-15).

Hilton and Merrill provide examples of effective hyperlinks (sec. 1).

If an electronic source includes no numbers distinguishing one part from another, you should cite the entire source. In this case, to establish that you have not accidentally omitted a number, avoid using a parenthetical citation by providing what information you have within the sentence that introduces the material.

Raymond Lucero's *Shopping Online* offers useful advice for consumers who are concerned about transmitting credit card information over the Internet.

(2) Guidelines for in-text citations and quotations

(a) Placement of in-text citations

When you acknowledge your use of a source by placing the author's name and a relevant page number in parentheses, insert this parenthetical citation directly after the information you used, generally at the end of a sentence but *before* the final punctuation mark (a period, question mark, or exclamation point).

Oceans store almost half the carbon dioxide released by humans into the atmosphere (Wall 28).

However, you may need to place a parenthetical citation earlier in a sentence to indicate that only the first part of the sentence contains borrowed material. Place the citation after the clause containing the material but before a punctuation mark (a comma, semicolon, or colon).

Oceans store almost half the carbon dioxide released by humans into the atmosphere (Wall 28), a fact that provides hope for scientists studying global warming but alarms scientists studying organisms living in the oceans.

If you cite the same source more than once in a paragraph, with no intervening citations of another source, you can place one parenthetical citation at the end of the last sentence in which the source is used: (Wall 28, 32).

(b) Lengthy quotations

When a quotation is more than four lines long, set it off from the surrounding text by indenting all lines one inch from the left margin. The first line should not be indented further than the others. The right margin should remain the same. Double-space the entire quotation and do not begin and end it with quotation marks.

In *Nickel and Dimed*, Barbara Ehrenreich describes the dire living conditions of the working poor:

> The lunch that consists of Doritos or hot dog rolls, leading to faintness before the end of the shift. The "home" that is also a car or a van. The illness or injury that must be "worked through," with gritted teeth, because there's no sick pay or health insurance and the loss of one day's pay will mean no groceries for the next. These experiences are not part of a sustainable lifestyle, even a lifestyle of chronic deprivation and relentless low-level punishment. They are, by almost any standard of subsistence, emergency situations. And that

> is how we should see the poverty of millions of low-wage
>
> Americans—as a state of emergency. (214)

A problem of this magnitude cannot be fixed simply by raising the minimum

wage.

Note that the period precedes the parenthetical citation at the end of an indented (block) quotation. Note, too, how the writer introduces and then comments on the block quotation from Ehrenreich, explaining the signficance of the quotation to the larger essay.

Rarely will you need to quote more than a paragraph, but if you do, indent the first line of each paragraph an extra quarter of an inch.

(c) Punctuation within citations and quotations

Punctuation marks clarify meaning in quotations and citations. The following list summarizes their common uses.

- A colon separates volume numbers from page numbers in a parenthetical citation.

  (Raine 2: 247)

- A comma separates the author's name from the title when it is necessary to list both in a parenthetical citation.

  (Kingsolver, *Animal Dreams*)

  A comma also indicates that page or line numbers are not sequential.

  (44, 47)

- Ellipsis points indicate an omission within a quotation.

  "They lived in an age of increasing complexity and great hope; we in

  an age of . . . growing despair" (Krutch 2).

- A hyphen indicates a continuous sequence of pages or lines.

  (44-47)

- A period separates acts, scenes, and lines of dramatic works.

  (3.1.56)

  A period also distinguishes chapters from verses in biblical citations.

  (Gen. 1.1)

- A question mark placed inside the final quotation marks indicates that the quotation is a question. Notice that the period after the parenthetical citation marks the end of the sentence.

  Peter Elbow asks, "What could be more wonderful than the pleasure of creating or appreciating forms that are different, amazing, outlandish, useless—the opposite of ordinary, everyday, pragmatic?" (542).

  When placed outside the final quotation marks, a question mark indicates that the quotation has been incorporated into a question posed by the writer of the paper.

  What does Kabat-Zinn mean when he advises people to practice mindfulness "as if their lives depended on it" (305)?

- Square brackets enclose words that have been added to the quotation as clarification and are not part of the original material.

  "The publication of this novel [*Beloved*] establishes Morrison as one of the most important writers of our time" (Boyle 17).

33b MLA list of works cited

All of the works you cite should be listed at the end of your paper, beginning on a separate page with the heading "Works Cited." Use the following tips as you prepare your list.

MLA

TIPS FOR PREPARING A LIST OF WORKS CITED

- Center the heading "Works Cited" (not enclosed in quotation marks) one inch from the top of the page.
- Arrange the list of works alphabetically by the author's last name.
- If a source has more than one author, alphabetize the entry according to the last name of the first author.
- If you use more than one work by the same author, alphabetize the works by the first major word in each title. For the first entry, provide the author's complete name (last name given first), but substitute three hyphens (---) for the author's name in subsequent entries. If that author is also the first author in a collaboration, write out the author's name in full.
- For a work without an author or editor, alphabetize the entry according to the first important word in the title.
- Type the first line of each entry flush with the left margin and indent subsequent lines one-half inch (a hanging indent).
- Double-space equally throughout—between lines of an entry and between entries.

Directory of MLA-Style Entries for a Works-Cited List

PRINT PUBLICATIONS

Print Articles

Print Books

Other Print Texts

Other Online Documents

Online Recordings and Images

OTHER COMMON SOURCES

Live and Recorded Performances

Works of Visual Art

When writing down source information for your bibliography, be sure to copy the information directly from the source.

PRINT PUBLICATIONS

Print Articles

A **journal** is a publication written for a specific discipline or profession. **Magazines** and **newspapers** are written for the general public. You can find most of the information required for a works-cited entry for a journal article on the first page of the journal (fig. 33.1) or at the bottom of the first page of the article you are citing.

Title of article and name of periodical

Put the article title in quotation marks with a period inside the closing quotation marks. Italicize the name of the periodical; do not add any punctuation following the name. Capitalize all major words (nouns, pronouns, verbs, adjectives, adverbs, and subordinating conjunctions). Omit the word *A*, *An*, or *The* from the beginning of the name of a periodical.

"Into the Void." *New Scientist*

Date of publication

Volume number

Issue number

Spring/Summer 2008
Volume 20
Number 1–2

American
Literary
History

Name of journal

Twenty Years of American Literary History: The Anniversary Volume

Title of article

Author

What Good Can Literary History
Do? **1** — Initial page number
Jonathan Arac

A Response to Jonathan Arac   **12**
Jonathan Elmer

Antipodean American Literature:
Franklin, Twain, and the Sphere of
Subalternity   **22**
Paul Giles

Can the Antipodean Speak?
A Response to Paul Giles   **51**
Lauren M. E. Goodlad

Women, Blood, and Contract   **57**
Shirley Samuels

Blood, Republicanism, and the Return
of George Washington: A Response to
Shirley Samuels   **76**
Andy Doolen

The Rise of the New Atlantic Studies
Matrix   **83**
William Boelhower

Oceanic, Traumatic, Post-
Paradigmatic: A Response to William
Boelhower   **102**
Jed Esty

National Treasure, Global Value, and
American Literary Studies   **108**
Eric Lott

Blood and Treasure: A Response to
Eric Lott   **124**
Susan M. Ryan

The Unkillable Dream of the Great
American Novel: *Moby-Dick* asTest
Case   **132**
Lawrence Buell

A Response to Lawrence Buell   **156**
Robert Milder

Border Literary Histories,
Globalization, and Critical
Regionalism   **160**
José E. Limón

Glocal Matters: A Response to José
E. Limón **183**
Richard T. Rodríguez

Figure 33.1. First page of a journal.

Volume and issue numbers

In an entry for an article from a journal, provide the volume number. If the issue number is available, put a period after the volume number and add the issue number.

Contemporary Review 194   *Studies in the Literary Imagination* 26.3

Date

For journals, place the year of publication in parentheses after the volume or issue number. For magazines and newspapers, provide the date of issue after the name of the periodical. Note the day first (if provided), followed by the month (abbreviated except for May, June, and July) and year.

Journal	*American Literary History* 20.1-2 (2008)
Magazine	*Economist* 13 Aug. 2005
Newspaper	*Chicago Tribune* 24 July 2002

Page numbers

Use a colon to separate the date from the page number(s). Note all the pages on which the article appears, separating the first and last page with a hyphen: 21-39. If the page numbers have the same hundreds or thousands digit, do not repeat it when listing the final page in the range: 131-42 or 1680-99. Magazine and newspaper articles are often interrupted by advertisements or other articles. If the first part of an article appears on pages 45 through 47 and the rest on pages 92 through 94, give only the first page number followed by a plus sign: 45+.

Medium of publication

Be sure to include the medium of publication (*Print*) at the end of the entry. Do not italicize the medium of publication.

1. Article in a journal

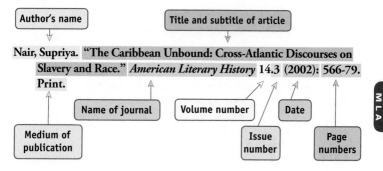

Author's name

Title and subtitle of article

Nair, Supriya. "The Caribbean Unbound: Cross-Atlantic Discourses on Slavery and Race." *American Literary History* 14.3 (2002): 566-79. Print.

Name of journal

Volume number

Date

Medium of publication

Issue number

Page numbers

2. Article in a monthly magazine

Keizer, Garret. "How the Devil Falls in Love." *Harper's* Aug. 2002: 43-51. Print.

3. Article in a weekly magazine or newspaper

Chown, Marcus. "Into the Void." *New Scientist* 24 Nov. 2007: 34-37. Print.

4. Article in a daily newspaper

Moberg, David. "The Accidental Environmentalist." *Chicago Tribune* 24 Sept. 2002, final ed., sec. 2: 1+. Print.

When the name of the city is not part of a locally published newspaper's name, it should be given in brackets after the title: *Star Telegram* [Fort Worth]. If a specific edition is not identifed on the masthead, put a colon after the date and then provide the page reference. Specify the section by inserting the letter and/or number as it appears in the newspaper (A7 or 7A, for example).

5. Unsigned article or wire service article

"View from the Top." *National Geographic* July 2001: 140. Print.

6. Editorial in a newspaper or magazine

Beefs, Anne. "Ending Bias in the Human Rights System." Editorial.

New York Times 22 May 2002, natl. ed.: A27. Print.

7. Book or film review in a magazine

Denby, David. "Horse Power." Rev. of *Seabiscuit*, dir. Gary Ross.

New Yorker 4 Aug. 2003: 84-85. Print.

Include the name of the reviewer, the title of the review (if any), the phrase *Rev. of* (for "Review of"), the title of the work being reviewed, and the name of the editor, author, or director.

8. Book or film review in a journal

Graham, Catherine. Rev. of *Questionable Activities: The Best*, ed. Judith

Rudakoff. *Canadian Theatre Review* 113 (2003): 74-76. Print.

Print Books

9. Book by one author

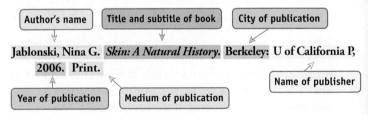

The title page and copyright page of a book (see figs. 33.2 and 33.3) provide the information needed to create a bibliographic entry. If more than one city is listed on the title page, mention only the first. Place a colon after the name of

Figure 33.2. A title page includes most, if not all, of the information needed for a bibliographic entry. In this case, the title page omits the publication date.

the city, followed by a shortened form of the publisher's name with a comma after it and then the copyright date. Place a period after the date. Be sure to include the medium of publication at the end of the entry, followed by a period.

University of California Press, one of the most distinguished
university presses in the United States, enriches lives around the
world by advancing scholarship in the humanities, social sciences,
and natural sciences. Its activities are supported by the UC Press
Foundation and by philanthropic contributions from individuals
and institutions. For more information, visit www.ucpress.edu.

University of California Press
Berkeley and Los Angeles, California

University of California Press, Ltd.
London, England

———————————————— Copyright year

©2006 by Nina G. Jablonski

Figure 33.3. If the title page does not give the book's date of publication, turn to the copyright page, which is usually the page following the title page.

10. Book by two authors

West, Nigel, and Oleg Tsarev. *The Crown Jewels: The British Secrets at the
    Heart of the KGB Archives.* New Haven: Yale UP, 1999. Print.

Type the first author's name in inverted order, followed by a comma, the word *and*, and the name of the second author in normal order. The title and subtitle (if any) are italicized with all major words capitalized.

11. Book by three authors

Spinosa, Charles, Ferdinand Flores, and Hubert L. Dreyfus. *Disclosing New
    Worlds: Entrepreneurship, Democratic Action, and the Cultivation of
    Solidarity.* Cambridge: MIT P, 1997. Print.

12. Book by more than three authors

Bullock, Jane A., George D. Haddow, Damon Cappola, Erdem Ergin, Lissa
Westerman, and Sarp Yeletaysi. *Introduction to Homeland Security*.
Boston: Elsevier, 2005. Print.

OR

Bullock, Jane A., et al. *Introduction to Homeland Security*. Boston: Elsevier,
2005. Print.

13. Book by a corporate author

Institute of Medicine. *Blood Banking and Regulation: Procedures, Problems,
and Alternatives*. Washington: Natl. Acad., 1996. Print.

14. Book by an anonymous author

Primary Colors: A Novel of Politics. New York: Warner, 1996. Print.

Begin the entry with the title. Do not use *Anonymous* or *Anon.*

15. Book with an author and an editor

Stoker, Bram. *Dracula*. Ed. Glennis Byron. Peterborough: Broadview,
1998. Print.

Include both the name of the author and the name of the editor
(preceded by *Ed.*).

16. Book with an editor instead of an author

Kachuba, John B., ed. *How to Write Funny*. Cincinnati: Writer's Digest, 2000. Print.

17. Edition after the first

Murray, Donald. *The Craft of Revision*. 4th ed. Boston: Heinle, 2001. Print.

18. Introduction, preface, foreword, or afterword to a book

Olmos, Edward James. Foreword. *Vietnam Veteranos: Chicanos Recall the
War*. By Lea Ybarra. Austin: U of Texas P, 2004. ix-x. Print.

The name that begins the entry is that of the author of the section of the book, not of the entire book. The name is followed by the title of the section (Introduction, Preface, Foreword, or Afterword).

19. Anthology (a collection of works by different authors)

Buranen, Lisa, and Alice M. Roy, eds. *Perspectives on Plagiarism and*

Intellectual Property in a Postmodern World. New York: State U of

New York P, 1999. Print.

If an editor or editors are listed instead of an author or authors, include the abbreviation *ed.* or *eds.* (not italicized) following the name(s). For individual works within an anthology, consult the following two models.

20. A work originally published in an anthology

Rowe, David. "No Gain, No Game? Media and Sport." *Mass Media and*

Society. Ed. James Curran and Michael Gurevitch. 3rd ed. New York:

Oxford UP, 2000. 346-61. Print.

Use this form for an article, essay, story, poem, or play that was published for the first time in the anthology you are citing. Place the title of the anthology after the title of the individual work. Provide the name(s) of the editor(s) after the abbreviation *Ed.* for "edited by," and note the edition if it is not the first. List the publication data for the anthology and the range of pages on which the work appears.

If you cite more than one work from an anthology, provide only the name(s) of the author(s), the title of the work, the name(s) of the editor(s), and the inclusive page numbers in an entry for each work. Also include an entry for the entire anthology, which presents the publication data.

Clark, Irene L. "Writing Centers and Plagiarism." Buranen and Roy 155-67.

Howard, Rebecca Moore. "The New Abolitionism Comes to Plagiarism."

Buranen and Roy 87-95.

21. A work from a journal reprinted in a textbook or an anthology

Selfe, Cynthia L. "Technology and Literacy: A Story about the Perils of Not

　　Paying Attention." *College Composition and Communication* 50.3

　　(1999): 411-37. Rpt. in *Views from the Center: The CCCC Chairs'*

　　Addresses 1977-2005. Ed. Duane Roen. Boston: Bedford; Urbana:

　　NCTE, 2006. 323-51. Print.

Use the abbreviation *Rpt.* (not italicized) for "Reprinted." Two cities and publishers are listed in the sample entry because the collection was copublished.

22. A work from an edited collection reprinted in a textbook or an anthology

Brownmiller, Susan. "Let's Put Pornography Back in the Closet." *Take Back*

　　the Night: Women on Pornography. Ed. Laura Lederer. New York:

　　Morrow, 1980. 252-55. Rpt. in *Conversations: Readings for Writing*.

　　By Jack Selzer. 4th ed. New York: Allyn, 2000. 578-81. Print.

See item 20 for information on citing more than one work from the same anthology.

23. Translated book

Garrigues, Eduardo. *West of Babylon*. Trans. Nasario Garcia. Albuquerque:

　　U of New Mexico P, 2002. Print.

Place the abbreviation *Trans.* (not italicized) for "Translated by" before the translator's name.

24. Republished book

Alcott, Louisa May. *Work: A Story of Experience*. 1873. Harmondsworth: Penguin,

　　1995. Print.

After the title of the book, provide the original publication date, followed by a period.

25. Multivolume work

Young, Ralph F., ed. *Dissent in America*. 2 vols. New York: Longman-Pearson,

2005. Print.

Cite the total number of volumes in a work when you have used material from more than one volume. Include the year the volumes were published. If the volumes were published over a span of time, provide inclusive dates: 1997-99 or 1998-2004.

If you have used only one volume, include that volume's number (preceded by the abbreviation *Vol.*) in place of the total number of volumes.

Young, Ralph F., ed. *Dissent in America*. Vol. 1. New York: Longman-Pearson,

2005. Print.

Note that the publisher's name in this entry is hyphenated: the first name is the imprint; the second is the publisher.

26. Article in a multivolume work

To indicate a specific article in a multivolume work, provide the author's name and the title of the article in quotation marks. Note the page numbers for the article after the date of publication.

Baxby, Derrick. "Jenner, Edward." *Oxford Dictionary of National Biography*.

Ed. H. C. G. Matthew and Brian Harrison. Vol. 30. Oxford: Oxford UP,

2004. 4-8. Print.

If required by your instructor, include the number of volumes and the inclusive publication dates after the medium of publication: Print. 23 vols. 1962-97.

27. Book in a series

Sumner, Colin, ed. *Blackwell Companion to Criminology*. Malden: Blackwell,

2004. Print. Blackwell Companions to Sociology 8.

When citing a book that is part of a series, add the name of the series and, if one is listed, the number designating the work's place in it. The series name is not italicized. Abbreviate words in the series name according to the MLA guidelines; for example, the word *Series* is abbreviated *Ser.* (not italicized).

Other Print Texts

28. Dictionary entry

When citing a specific dictionary definition for a word, use the abbreviation *Def.* (for "Definition") and indicate which one you used if the entry has two or more.

"Reactive." Def. 2a. *Merriam-Webster's Collegiate Dictionary*. 10th ed. 2001. Print.

29. Sacred text

Begin your works-cited entry for a sacred text with the title of the work, rather than information about editors or translators.

New American Standard Bible. Anaheim: Foundation, 1997. Print.

The Qur'an. Trans. Muhammad A. S. Abdel Haleem. Oxford: Oxford UP,

2004. Print.

30. Government publication

United States. Office of Management and Budget. *A Citizen's Guide to the*

Federal Budget. Washington: GPO, 1999. Print.

When citing a government publication, list the name of the government (e.g., United States or Minnesota) and the agency that issued the work. Italicize the title of a book or pamphlet. Indicate the city of publication. Federal publications are usually printed by the Government Printing Office (GPO) in Washington DC, but be alert for exceptions.

When the name of an author, editor, or compiler appears on a government publication, you can begin the entry with that name, followed by the abbreviation *ed.* or *comp.* if the person is not the author. Alternatively, insert that name after the publication's title and introduce it with the word *By* or the abbreviation *Ed.* or *Comp*.

31. Law case

Chavez v. Martinez. 538 US 760. Supreme Court of the US. 2003. *United States Reports*. Washington: GPO, 2004. Print.

Include the last name of the first plaintiff, the abbreviation *v.* for "versus," the last name of the first defendant, data on the law report (volume, abbreviated name, and page or reference number), the name of the deciding court, and the year of the decision. Although law cases are italicized in the text of a paper, they are *not* italicized in works-cited entries.

32. Public law

No Child Left Behind Act of 2001. Pub. L. 107-10. 115 Stat. 1425-2094. 8 Jan. 2002. Print.

Include the name of the act, its public law number, its Statutes at Large cataloging number and page numbers, the date it was enacted, and the medium of publication. Notice the use of abbreviations in the example. Although no works-cited entry is needed for familiar sources such as the U.S. Constitution, an in-text citation should still be included.

33. Pamphlet or bulletin

Stucco in Residential Construction. St. Paul: Lath & Plaster Bureau, 2000. Print.

If the pamphlet has an author, begin with the author's name, as you would for a book.

34. Published dissertation

Fukuda, Kay Louise. *Differing Perceptions and Constructions of the Meaning
of Assessment in Education*. Diss. Ohio State U, 2001. Ann Arbor: UMI,
2002. Print.

After the title of the dissertation, include the abbreviation *Diss.*,
the name of the university granting the degree, the date of
completion, and the publication information. In the example,
UMI stands for "University Microfilms International," which
publishes many dissertations.

35. Published letter

In general, treat a published letter like a work in an anthology,
adding the date of the letter and the number (if the editor assigned one).

Jackson, Helen Hunt. "To Thomas Bailey Aldrich." 4 May 1883. *The Indian
Reform Letters of Helen Hunt Jackson, 1879-1885*. Ed. Valerie Sherer
Mathes. Norman: U of Oklahoma P, 1998. 258-59. Print.

Print Cartoons, Maps, and Other Visuals

36. Cartoon or comic strip

Cheney, Tom. Cartoon. *New Yorker* 9 June 2003: 93. Print.

Trudeau, Garry. "Doonesbury." Comic strip. *Daily Record* [Ellensburg]
21 Apr. 2005: A4. Print.

After the creator's name, place the title of the work (if given) in quotation marks and include the descriptor *Cartoon* or *Comic strip*.

37. Map or chart

Cincinnati and Vicinity. Map. Chicago: Rand, 2008. Print.

Include the title and the appropriate descriptor, *Map* or *Chart*.

38. Advertisement

Nu by Yves Saint Laurent. Advertisement. *Allure* June 2003: 40. Print.

The name of the product and/or that of the company being advertised is followed by the designation *Advertisement*.

ONLINE PUBLICATIONS

Many of the guidelines for documenting online sources are similar to those for print sources. For sources found online, provide electronic publication information and access information.

Electronic publication information

Indicate the author's name, the title of the work, the title of the Web site, the site's sponsoring organization (usually found at the bottom of the site's home page; see fig. 33.4), the date of publication, and the medium of publication (*Web*). All of this information precedes the access information.

Access information

When you document an online source, you must include the date of access: the day, month, and year on which you consulted the source. Either keep track of the date of access or print out the source so that you have a record.

You are not required to include the URL if your readers can easily locate the online source by searching for the author's name and the title of the work. For cases in which your readers cannot easily locate a source, you should provide the complete URL (between angle brackets), including the protocol (http, ftp, telnet, or news). When the URL does not fit on a single line, break it only after a slash. Make sure that the URL is accurate. Take care to distinguish between uppercase and lowercase letters and to include hyphens and

Title of site ———

Date of publication ———

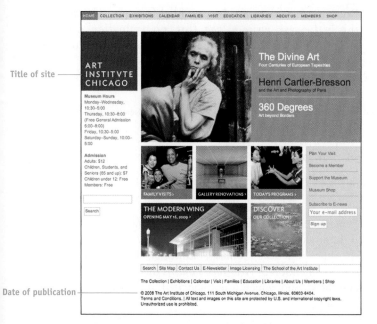

Figure 33.4. The home page for the Art Institute of Chicago indicates the title of the site (which is also the name of the sponsoring organization) and the date of publication.

underscores. The URL follows the date of access, appearing after a period and a space. The closing angle bracket should also be followed by a period.

Online Articles

The following formats apply to articles available only online.

39. Scholarly journal article

Harnack, Andrea, and Gene Kleppinger. "Beyond the MLA Handbook:

Documenting Sources on the Internet." *Kairos* 1.2 (1996): n. pag. Web.

14 Aug. 1997.

Page numbers may not be provided for online journals; if this is the case, write *n. pag.* (for "no pagination"). If they are provided, place them after the colon that follows the year of publication. The access date ends the entry.

40. Popular magazine article

Plotz, David. "The Cure for Sinophobia." *Slate.com.* Newsweek Interactive,

4 June 1999. Web. 15 June 1999.

41. Newspaper article

"Tornadoes Touch Down in S. Illinois." *New York Times.* New York Times,

16 Apr. 1998. Web. 20 May 1998.

When no author is identified, begin with the title of the article. If the article is an editorial, include *Editorial* (not italicized) after the title: "America's Promises." Editorial. (In the sample entry, the first mention of *New York Times* is the title of the Web site, and the second, which is not italicized, is the name of the site's sponsor.)

Online Books

42. Book available only online

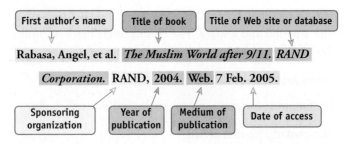

Because there are more than three authors, the abbreviation *et al.* has been used in the example, but listing all names is

also acceptable: Rabasa, Angel, Cheryl Benard, Peter Chalk, C. Christine Fair, Theodore W. Karasik, Rollie Lal, Ian O. Lesser, and David E. Thaler. Note that in this example the name of the sponsoring organization is in the title of the Web site.

43. Book available online and in print

Rohrbough, Malcolm J. *Days of Gold: The California Gold Rush and the American Nation.* Berkeley: U of California P, 1997. *History E-book Project.* Web. 17 Feb. 2005.

Begin the citation with print citation information: the author's name, the title of the work, city of publication, publisher, and date. Follow this information with the title of the database or Web site (italicized), the medium of publication (*Web*), and the date of access.

44. Part of an online book

Strunk, William, Jr. "Elementary Rules of Usage." *The Elements of Style.* Ithaca: Humphrey, 1918. N. pag. *Bartleby.com.* Web. 6 June 2003.

Online Databases

Many print materials are available online through a database (JSTOR, Project MUSE, ERIC, PsycINFO, Academic Universe, LexisNexis, ProQuest, InfoTrac, Silver Platter, or EBSCO). To cite material from an online database, begin with the author, the title of the article (in quotation marks), the title of the publication (in italics), the volume and issue numbers, the year of publication, and the page numbers (or the abbreviation *n. pag.*). Then add the name of the database (in italics), the medium of publication consulted (*Web*), and the date of access. You can find most of the information you need for a works-cited entry on the abstract page of the article you select (see fig. 33.5).

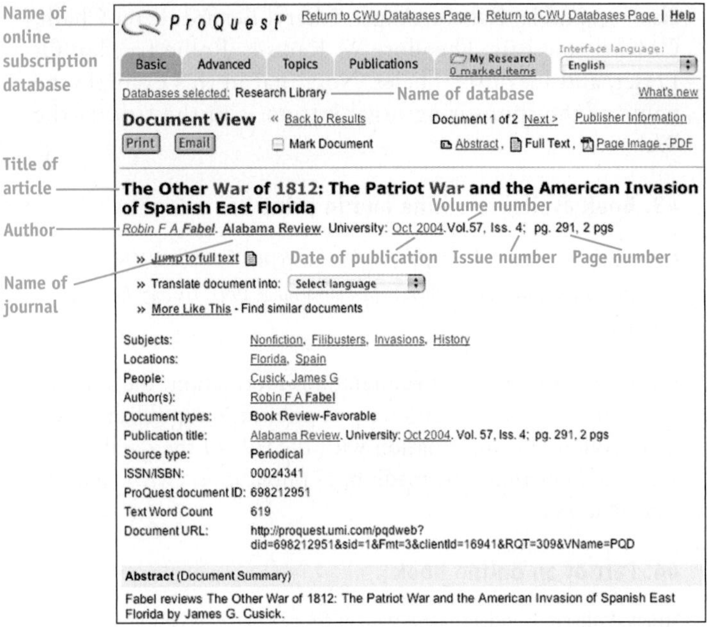

Name of
online
subscription
database

Title of
article

Author

Name of
journal

Figure 33.5. Abstract page from an online subscription database.

45. ERIC

Taylor, Steven J. "Caught in the Continuum: A Critical Analysis of the Principle
of the Least Restrictive Environment." *Research and Practice for Persons
with Severe Disabilities* 29.4 (2004): 218-30. *ERIC*. Web. 3 Mar. 2009.

46. EBSCO

Folks, Jeffrey J. "Crowd and Self: William Faulkner's Sources of Agency in
The Sound and the Fury." *Southern Literary Journal* 34.2 (2002): 30+.
EBSCO. Web. 6 June 2003.

For sources that list only the page number on which a work
begins, include that number followed by a plus sign.

47. LexisNexis

Suggs, Welch. "A Hard Year in College Sports." *Chronicle of Higher Education* 19 Dec. 2003: 37. *LexisNexis*. Web. 17 July 2004.

48. ProQuest

Fabel, Robin F. A. "The Other War of 1812: The Patriot War and the American Invasion of Spanish East Florida." *Alabama Review* 57.4 (2004): 291-92. *ProQuest*. Web. 8 Mar. 2005.

49. InfoTrac

Priest, Ann-Marie. "Between Being and Nothingness: The 'Astonishing Precipice' of Virginia Woolf's *Night and Day*." *Journal of Modern Literature* 26.2 (2002-03): 66-80. *InfoTrac*. Web. 12 Jan. 2004.

50. JSTOR

Blum, Susan D. "Five Approaches to Explaining 'Truth' and 'Deception' in Human Communication." *Journal of Anthropological Research* 61.3 (2005): 289-315. *JSTOR*. Web. 3 Mar. 2009.

51. Project MUSE

Muñoz, Alejandro Anaya. "Transnational and Domestic Processes in the Definition of Human Rights Policies in Mexico." *Human Rights Quarterly* 31.1 (2009): 35-58. *Project MUSE*. Web. 3 Mar. 2009.

52. Abstract from a subscription database

Landers, Susan J. "FDA Panel Findings Intensify Struggles with Prescribing of Antidepressants." *American Medical News* 47.37 (2004): 1-2. *ProQuest Direct*. Web. 7 Feb. 2005.

Online Communications and Web Sites

53. Web site

McGann, Jerome, ed. *The Complete Writings and Pictures of Dante Gabriel Rossetti*. Inst. for Advanced Technology in the Humanities, U of Virginia, n.d. Web. 16 Mar. 2009.

Include the name of the author, editor, compiler, director, or translator, followed by the title of the site (italicized), the version or edition (if given), the publisher or sponsor (if not available, use *N.p.*), the date of publication (if not available, use *n.d.*), the medium of publication (*Web*), and the date of access.

54. Web site with incomplete information

Breastcancer.org. N.p., 2 Feb. 2008. Web. 5 Feb. 2008.

If a Web site does not provide all the information usually included in a works-cited entry, list as much as is available.

55. Section of a Web site

Altman, Andrew. "Civil Rights." *Stanford Encyclopedia of Philosophy*. Ed. Edward N. Zalta. Center for the Study of Lang. and Information, Stanford U, 3 Feb. 2003. Web. 12 June 2003.

Mozart, Wolfgang Amadeus. "Concerto No. 3 for Horn, K. 447." *Essentials of Music*. Sony Music Entertainment, 2001. Web. 3 Mar. 2009.

56. Discussion group or forum

Schipper, William. "Re: Quirk and Wrenn Grammar." *Ansaxnet*. N.p., 5 Jan. 1995. Web. 12 Sept. 1996.

Provide the name of the forum (in this case, *Ansaxnet*) after the title of the work. If the posting is untitled, identify the genre (e.g., *Online posting*) instead of providing the title.

57. Newsgroup

May, Michaela. "Questions about RYAs." *Generation X.* N.p., 19 June 1996.

Web. 29 June 1996.

The name of a newsgroup (*Generation X*) takes the place of the title of the Web site.

58. Web log (blog)

Cuthbertson, Peter. "Are Left and Right Still Alright?" *Conservative*

Commentary. N.p., 7 Feb. 2005. Web. 18 Feb. 2005.

Other Online Documents

59. Online encyclopedia entry

"Iran." *Encyclopaedia Britannica Online.* Encyclopaedia Britannica, 2002.

Web. 6 Mar. 2004.

60. Online congressional document

United States. Cong. Senate. Special Committee on Aging. *Global Aging:*

Opportunity or Threat for the U.S. Economy? 108th Cong., 1st sess. S.

Hrg. 108-30. Washington: GPO, 2003. *GPO Access.* Web. 7 Jan. 2005.

Provide the number and session of Congress and the type and number of publication. (*S* stands for "Senate"; *H* or *HR* stands for "House of Representatives.")

Bills	S 41, HR 82
Reports	S. Rept. 14, H. Rept. 18
Hearings	S. Hrg. 23, H. Hrg. 25
Resolutions	S. Res. 32, H. Res. 52
Documents	S. Doc. 213, H. Doc. 123

MLA

61. Online document from a government office

United States. Dept. of State. Bur. of Democracy, Human Rights, and Labor.

 Guatemala Country Report on Human Rights Practices for 1998. Feb.

 1999. Web. 1 May 1999.

Begin with the name of the country, state, or city whose government is responsible for the document and the department or agency that issued it. If a subdivision of the larger organization is responsible, name the subdivision. If an author is identified, provide the name, preceded by the word *By*, between the title and the date of issue of the document.

62. Online law case

Tennessee v. Lane. 541 US 509. Supreme Court of the US. 2004. *Supreme*

 Court Collection. Legal Information Inst., Cornell U Law School, n.d.

 Web. 28 Jan. 2005.

63. Online public law

Individuals with Disabilities Education Act. Pub. L. 105-17. 104 Stat.

 587-698. *Thomas*. Lib. of Cong., 4 June 1997. Web. 29 Jan. 2005.

64. Online sacred text

Sama Veda. Trans. Ralph T. H. Griffith. 1895. *Sacred-Texts.com*. Ed. John B.

 Hare. N.p., 2008. Web. 6 Mar. 2008.

Online Recordings and Images

65. Online music

Moran, Jason. "Jump Up." *Same Mother*. Blue Note, 2005. *Blue Note*. Blue

 Note Records. Web. 7 Mar. 2005.

In this entry, "Blue Note" is the manufacturer of the CD, *Blue Note* is the title of the Web site where the song was accessed, and "Blue Note Records" is the sponsor of that site.

66. Online speech

Malcolm X. "The Ballot or the Bullet." Detroit. 12 Apr. 1964. *American*

> *Rhetoric: Top One Hundred Speeches*. Ed. Michael E. Eidenmuller.
>
> N.p., 2005. Web. 14 Jan. 2005.

"12 Apr. 1964" is the date the speech was delivered, "2005" is the year of the speech's electronic publication, and "14 Jan. 2005" is the date of access.

67. Online video

Riefenstahl, Leni, dir. *Triumph of the Will*. Reichsparteitag-Film, 1935.

> *Movieflix.com*. MovieFlix, 2005. Web. 17 Feb. 2005.

"1935" is the year in which the movie was originally released, "2005" is the year in which it was made available online, and "17 Feb. 2005" is the date of access.

68. Online television or radio program

"Religion and the American Election." Narr. Tony Hassan. *The Religion*

> *Report*. ABC Radio National, 3 Nov. 2004. Web. 18 Feb. 2005.

69. Online interview

McLaughlin, John. Interview by Wolf Blitzer. *CNN.com*. Cable News

> Network, 14 July 2004. Web. 21 Dec. 2004.

70. Online work of art

Vermeer, Johannes. *Young Woman with a Water Pitcher*. c. 1660.

> Metropolitan Museum of Art, New York. *The Metropolitan Museum*
>
> *of Art*. Web. 2 Oct. 2002.

71. Online photograph

Marmon, Lee. *Engine Rock*. 1985. *Lee Marmon Gallery*. Web. 9 Feb. 2009.

72. Online map or chart

"Virginia 1624." Map. *Map Collections 1544-1996*. Lib. of Cong. Web.
    26 Apr. 1999.

United States. Dept. of Health and Human Services. Centers for Disease
    Control and Prevention. "Daily Cigarette Smoking among High School
    Seniors." Chart. 27 Jan. 2005. *National Center for Health Statistics*.
    Web. 25 Feb. 2005.

73. Online advertisement

Milk Processor Education Program. "Got Milk?" Advertisement. *MilkPEP.*
    MilkPEP, n.d. Web. 16 Feb. 2005.

74. Online cartoon or comic strip

Cagle, Daryl. "Social Security Pays 3 to 2." Cartoon. *Slate.com*. Newsweek
    Interactive, 4 Feb. 2005. Web. 5 Feb. 2005.

OTHER COMMON SOURCES

Live and Recorded Performances

75. Play performance

Proof. By David Auburn. Dir. Daniel Sullivan. Walter Kerr Theater, New York.
    8 Oct. 2002. Performance.

Cite the date of the performance you attended.

76. Lecture or presentation

Guinier, Lani. Barbara Jordan Lecture Ser. Schwab Auditorium, Pennsylvania
    State U, University Park. 4 Oct. 2004. Address.

Scharnhorst, Gary. English 296.003. Dane Smith Hall, U of New Mexico,

>Albuquerque. 30 Apr. 2008. Class lecture.

Identify the site and the date of the lecture or presentation. Use the title if available; otherwise, provide a descriptive label.

77. Interview

Furstenheim, Ursula. Personal interview. 16 Jan. 2003.

Sugo, Misuzu. Telephone interview. 20 Feb. 2003.

For an interview you conducted, give only the name of the person you interviewed, the type of interview, and the date of the interview. If the interview was conducted by someone else, add the name of the interviewer, a title or a descriptive label, and the name of the source.

Harryhausen, Ray. Interview by Terry Gross. *Fresh Air*. Natl. Public Radio.

>WHYY, Philadelphia, 6 Jan. 2003. Radio.

78. Film

My Big Fat Greek Wedding. Dir. Joel Zwick. IFC, 2002. Film.

The name of the company that produced or distributed the film (IFC, in this case) appears before the year of release. It is not necessary to cite the city in which the production or distribution company is based.

When you want to highlight the contribution of a specific person, list the contributor's name first. Other supplementary information may be included after the title.

Gomez, Ian, perf. *My Big Fat Greek Wedding*. Screenplay by Nia Vardalos.

>Dir. Joel Zwick. IFC, 2002. Film.

79. Radio or television program

When referring to a specific episode, place quotation marks around its title. Italicize the title of the program.

"'Barbarian' Forces." *Ancient Warriors*. Narr. Colgate Salsbury. Dir. Phil
   Grabsky. Learning Channel. 1 Jan. 1996. Television.

To highlight a specific contributor or contributors, begin the entry
with the name or names and note the nature of the contribution.

Abumrad, Jad, and Robert Kulwich, narrs. "Choice." *Radiolab*. New York
   Public Radio. WNYC, New York, 14 Nov. 2008. Radio.

Works of Visual Art

80. Painting

Gauguin, Paul. *Ancestors of Tehamana*. 1893. Oil on canvas. Art Inst. of
   Chicago, Chicago.

Identify the artist's name, the title of the work (italicized), the
date of composition (if known; otherwise, write *N.d.*), the
medium of composition, the organization or individual holding the work, and the city in which the work is located. For a
photograph or reproduction of a work of art, provide the preceding information followed by complete publication information for the source, including medium of publication.

81. Photograph

Marmon, Lee. *White Man's Moccasins*. 1954. Photograph. Native American
   Cultural Center, Albuquerque.

Digital Sources

82. CD-ROM

"About *Richard III*." *Cinemania 96*. Redmond: Microsoft, 1996. CD-ROM.

Indicate which part of the CD-ROM you are using, and then
provide the title of the CD-ROM. Begin the entry with the
name of the author if one has been provided.

Jordan, June. "Moving towards Home." *Database of Twentieth-Century African American Poetry on CD-ROM.* Alexandria: Chadwyck-Healey, 1999. CD-ROM.

83. Work from a periodically published database on CD-ROM

Parachini, John V. *Combating Terrorism: The 9/11 Commission Recommendations and the National Strategies.* CD-ROM. *RAND Electronically Distributed Documents.* RAND. 2004. Disc 8.

84. DVD

A River Runs through It. Screenplay by Richard Friedenberg. Dir. Robert Redford. 1992. Columbia, 1999. DVD.

Cite relevant information about the title and director as you would for a film. Note the original release date of the film and the release date for the DVD. If the original company producing the film did not release the DVD, list the company that released the DVD instead.

85. Sound recording on CD

Franklin, Aretha. *Amazing Grace: The Complete Recordings.* Atlantic, 1999. CD.

For a sound recording on another medium, identify the type (*Audiocassette* or *LP*).

Raitt, Bonnie. *Nick of Time.* Capitol, 1989. Audiocassette.

When citing a recording of a specific song, begin with the name of the performer and place the song title in quotation marks. Identify the author(s) after the song title. If the performance is a reissue from an earlier recording, provide the original date of recording (preceded by *Rec.* for "Recorded").

Horne, Lena. "The Man I Love." By George Gershwin and Ira Gershwin. Rec. 15 Dec. 1941. *Stormy Weather.* BMG, 1990. CD.

33c   Sample MLA-style paper

(1) Submit a title page if your instructor requires one
The MLA recommends omitting a title page and instead providing identifying information on the first page of the paper. However, if your instructor requires a title page, type the title of the paper, your name, the instructor's name, the name of the course with its section number, and the date—all centered on the page.

(2) Sample MLA-style paper
Interested in the controversy surrounding genetically modified foods, Marianna Suslin explores both sides of the debate as she comes to her conclusion in the MLA-documented paper that follows.

TIPS FOR PREPARING AN MLA-STYLE PAPER

- Number all pages (including the first one) with an arabic numeral in the upper-right corner, one-half inch from the top. Put your last name before the page number.

- On the left side of the first page, one inch from the top, type a heading that includes your name, the name of your professor, the course number, and the date of submission.

- Double-space between the heading and the title of your paper, which should be centered on the page. If your title consists of two or more lines, double-space them and center each.

- Double-space between your title and the first line of text.

- Indent the first paragraph, and every subsequent paragraph, one-half inch.

- Double-space throughout.

1 inch

1/2 inch

Suslin 1   The writer's
last name
Marianna Suslin   and the page
number
Professor Squier

Sociology 299, Section 1   — Heading

27 November 2007

Genetically Modified Foods and Developing Countries   Center the
title.
Since the 1960s, thousands of genetically modified plants,

also referred to as "genetically modified organisms" (GMOs)

and "transgenic crops," have been introduced to global markets.   Double-
space
Those who argue for the support of genetic modification claim that   throughout.

the crops have higher yield, grow in harsher conditions, benefit

the ecology, and hold great potential for benefiting poor farmers

in developing countries. Despite these claims, the practice of

genetic engineering—of inserting genetic material into the DNA   Use
one-inch
of a plant—continues to be controversial, with no clear answers   margins
on both
as to whether genetically engineered foods can be the answer for   sides of
the page.
developing countries.

One of the most important potential benefits of the technology   Thesis

to both proponents and opponents of genetic engineering is its

potential to improve the economies of developing countries.

According to Sakiko Fukuda-Parr, "Investing in agricultural

technology increasingly turns up these days on the lists of the top ten

practical actions the rich world could take to contribute to reducing

1 inch

Suslin 2

global poverty." Agriculture is the source of income for the world's poorest—70 percent of those living on less than a dollar a day support themselves through agriculture. These farmers could benefit greatly from higher yield crops that could grow in nutrient poor soil. Genetic modification "has shown how high-yielding varieties developed at international centers can be adapted to local conditions, dramatically increasing yields and farm incomes" (Fukuda-Parr 3).

Theoretically, genetic engineering can bring about an increase in farm productivity that would give people in developing countries the chance to enter the global market on better terms. Developing countries are often resource poor and thus have little more than labor to contribute to the world economy. Farming tends to be subsistence level, as farmers can grow only enough on the land—which tends to be nutrient poor—to feed themselves. But the higher yield of

genetically modified crops, along with their resistance to pests and ability to thrive in nutrient poor soil, can enable the farmers to produce more crops, maybe to the point of exporting extra crops not needed for subsistence (Fukuda-Parr 1). Genetic modification can also help poor farmers by using genetics to delay the ripening process and thereby allowing the farmer to store the crops longer, have more time in which to sell the crops without fear of spoilage,

Suslin 3

and avoid the heavy losses caused by "uncontrolled ripening and spoiling of fruits and vegetables" (Royal Society et al. 238).

Citation of a work by an organization

Today, eighteen percent of people living in developing countries do not have enough food to meet their needs (Royal Society et al. 235). "Malnutrition plays a significant role in half of the nearly 12 million deaths each year of children under five in developing countries" (UNICEF, qtd. in Royal Society et al. 235). Genetically modified foods producing large yields in nutrient poor soils could help feed the world's increasing population and combat malnutrition, since scientists are working on ways to make the genetically modified foods more nutritious than unmodified crops. Genetically modified rice, for example, has already been created that "exhibits an increased production of beta-carotene," which is a precursor to vitamin A (Royal Society et al. 240). Because vitamin A deficiencies are common in developing countries and contribute to half a million children becoming partially or totally blind each year, advances in genetic engineering offer hope for millions of people who live with nutrient deficiencies (Royal Society et al. 239).

Proponents of genetic engineering have also argued that genetically modified crops have the potential to decrease the amount of damage modern farming technologies have on ecology at the

Suslin 4

same time that they improve the economy. For example, genetically modified plants with resistance to certain insects would decrease the amount of pesticides that farmers have to use. Genes for insect resistance have already been introduced into cotton, making possible a huge decrease in insecticide use (Royal Society et al. 238). A decrease in the amount of pesticides used is good from an ecological perspective.[1] Pesticides not only can be washed into streams and be harmful to wildlife but have also been known to appear in groundwater, thus potentially causing harm to humans.

Scientists have argued that genetic engineering is only the latest step in the human involvement in plant modification that has been going on for thousands of years.[2] Since the dawn of the agricultural revolution, people have been breeding plants for desirable traits and thus altering the genetic makeup of plant populations. Genetic engineering, however, produces plants with the desirable trait much faster (Fukuda-Parr 5).

While there are many potential benefits that can come from genetic engineering for farmers in developing countries and even in the United States, many people remain skeptical about this new technology. Many Americans are uneasy about consuming foods that have been genetically enhanced, citing the potential risks of consuming GMOs, which outweigh the benefits

A super-script number indicates an endnote.

MLA

Suslin 5

of this new technology (Brossard, Shanahan, and Nesbitt 10).
Considering the risks of genetically modified foods, people
in developing countries are likely to feel the same way: that
the risks outweigh the benefits. No matter how many potential
benefits genetically modified crops may bring, if they are not
safe for consumption, they will not help but hurt the economies
of developing countries.

In "Genetically Modified Food Threatens Human Health,"
Jeffrey Smith argues that inserting foreign genetic material into
food is extremely dangerous because it may create unknown toxins
or allergens. Smith points to the fact that gene insertion could
also damage a plant's DNA in unpredictable ways. For example,
when scientists were working with the soybean plant, the process
of inserting the foreign gene damaged a section of the plant's own
DNA, "scrambling its genetic code" (105). The sequence of the gene
that was inserted had inexplicably rearranged itself over time. The
protein the gene creates as a result of this rearrangement is likely to be
different, and since this new protein has not been evaluated for safety,
it could be harmful or toxic (105).

In *Genetically Modified Food: A Short Guide for the
Confused*, Andy Rees argues a similar point: genetically modified
foods carry unpredictable health risks. He cites the 1989 incident in

The writer describes disadvantages of eating genetically modified foods.

Direct quotation of a phrase from a cited work

Suslin 6

which bacteria genetically modified to produce large amounts of
the food supplement L-tryptophan "yielded impressively toxic
contaminants that killed 37 people, partially paralyzed 1,500 and
temporarily disabled 5,000 in the US" (75). Rees also argues that
genetically modified foods have possible carcinogenic effects:
"Given the huge complexity of genetic coding, even in very
simple organisms such as bacteria, no one can possibly predict
the overall, long-term effects of GM [genetically modified] foods
on the health of those who eat them" (78). Rees cites the 1999
study on male rats fed genetically modified potatoes, explaining
that the genetically modified potatoes had "a powerful effect on
the lining of the gut (stomach, small bowel, and colon)" leading
to a proliferation of cells, which according to histopathologist
Stanley Ewen, is then likely to "act on any polyp present in the
colon . . . and drastically accelerate the development of cancer in
susceptible persons" (qtd. in Rees 78).

In addition to the health risks involved in consuming
genetically modified foods, some experts also argue that such
foods will not benefit farmers in developing countries but will
aid big corporations here in the United States. In "The Emperor's
New Crops," Brian Halweil brings up the fact that global sales for
genetically modified crops grew from seventy-five million dollars

Three ellipsis points mark an omission in quoted material.

Suslin 7

in 1995 to one and a half billion dollars in 1998. Genetically modified crops are obviously lucrative for large companies. In addition, of the fifty-six transgenic products approved for commercial planting in 1998, thirty-three belonged to just four corporations (Halweil 256).

The spread of genetic engineering can change power relations between nations (Cook 3). The big American corporations that sell genetically modified seeds can hold power over the governments of developing countries, hindering their further economic development. Because all transgenic seeds are patented, it is illegal for farmers to practice "seed saving" (reserving a certain amount of seeds from the harvest to plant in the next growing season). Farmers thus have to depend entirely on the big corporations for their seeds. Since these corporations have a monopoly on genetically modified seeds, the prices for these seeds are likely to remain high, and poor farmers are unlikely to be able to afford them. Genetically altered seeds can then become just one more way that rich countries and their corporations exploit the people of developing countries. Thus, genetic engineering could become one more way of hindering the development of poor countries—not the opportunity for economic improvement and increased social equality that its proponents claim it is. Unscrupulous companies could also use the economic vulnerability of developing countries to develop and test genetically modified products that have

The writer focuses on social issues related to genetically modified foods.

Suslin 8

been rejected in the United States or Europe (Newell 68), thereby
rendering harm to people in developing countries.

With many concerned about the health risks associated with
GMOs, international organizations such as Greenpeace and Friends
of the Earth have advocated food labeling, believing that consumers
should have the right to choose whether or not to buy and expose
themselves to the risks associated with consuming GMOs (Huffman 3).
The FDA, however, contends that scientific studies "detect no
substantial difference between food from traditional crops and GM
crops" (*Federal Register*) and regards genetic modification as not
altering the product enough to require labeling. Interestingly, one
of the reasons for not labeling genetically modified food is the
concern that consumers will shun the products with the GMO label,
and thus the industry producing genetic modifications will suffer
(Weirich 17). The interests of corporate giants, therefore, appear to
be able to influence decision making in the United States, where the
government and economy are comparatively strong. The impact of
corporations on the governments of poorer countries, then, is likely
to be much more pronounced, and poorer countries are likely to be
victimized by big corporations.

Moreover, there is some evidence that genetically modified
foods do not live up to their promise and, therefore, lack the

The writer
continues to
explore both
sides of the
controversy.

M L A

benefits that could help farmers in poor countries. Rees argues that genetically modified crops will not be able to ameliorate world hunger. Rather, he believes that more than enough food is produced to feed everyone in the world without these crops and that people go hungry because they cannot afford to buy from the plenty around them for socioeconomic reasons (49). Rees also argues that genetically modified crops have not increased farmers' incomes, regardless of what proponents of genetic engineering may claim. He points to a 2003 study by Professor Caroline Saunders at Lincoln University, New Zealand, which found that "GM food releases have not benefited producers anywhere in the world" and that "the soil association's 2002 'Seeds of Doubt' report, created with feedback from farmers and data from six years of commercial farming in North America, shows that GM soy and maize crops deliver less income to farmers (on average) than non-GM crops" (50-51). The potential benefit of genetically modified crops thus remains uncertain.

While proponents of genetic engineering insist that genetically modified crops can increase yield and help feed the hungry, opponents point to health risks and challenge the research that appears to prove that genetically modified foods are beneficial. However, even if genetically modified crops do prove to be as beneficial as proponents claim, there is nothing to ensure that this

Suslin 10

technology would benefit poor farmers in developing countries.

Since large corporations hold patents on all genetically modified

seeds, there is nothing to guarantee that poor farmers would have

access to these seeds, no matter how advanced or beneficial the

technology turns out to be. As of now, developing countries continue

to be at a disadvantage despite the creation and wide distribution of

genetically modified crops. Therefore, it is far from certain whether

this new technology will benefit developing nations in the dramatic

way that proponents of genetic engineering assert.

The writer's conclusion is drawn from research reported on the previous pages.

Suslin 11

Notes

Center the heading.

1. There is some concern, however, about the long-term effects of crops genetically engineered for pest resistance. Since these plants are engineered to continually produce a form of the pesticide used to combat the pest problem, insects are constantly exposed to the chemical used to kill them. Such exposure increases the likelihood that the insects will develop a tolerance for this chemical, making the pesticide ineffective.

2. The main difference between genetic engineering and the breeding of plants for desired traits that people have practiced for thousands of years is that genetic engineering actually alters the DNA of a particular plant. Traditional breeding cannot alter the DNA of an individual plant but instead seeks to increase the number of plants that have a trait that occurs naturally. While the end product of both genetic engineering and selective breeding is similar in that both produce plants with desirable traits, the actual processes are radically different.

Numbers on notes match the superscript numbers in the body of the paper.

MLA

The writer continues to explore both sides of the controversy.

Center the heading.

Works Cited

Alphabetize the entries according to the authors' last names.

Brossard, Dominique, James Shanahan, and T. Clint Nesbitt, eds. *The*

Public, the Media, and Agricultural Biotechnology. Cambridge:

CABI, 2007. Print.

Cook, Guy. *Genetically Modified Language: The Discourse of*

Indent second and subsequent lines of each entry one-half inch.

Arguments for GM Crops and Food. New York: Routledge,

2005. Print.

Easton, Thomas A., ed. *Taking Sides: Clashing Views on*

Controversial Environmental Issues. 11th ed. Dubuque:

McGraw, 2005. Print.

Federal Register 54.104 (1992): 22991. Print.

Fukuda-Parr, Sakiko, ed. *The Gene Revolution: GM Crops and*

Unequal Development. Sterling: Earthscan, 2007. Print.

The medium is provided in the Easton entry and is not repeated in the entries for works included in that book.

Halweil, Brian. "The Emperor's New Crops." Easton 249-59.

Huffman, W. E. "Production, Identity Preservation, and Labeling in

a Marketplace with Genetically Modified and Non-Genetically

Modified Foods." *Plant Physiology* 134 (2004): 3-10. Web. 5 Nov.

2007.

Newell, Peter. "Corporate Power and 'Bounded Autonomy' in the

Global Politics of Biotechnology." *The International Politics of*

Genetically Modified Food: Diplomacy, Trade, and Law. Ed.

Robert Falkner. Hampshire: Palgrave, 2007. 67-84. Print.

Rees, Andy. *Genetically Modified Food: A Short Guide for the Confused*. Ann Arbor: Pluto, 2006. Print.

Royal Society et al. "Transgenic Plants and World Agriculture." Easton 234-45.

Smith, Jeffrey M. "Genetically Modified Food Threatens Human Health." *Humanity's Future*. Ed. Louise I. Gerdes. Detroit: Gale, 2006. 103-08. Print.

Weirich, Paul, ed. *Labeling Genetically Modified Food: The Philosophical and Legal Debate*. New York: Oxford UP, 2007. Print.

34 Writing in the Social Sciences

The **social sciences** include such disciplines as psychology, anthropology, sociology, political science, and economics. Researchers in these disciplines study how humans behave as members of groups—families, peer groups, ethnic communities, political parties, and many others. The goal of research in the social sciences is to examine and explain behavior occurring under a particular set of circumstances. For example, Danielle Dezell, the student whose report is featured later in this chapter, investigated whether students depend on gender stereotypes to assign status to certain occupations. Typical assignments in the social sciences are library research papers, case studies, and laboratory or field reports.

34a Audience, purpose, and the research question

The first step toward completing a writing assignment for a course in the social sciences is to determine your audience and purpose. Your audience will always include your instructor, but it could include students in your class and sometimes people outside your class. Identifying your audience will help you decide how much background information to present, how much technical language to include, and what types of reasoning and sources to use.

Once you know what your purpose is and to whom you are writing, you can craft a research question that will help you find sources, evaluate them, and use them responsibly. Here are some examples of types of research questions that could be posed about the topic of community service performed by students:

Question about causes or purposes

Why do students perform community service?

Question about consequences

What do students believe they have learned through their community service?

Question about process

How do college instructors help students get involved in community service?

Question about definitions or categories

What does community service entail?

Question about values

What values do instructors hope to cultivate by encouraging students to perform community service?

34b Evidence, sources, and reasoning

Researchers in the social sciences study the behavior of humans and other animals. To make accurate observations of their subjects' activities, these researchers either design controlled laboratory experiments or conduct field research. Interviews and surveys are the two most common techniques for gathering data in the field, although observations are also widely used. Both laboratory experiments and field research yield data that social-science researchers can use as evidence to make statements (or claims) about the behavior of humans and other animals.

Researchers in the social sciences distinguish between quantitative studies and qualitative studies. **Quantitative studies,** such as laboratory experiments and surveys, yield data that can be presented in numerical form, as statistics. Using statistical data and formulas, researchers show how likely it is for a behavior to occur or to have certain consequences. If you decide to undertake a quantitative study, you should turn your research question into a **hypothesis,** an objective prediction of what the results of your experiment or survey will be. The results of your study will either prove or disprove your hypothesis. Be prepared to provide possible explanations for either outcome.

Hypotheses are best formed after a sustained period of observation and preliminary research. When presenting her hypothesis about gender stereotypes and occupational status, Danielle Dezell states her prediction in the context of existing research.

> Although studies have not correlated participant gender and occupational status (Parker et al., 1989), Teig and Susskind (2008) found that occupational gender did correlate with occupational status. The current study expects to find that people's ranking of occupational status correlates with the stereotyped gender of the occupation.

Researchers who perform **qualitative studies,** such as observations and interviews, are interested in interpreting behavior by first watching, listening to, or interacting with individuals or a group. If you decide to conduct a qualitative study, you will not reason *from* a hypothesis but will reason *to* a hypothesis. You will observe a phenomenon and note what you see or hear. Then, instead of reporting numbers as evidence, you will provide detailed descriptions and discuss their significance.

Researchers in the social sciences recognize that some studies have both quantitative and qualitative features. They also expect to use both primary and secondary sources in many of their research projects. Primary sources consist of data derived from experiments, observations, surveys, or interviews. Secondary sources are articles or case studies written about a research topic.

34c Conventions of language and organization

(1) Style guidelines

Most of the social sciences follow the guidelines presented in the *Publication Manual of the American Psychological Association*. This manual stresses the importance of writing prose that is clear, concise, unbiased, and well organized. The following specific tips can help you write in the style recommended by the manual.

TIPS FOR PREPARING A PAPER IN THE SOCIAL SCIENCES

- Use the active voice as often as possible, although the passive voice may be acceptable for describing methodology.

- Choose verb tenses carefully. Use the present tense to discuss results and report conclusions (as in "The findings suggest . . ."). Reserve the past tense for referring to specific events in the past and for describing your procedures (as in "Each participant signed a consent form . . .").

- Use a first-person pronoun rather than referring to yourself or to any coauthor(s) and yourself in the third person.

  We
  ∧ ~~The experimenters~~ retested each participant after a rest period.

- Clarify noun strings by placing the main noun first.

  the method for testing literacy NOT the literacy testing method

---

(2) Organization

Assignments in the social sciences will generally require you to (1) state a research question, thesis, or hypothesis; (2) discuss research that has already been published about your topic; (3) describe your methodology; and (4) present your conclusions or results.

To organize the information they are presenting, writers in the social sciences use tables and graphs as well as headings, which are designed to signal levels of importance. Danielle Dezell includes a table to display her results (see page 365). If you decide to use a table in your paper, be sure to refer to the table by number (for example, Table 1) and explain the significance of the information it provides. Without a brief discussion of the table, your readers may have difficulty understanding why you included it.

Graphs provide a visual representation of data. Danielle uses line graphs to highlight her comparison of gender stereotypes and perceptions of occupational status (see page 367). Graphs are labeled as numbered figures. Like tables, they should be discussed in the text.

(3) Reference list

At the end of any paper you write for a course in the social sciences, you should include a list of all the sources you used. You can find sample lists of references on pages 370–371 and 400.

34d Examples of writing in the social sciences

(1) Library research report

Library research reports are written by both students and professionals. The purpose of such reports is to bring together several related sources on a specific topic in order to examine that topic closely. Writing such a report will require you to read a number of sources and then summarize, critique, and synthesize those sources. Library research reports generally include the following elements:

- Statement of the research question or thesis
- Presentation of background information, using sources
- Discussion of major findings presented in the sources
- Application of those findings to the specific research question
- Conclusions
- References

An excerpt from a library research report is shown in figure 34.1. In the report's introduction, authors Matthew

The first paragraph presents past studies on the topic.

The next paragraph discusses gaps in the research.

INTRODUCTION

LAUGHTER AND HUMOR were accorded high evolutionary significance by Darwin (1872) and have received increasing attention from biologists and psychologists during the last 30 years. This attention has resulted in myriad empirical advances and has left laughter and humor well characterized on multiple proximate levels (see Provine 2000; Vaid 2002; Bachorowski and Owren 2003; van Hooff and Preuschoft 2003; Wild, Rodden et al. 2003). Laudably, this research has spawned a number of hypotheses attempting to explain the ultimate evolutionary origins of laughter and humor (e.g., Eibl-Eibesfeldt 1989; Weisfeld 1994; Pinker 1997; Ramachandran 1998; Harris 1999; Miller 2000; Provine 2000; Owren and Bachorowski 2001; Caron 2002; Howe 2002; Jung 2003; Storey 2003). Nevertheless, the scientific study of laughter and humor is still in its infancy relative to other comparable subjects in emotions and communication research.

Many empirical questions about laughter and humor remain unanswered or neglected. For example, most researchers (e.g., Provine 2000; Owren and Bachorowski 2003; Vettin and Todt 2004) have failed to make the important distinction between Duchenne (stimulus-driven and emotionally valenced) and non-Duchenne (self-generated and emotionless) laughter (Keltner and Bonanno 1997; see also Wild, Rodden et al. 2003). While laughter has recently been found to occur most frequently during casual conversation and not following deliberate humor (Provine 1993; LaGreca et al. 1996; Vettin and Todt 2004), researchers have yet to question whether such conversational laughter is different in kind from that following humor. This oversight might well be the root cause of the widespread confusion concerning the diversity of forms and functions that characterizes laughter today (Keltner and Bonanno 1997).

Figure 34.1. An excerpt from the introduction of a library research report.

Gervais and David Sloan Wilson present background information for their study. Notice that the authors maintain a neutral stance that conveys an impression of impartiality, although they clearly and strongly state their point of view.

(2) Case study

A case study is a qualitative project that requires a researcher to describe a particular participant or group of participants. The researcher refrains from making generalizations about the participant(s) in the study and instead focuses on the behavior of the participant(s). After describing the behavior, the researcher usually suggests a solution to the problem faced by the participant(s). Most case studies include the following information:

- An introduction to the participant(s)
- A description of the problem
- Observations
- A presentation of strategies to solve the problem

Figure 34.2 is an excerpt from a case study, one of many that can be found on the Web site *Improving Provision for Disabled Psychology Students.*

Introduction of the participant and description of the problem

> Bill is a . . . psychology student with dyslexia. In addition to difficulties with arithmetic and organisational skills, he has particular problems with short-term memory. . . .
>
> He has always found psychology a fascinating subject. Though he doesn't feel that his impairment directed his decision to study psychology, he suggests that it may be one reason why he was interested in "how the mind works."

Observations

> Bill finds that he has to work harder than most people to achieve the same level of performance. Since reading takes him a long time, he has found it difficult to keep up with all the allocated work necessary for the degree, and feels overwhelmed by the sheer volume and rate of work he has to get through. The biggest barrier he has to overcome is only having a period of one week to submit some of his laboratory reports: "I can't even get the reading for lab reports done in the week we have to complete reports, never mind getting the actual report written up!"

Strategies for solving the problem

> In terms of more positive experiences, he has found it particularly beneficial when lecturers put their lecture slides on the web before classes, giving him adequate time to print them out and thus enabling him to make notes on the printed-out slide during the lecture. This saves him from having to take so many notes, and allows him time to take in the material that is being taught.

Figure 34.2. An excerpt from a case study posted online.

34e Laboratory or field (observation) report

Social science students and professionals often conduct research in a laboratory or in the field (that is, in a natural setting). Reports based on this type of research contain standard sections: introduction, method, results, and discussion. An example of a laboratory report is Danielle Dezell's paper on gender stereotypes and occupations. Written according to the style guidelines of the American Psychological Association (APA), her report includes all the standard sections. Because Danielle asked fellow students to participate in her study, she was required to submit a proposal for her study and a consent form to the institutional review board at her university for approval. Although Danielle collaborated with Cameron Dooley and Elaine Acosta on the experiment described in the report, she wrote the report on her own.

Gender Stereotypes and Perceptions of Occupational Status

Among University Students

Danielle Dezell

Central Washington University

Abstract

The writer introduces the purpose of the study.

This study investigated whether the gender of participants affected their view of certain occupations and whether the gender typically associated with an occupation affected participants' ranking of the status of that occupation. Participants were asked (1) to write a response to a prompt designed to elicit gender-specific pronouns and (2) to rate the status of one of three occupations typically associated with a gender. The results were compared to see whether the interaction between participant gender and stereotypical occupational gender influenced the perception of the status of the occupation and to discover whether participant gender influenced the perception of occupational gender.

GENDER STEREOTYPES AND PERCEPTIONS   3

Gender Stereotypes and Perceptions of Occupational Status

Among University Students

Occupational gender stereotypes are important to examine
for their possible influence not only on a person's occupational
choice but also on perceptions of status associated with
occupations. When university-age students consider possible
careers, they often choose one based on their own gender and
on the stereotypical gender assigned to an occupation (Evans &
Diekman, 2009). They may also choose an occupation
according to the status they believe it to have. An investigation
into gender stereotypes about occupations is a first step in
limiting their influence on students' career choices.

Gender stereotypes begin in early childhood, when
children see how society views certain professions. These
societal influences can have long-term effects on how children may
stereotype various occupations (Firestone, Harris, & Lambert,
1999). Several studies using school-age children as participants
have examined the strength of these early stereotypes. Miller
and Hayward (2006) showed that participants often preferred
occupations that were stereotyped to their own gender (i.e.,
boys preferred stereotypically male jobs, and girls preferred
stereotypically female jobs). Another study conducted by Teig

The writer establishes the importance of her report.

By discussing the work of other researchers, the writer not only provides readers with necessary information but also demonstrates her credibility.

GENDER STEREOTYPES AND PERCEPTIONS   4

and Susskind (2008) looked at both status and stereotypes. When participants were asked to rate the status of jobs, the researchers found that out of the 18 highest ranked jobs, only 3 were classified as feminine. Of all the occupations, 27.8% of masculine occupations had a high status ranking, while 15.4% of feminine occupations had a high status ranking. Participants in this study classified both *librarian* and *elementary school teacher* as stereotypically feminine occupations. The researchers found that there was a significant correlation between the gender of the participant and how he or she ranked the status of an occupation. However, the researchers pointed out that as girls grew older, their tendency to stereotype lessened. Boys, though, continued to carry gender stereotypes into adulthood. Miller and Hayward (2006) noted that men generally prefer occupations traditionally performed by men.

In a study whose participants were college-age students, Shinar (1975) looked at how the participants rated the masculinity and femininity of various occupations on a 1-to-7 Likert scale (1 being *masculine* and 7 being *feminine*). The study showed that both men and women held gender stereotypes about certain occupations. The participants rated *miner* as a fully masculine job (mean rating of 1.000) and *manicurist* as a mostly

The writer refers to previous studies and synthesizes their findings.

GENDER STEREOTYPES AND PERCEPTIONS   5

feminine job (mean rating of 6.667). Shinar also reported that
head librarian had a mean rating of 5.583, *high school teacher* a
mean rating of 4.000, and *carpenter* a mean rating of 1.667. What
is interesting is that Shinar showed that both women and men
demonstrated gender stereotyping, whereas, over 30 years later,
Seguino (2007) and Miller and Hayward (2006) found that men had
much stronger stereotypes than women. Miller and Hayward also
suggested that women grow out of a stereotyping mindset by age 18.

   Although certain occupations clearly seem to be gender
stereotyped, occupational status is not always related to gender.
Parker, Chan, and Saper (1989) found that there was no significant
correlation between participant gender and occupational status
ratings. It might be tempting to believe that jobs associated with
masculinity would be ranked as having higher social status, but
these researchers showed that the status of many traditionally
masculine jobs (e.g., *heavy equipment operator*) was considered
low. This finding is especially interesting because it suggests
that when people choose an occupation, they might rely more
on the perception of the gender associated with an occupation
than on the perception of status.

   One way to test how people stereotype a job according
to gender is to ask them to assign a pronoun to a certain

The writer adds
her own voice to
the discussion
of gender
stereotypes.

GENDER STEREOTYPES AND PERCEPTIONS   6

occupation. This simple test provides insight into how gender

stereotypes of occupations work and whether males or females

are more likely to hold such stereotypes. A study looking at the

gender people attributed to different gender-neutral characters

introduced in a dialogue script found that both men and women

were more likely to assume that a character was male. The same

study also found that men and women had equal biases toward

gender assumptions (Merritt & Kok, 1995). In a similar study,

participants were asked to attribute a gender to various stuffed

animals. Both children and adults used the male pronoun to

describe stuffed animals that were gender-neutral (Lambdin,

Greer, Jibotian, Wood, & Hamilton, 2003).

This study aims to discover both whether participants

stereotype certain occupations as being either male or female

and whether participants rate the status of an occupation based

on whether the occupation has historically been a masculine,

feminine, or gender-neutral occupation. The findings of previous

studies suggest that both males and females do stereotype certain

occupations. Although studies have not correlated participant

gender and occupational status (Parker et al., 1989), Teig and

Susskind (2008) found that occupational gender did correlate

with occupational status. The current study expects to find

After reporting the work of other researchers in previous paragraphs, the writer now introduces her hypothesis.

GENDER STEREOTYPES AND PERCEPTIONS 7

that people's ranking of occupational status correlates with the

stereotyped gender of the occupation.

Method

Participants

A total of eight groups participated in the study. Numbers

of participants in each group varied. Overall, there were 40

participants, 11 males and 29 females. All participants were

students at Central Washington University and were 19 years old

or older. The participants were all volunteers and were randomly

assigned to one of three experimental conditions.

Materials

The materials for each experimental condition were a sheet

of paper that presented one of three different writing prompts and

asked for four pieces of demographic information. A script from

which the researcher read was also used. Each writing prompt

was a scenario about an employee of a school who had a problem;

however, the employee's occupation in each prompt differed. The

occupations and their associated gender stereotypes were as follows:

librarian (female), *woodshop teacher* (male), and *high school*

teacher (gender neutral). The occupations were chosen based on the

percentage of females employed in each occupation, according to

statistics from the Bureau of Labor Statistics (Bureau of Labor

Information on methodology helps readers decide whether the researcher's findings are reliable and valid.

GENDER STEREOTYPES AND PERCEPTIONS   8

Statistics, 2010). The statistics showed that *high school teacher* was

the most gender-neutral occupation (54.9% female). The occupation

librarian was found to be gender segregated toward females (81.8%

female). There were no statistics for *woodshop teacher*, though there

were statistics for *carpenter* (1.6% female). Because most carpenters

are male, it is quite likely that most people would stereotype the

occupation of woodshop teacher as male. A focus on jobs that were

all in a school environment prevented the creation of confounds

based on the status of a work environment.

The writing prompts excluded any language that might

allow the participant to infer the gender of the person in the

prompt (e.g., no pronouns were used). A five-point Likert

scale was used to measure how participants rated the status

of an occupation. Each of the three prompt sheets used

identical wording in the directions, prompts, Likert scale, and

demographic items (i.e., gender, age, class standing, and major);

the only difference among the prompts was the occupation used.

Procedure

Each group of participants had two administrators. The study

took approximately 15 minutes. One administrator passed out

consent forms, collected them, and then distributed the prompts,

while the other administrator read the appropriate directions from

GENDER STEREOTYPES AND PERCEPTIONS 9

the script. Once the participants had the prompt, they were given 10 minutes to complete the story. After the administrators collected the stories, participants were debriefed and provided with the opportunity to ask questions.

Results

The descriptive statistics can be found in Table 1. A two-way between-subjects ANOVA with $\alpha = .05$ showed that the interaction between participant gender and occupation in the prompts was not significant, $F(2, 34) = .88$, $p > .05$. Of the two main effects,

Statistics are used to report results.

Table 1
Descriptive Statistics

Gender of Participant	Occupation in Prompt	Mean	Std. Deviation	N
F	Librarian	2.75	.452	12
	High School Teacher	2.75	.463	8
	Woodshop Teacher	2.56	.527	9
	Total	2.69	.471	29
M	Librarian	5.00	.545	1
	High School Teacher	3.20	1.304	5
	Woodshop Teacher	3.20	.837	5
	Total	3.36	1.120	11
Total	Librarian	2.92	.760	13
	High School Teacher	2.92	.862	13
	Woodshop Teacher	2.79	.699	14
	Total	2.88	.757	40

GENDER STEREOTYPES AND PERCEPTIONS   10

only gender was significant, $F(1, 34) = .001$, $p < .05$. However, occupation had a nonsignificant main effect, $F(2, 34) = .052$, $p > .05$. The averages of means are graphed in Figure 1. The homogeneity of variance test was significant, $F(5, 34) = .003$, $p < .05$. The first chi-square test, which was run on the interaction between participant gender and type of pronoun used by the participant in responding to the prompt, had a Pearson's correlation of .267, which is not significant. The second chi-square test between occupation in the prompt and pronoun type had a highly significant Pearson's correlation of .000.

Discussion

The statistics reported in the previous section are explained in this section.

The results of the study showed that there was no interaction between the status ranking of an occupation and the gender stereotyping of that occupation. This is contrary to the findings of Teig and Susskind (2008), who found that the gender stereotype of an occupation affects the rating of its status. However, it is similar to the findings of Parker et al. (1989), who showed that the gender of a participant had no bearing on occupational status. All three occupations were ranked on average as having medium status (mean of 2.875). *Librarian* had a mean status of 2.92; *high school teacher*, a mean status of 2.92; and *woodshop teacher*, a mean status of 2.79. While there may

GENDER STEREOTYPES AND PERCEPTIONS   11

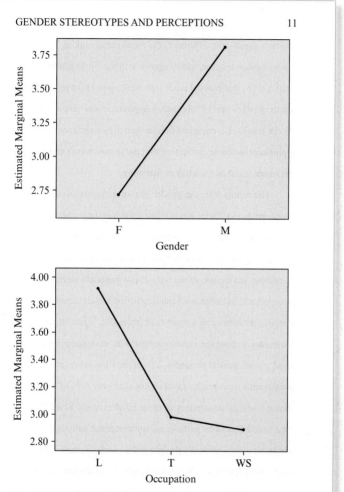

Figure 1. Means for main effects.

GENDER STEREOTYPES AND PERCEPTIONS   12

not be a significant difference, the mean status ranking is lowest

for *woodshop teacher*, which agrees with the finding of Parker

et al. (2008) that manual labor jobs were rated as having a lower

status. Neither part of this study's hypothesis was supported

by the results. Levene's test of homogeneity of variance had a

significant outcome, indicating that the groups were unequal and

the result is not due to random sampling.

The results from the gender-stereotyping tests were

more intriguing. There was a significant correlation between

the occupation mentioned in the prompt and the type of

pronoun chosen by the participant to respond to the prompt

(feminine, masculine, or neutral). Participants did stereotype the

occupations, but what is interesting is that females used gender-

specific pronouns much more than males did. When writing

their stories about the various occupations, male participants

used gender-neutral pronouns 72% of the time, whereas female

participants used gender-neutral pronouns only 41% of the time.

The writer compares her results with those of other researchers.

These findings are contrary to those of Merritt and Kok (1995),

who found that when participants are presented with unspecified

characters, they generally designate the gender as male. The

findings of this study also contradict the occupational-stereotype

findings of Shinar (1975), who stated that men use stereotypes

GENDER STEREOTYPES AND PERCEPTIONS   13

more than women, and of Miller and Hayward (2006), who
reported that females tend to use fewer stereotypes once they are
enrolled in college.

One of the biggest limitations of the study was that there
were so few participants, especially men. Data elicited from a
larger number of male participants would have provided a more
accurate picture of how men view occupational stereotypes.
The prompts could also have been worded better. Because of
the awkward wording of the prompts, participants had a good
idea of what the study was looking for and so may have adjusted
their responses. Another limitation is that there were only
three occupations. Including a greater number of occupations
would have made it possible to state conclusions about gender
stereotypes more firmly. Future studies should include not only
more occupations but also occupations that obviously have
different statuses. This study chose occupations that were all in
the same environment in order to avoid confounds; however, if
there were many different types of occupations from a variety
of environments, participants might not be able to determine
as easily the researcher's intent. Despite these limitations, this
study suggests that people are starting to have fewer assumptions
about the relation between gender and occupation.

The writer
acknowledges
some
limitations of
the study.

References

Bureau of Labor Statistics. (2010). *Household data: Annual averages* [Data file]. Retrieved from http://www.bls.gov/cps/cpsaat11

Evans, C., & Diekman, A. (2009). On motivated role selection: Gender beliefs, distant goals, and career interest. *Psychology of Women Quarterly*, *33*(2), 235–249. doi:10.1111/j.1471-6402.2009.01493.x

Firestone, J., Harris, R., & Lambert, L. (1999). Gender role ideology and the gender based differences in earnings. *Journal of Family and Economic Issues*, *20*(2), 191–215. doi:10.1023/A:1022158811154

Lambdin, J. R., Greer, K. M., Jibotian, K. S., Wood, K. R., & Hamilton, M. C. (2003). The animal = male hypothesis: Children's and adult's beliefs about the sex of non-sex-specific stuffed animals. *Sex Roles, 48*(11/12), 471–482. doi:10.1023/A:1023567010708

Merritt, R. D., & Kok, C. J. (1995). Attribution of gender to a gender-unspecified individual: An evaluation of the people = male hypothesis. *Sex Roles, 33*(3/4), 145–157. doi:10.1007/BF01544608

Miller, L., & Hayward, R. (2006). New jobs, old occupational stereotypes: Gender and jobs in the new economy. *Journal*

GENDER STEREOTYPES AND PERCEPTIONS   15

    of Education & Work, 19(1), 67–93. doi:10.1080

    /13639080500523000

Parker, H., Chan, F., & Saper, B. (1989). Occupational

    representativeness and prestige rating: Some observations.

    Journal of Employment Counseling, 26(3), 117–131.

    Retrieved from http://www.employmentcounseling.org

Seguino, S. (2007). Plus ça change? Evidence on global trends in

    gender norms and stereotypes. *Feminist Economics, 13*(2),

    1–28. doi:10.1080/13545700601184880

Shinar, E. (1975). Sexual stereotypes of occupations. *Journal of*

    Vocational Behavior, 7(1), 99–111. Retrieved from http://www

    .sciencedirect.com/science/journal/00018791

Teig, S., & Susskind, J. (2008). Truck driver or nurse? The impact of

    gender roles and occupational status on children's occupational

    preferences. *Sex Roles, 58*(11/12), 848–863. doi:10.1007

    /s11199-008-9410-x

APA

35 APA Documentation

The American Psychological Association (APA) publishes a style guide entitled *Publication Manual of the American Psychological Association*. Its documentation system (called an *author-date system*) is used in psychology and many other disciplines, including education, economics, and sociology.

35a APA-style in-text citations

APA-style in-text citations usually include just the last name(s) of the author(s) of the work and the year of publication. However, be sure to specify the page number(s) for any quotations you use in your paper. The abbreviation *p.* (for "page") or *pp.* (for "pages") should precede the number(s). If you do not know the author's name, use a shortened version of the source's title instead. The following examples are representative of the types of in-text citations you can expect to use.

1. Work by one author

Yang (2006) admits that speech, when examined closely, is a "remarkably messy means of communication" (p. 13).

OR

When examined closely, speech is "a remarkably messy means of communication" (Yang, 2006, p. 13).

Use commas to separate the author's name from the date and the date from the page number. Include page numbers only when quoting from the source.

2. Work by two authors

Darvas and Walsh (2002) claim that, regardless of whether children spend time in day care, their development in early childhood is determined primarily by the nature of the care they receive from parents.

OR

Regardless of whether children spend time in day care, their development in early childhood is determined primarily by the nature of the care they receive from parents (Darvas & Walsh, 2002).

When the authors' names are in parentheses, use an ampersand (&) to separate them.

3. Work by more than two authors

The speech of Pittsburgh, Pennsylvania, is called *Pittsburghese* (Johnstone, Bhasin, & Wittkofski, 2002).

For works with three to five authors, cite all the authors the first time the work is referred to, but in subsequent references give only the last name of the first author followed by *et al.* (meaning "and others").

According to Johnstone et al. (2002), newspapers published in Pittsburgh frequently use nonstandard spelling to represent the pronunciation of /aw/.

For works with six or more authors, provide only the last name of the first author followed by *et al.* in both the first and subsequent citations.

4. Anonymous work

Use a shortened version of the title to identify an anonymous work.

Chronic insomnia often requires medical intervention ("Sleep," 2009).

This citation refers to an article identified in the bibliography as "Sleep disorders: Standard methods of treatment."

If the word *Anonymous* is used in the source itself to designate the author, it appears in place of an author's name.

The documents could damage the governor's reputation (Anonymous, 2009).

5. Two or more works by different authors in the same parenthetical citation

Smokers frequently underestimate the long-term effects of smoking (O'Conner, 2005; Polson & Truss, 2007).

Arrange the citations in alphabetical order, using a semicolon to separate them.

6. Two or more works by the same author in the same parenthetical citation

The amygdala is active when a person experiences fear or anger (Carey, 2001, 2002).

Jameson (2007a, 2007b) has proposed an anxiety index for use by counselors.

Order the publication dates of works by the same author from earliest to most recent; however, if the works have the same publication date, distinguish the dates with lowercase letters (a, b, c, and so on) assigned according to the order in which the entries for the works are listed in your bibliography.

7. Personal communication

State educational outcomes are often interpreted differently by teachers in the same school (J. K. Jurgensen, personal communication, May 4, 2009).

Letters, memos, e-mail messages, interviews, and telephone conversations are cited in the text only, not in the reference list.

8. Indirect source

Korovessis (2002, p. 63) points out Toqueville's description of the "strange melancholy" exhibited by citizens living amid abundance.

Toqueville (as cited in Korovessis, 2002, p. 63) observed the "strange melancholy" exhibited by citizens living amid abundance.

In the reference list, include a bibliographic entry for the source read, not for the original source. Use an indirect source only when you are unable to obtain the original.

35b   APA-style reference list

All of the works you cite should be listed at the end of your paper, beginning on a separate page with the heading "References." The following tips will help you prepare your list.

TIPS FOR PREPARING A REFERENCE LIST

■ Center the heading "References" one inch from the top of the page.

■ Include entries for only those sources you explicitly cite in your paper but not for personal communications or original works cited in indirect sources.

■ Arrange the list of works alphabetically by the author's last name or by the last name of the first author.

■ If you use more than one work by the same author(s), arrange the entries according to the date of publication, placing the entry with the earliest date first. If two or more works by the same author(s) have the same publication date, the entries are arranged so that the titles of the works are in alphabetical order, according to the first important word in each title; lowercase letters are then added to the date (e.g., 2008a, 2008b) to distinguish the works.

■ When an author's name appears both in a single-author entry and as the first name in a multiple-author entry, place the single-author entry first.

■ For a work without an author, alphabetize the entry according to the first important word in the title.

■ Type the first line of each entry flush with the left margin and indent subsequent lines one-half inch or five spaces (a hanging indent).

■ Double-space between lines of each entry and between entries.

Directory of APA-Style Entries for the Reference List

BOOKS

When preparing an entry for the reference list, be sure to copy the bibliographic information directly from the title page of a book (see fig. 35.1).

1. Book by one author

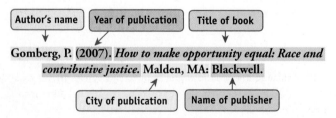

Gomberg, P. (2007). *How to make opportunity equal: Race and contributive justice.* Malden, MA: Blackwell.

Invert the author's last name and his or her initials; place a comma after the last name. Capitalize only the first word

Title — Working with People
with Learning Disabilities

Subtitle — Theory and Practice

Authors — *David Thomas and Honor Woods*

Publisher — Jessica Kingsley Publishers
Cities of publication — London and New York

Figure 35.1. The title page of a book provides most of the information necessary for creating a bibliographic entry for a research paper.

and any proper nouns in the title and subtitle (if there is one). Italicize both title and subtitle. Include the city of publication and the United States Postal Service two-letter state abbreviation.

2. Book by two or more authors

Thomas, D., & Woods, H. (2003). *Working with people with disabilities:*

　　　Theory and practice. London, England: Jessica Kingsley.

Invert the last names and initials of all authors. Use a comma after each last name and after each set of initials except the last. Use an ampersand (in addition to the comma) before the last author's name. If there are more than seven authors, list the first six names followed by a comma and three ellipsis points and then the last author's name. When a work has been published in a city outside the United States, include the name of the country.

3. Book with editor(s)

Wolfe, D. A., & Mash, E. J. (Eds.). (2005). *Behavioral and emotional disorders*

　　　in adolescents: Nature, assessment, and treatment. New York, NY:

　　　Guilford Press.

Provide only enough of the publisher's name so that it can be identified clearly. Omit words such as *Publishers* and abbreviations such as *Inc.* However, include *Books* and *Press* when they are part of the publisher's name.

4. Book with a corporate or group author

U.S. War Department. (2003). *Official military atlas of the Civil War*.

　　　New York, NY: Barnes & Noble.

When the author and the publisher of a book are the same, use the publisher's name at the beginning of the entry and *Author* at the end.

American Psychiatric Association. (1995). *American Psychiatric Association*

　　　capitation handbook. Washington, DC: Author.

5. Edition after the first

Lycan, W., & Prinz, J. (Eds.). (2008). *Mind and cognition* (3rd ed.). Malden,
MA: Blackwell.

If a work has an editor or editors, include the abbreviation
Ed. for "editor" or *Eds.* for "editors." Identify the edition in
parentheses immediately after the title. Use abbreviations: *2nd,*
3rd, and so on for the edition number and *ed.* for "edition."

6. Translation

Rank, O. (2002). *Psychology and the soul: A study of the origin, conceptual*
evolution, and nature of the soul (G. C. Richter & E. J. Lieberman,
Trans.). Baltimore, MD: Johns Hopkins University Press. (Original work
published 1930)

A period follows the name of the publisher but not the
parenthetical note about the original publication date.

7. Multivolume work

Doyle, A. C. (2003). *The complete Sherlock Holmes* (Vols. 1–2). New York, NY:
Barnes & Noble.

If the multivolume work was published over a period of more
than one year, use the range of years for the publication date.

Hawthorne, N. (1962–1997). *The centenary edition of the works of Nathaniel*
Hawthorne (Vols. 1–23). Columbus: Ohio University Press.

If the publisher is a university press whose name mentions a
state, do not include the state abbreviation.

8. Government report

Executive Office of the President. (2003). *Economic report of the President,*
2003 (GPO Publication No. 040-000-0760-1). Washington, DC: U.S.
Government Printing Office.

9. Selection from an edited book

Empson, R. (2007). Enlivened memories: Recalling absence and loss
in Mongolia. In J. Carsten (Ed.), *Ghosts of memory: Essays on
remembrance and relatedness* (pp. 58–82). Malden, MA:
Blackwell.

Italicize the book title but not the title of the selection.

10. Selection from a reference book

Wickens, D. (2001). Classical conditioning. In *The Corsini encyclopedia of
psychology and behavioral science* (Vol. 1, pp. 293–298). New York,
NY: John Wiley.

ARTICLES IN PRINT

11. Article with one author in a journal with continuous pagination

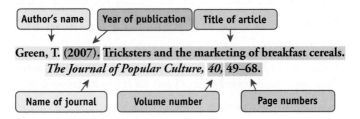

Italicize the name of the journal; capitalize all major words,
as well as any other words consisting of four or more letters. Do
not italicize the title of the article; capitalize only the first word
of the title and subtitle (if there is one) and any proper nouns.
Figure 35.2 shows where the information for this type of entry
is found on the first page of an article.

Tricksters and the Marketing of —— Title
Breakfast Cereals

THOMAS GREEN —— Author

B REAKFAST CEREALS ARE SOLD BY TRICKSTERS. FROM LUCKY THE Leprechaun to the Cookie Crook to the mischievous live-action squirrels who vend General Mills Honey Nut Clusters, an astounding number of Saturday morning television commercials feature 30-second dramatizations of trickster tales that are designed to promote breakfast cereals. True, breakfast cereals are not the only products sold by tricksters, and not all cereals are sold by tricksters—especially in the last decade. But the association is common enough to persist as an unexamined assumption that seems obvious to most Americans once it is pointed out. Naturally, breakfast cereals are often sold by animated tricksterish mascot characters, and naturally such commercials feature motifs and narrative patterns that are common in trickster tales. But the perception of an inherent internal logic in this scheme overlooks a couple of key questions. Why, for example, are tricksters considered a particularly appropriate or effective means of marketing breakfast cereals? And why breakfast cereals in particular (and a few other breakfast products), almost to the exclusion of tricksters in other types of marketing campaigns? The answers to these questions, it turns out, may lie back in the semi-mystical, pseudoreligious origins of prepared breakfast foods and the mating of the mythology of those foods with the imperatives of the competitive, prepared-foods marketplace.

Name of journal | Volume number | Issue number | Year of publication

The Journal of Popular Culture, Vol. 40, No. 1, 2007
© 2007, Copyright the Authors
Journal compilation © 2007, Blackwell Publishing, Inc.

Figure 35.2. The first page of a journal article provides the information needed to complete a bibliographic entry for that source.

12. Article with two authors in a journal with each issue paginated separately

Rudisill, J. R., & Edwards, J. M. (2002). Coping with job transitions.

Consulting Psychology Journal, 54(1), 55–62.

When you use an article from a journal paginated separately (that is, a journal whose every issue begins on page 1), provide the issue number (placed in parentheses) directly after the volume number (italicized). Do not insert a space between the volume and issue numbers.

13. Article with three to seven authors

Frost, R. O., Steketee, G., & Williams, L. (2002). Compulsive buying,

compulsive hoarding, and obsessive-compulsive disorder. *Behavior

Therapy, 33*(2), 201–213.

14. Article with more than seven authors

Reddy, S. K., Arora, M., Perry, C. L., Nair, B., Kohli, A., Lytle, L. A., … Stigler, M.

(2002). Tobacco and alcohol use outcomes of a school-based intervention

in New Delhi. *American Journal of Health Behavior, 26,* 173–181.

15. Article in a monthly, biweekly, or weekly magazine

Winson, J. (2002, June). The meaning of dreams. *Scientific American, 12,* 54–61.

For monthly publications, provide both the year and the month, separated by a comma. For magazines published weekly or biweekly, add the day of the issue: (2003, May 8).

16. Article in a newspaper

Simon, S. (2007, October 14). Winning hearts, minds, homes. *Los Angeles

Times,* p. A1.

Include both the section letter and the page number.

17. Letter to the editor

Mancall, M. (2002, June 17). Answer to cynicism [Letter to the editor]. *The New York Times,* p. A20.

Indicate within brackets that the work is a letter to the editor.

18. Book review

Orford, J. (2007). Drug addiction and families [Review of the book *Drug addiction and families*]. *Addiction, 102,* 1841–1842.

If the review has its own title, use that instead of the title of the book. Retain the bracketed information.

SOURCES PRODUCED FOR ACCESS BY COMPUTER

The APA guidelines for electronic sources are similar to those for print sources. Exceptions are explained after the sample entries that follow. Information about when and/or how a source was retrieved appears at the end of the entry. The period that normally ends an entry is omitted after a URL because it could cause difficulty in retrieving a file. If a URL has to continue on a new line, break it before a punctuation mark or other special character. Note that many scholarly journals now use a Digital Object Identifier (DOI) to simplify searching for an article. Whenever possible, use a DOI (without a period following it) instead of a URL at the end of an entry. The DOI will appear on the first page of the article, which usually contains the abstract. Figure 35.3 shows the location of a DOI and other pertinent bibliographic information on the first page of an online journal article.

Journal of Experimental Psychology: Applied —— Name of journal
2001, Vol. 7, No. 1, 27–50

Page numbers

Volume and issue number

Year of publication

Copyright 2001 by the American Psychological Association, Inc.
1076-898X/01/$5.00 DOI: 10.1037//1076-898X.7.1.27

DOI

Children's Eyewitness Reports After Exposure to Misinformation From Parents

Title of article

Debra Ann Poole
Central Michigan University

Authors of article

D. Stephen Lindsay
University of Victoria

This study examined how misleading suggestions from parents influenced children's eyewitness reports. Children (3 to 8 years old) participated in science demonstrations, listened to their parents read a story that described experienced and nonexperienced events, and subsequently discussed the science experience in two follow-up interviews. Many children described fictitious events in response to open-ended prompts, and there were no age differences in suggestibility during this phase of the interview. Accuracy declined markedly in response to direct questions, especially for the younger children. Although the older children retracted many of their false reports after receiving source-monitoring instructions, the younger children did not. Path analyses indicated that acquiescence, free recall, and source monitoring all contribute to mediating patterns of suggestibility across age. Results indicate that judgments about the accuracy of children's testimony must consider the possibility of exposure to misinformation prior to formal interviews.

During the past decade, there has been keen interest in young children's performance when interviewed about autobiographical events. This interest was sharpened by broad social changes that led the public to be more concerned about crimes to which child victims are often the sole witnesses (e.g., child sexual abuse), but it also reflected a movement in psychology away from relatively artificial research paradigms (e.g., studies of memory for word lists) and toward more naturalistic and multifaceted approaches to research. Although the field of eyewitness testimony receives considerable attention for its forensic implications, researchers increasingly view eyewitness paradigms as tools for studying basic issues in memory and cognition.

There have been several recent reviews of the literature on interviewing children for forensic purposes (e.g., Ceci & Bruck, 1995; Poole & Lamb, 1998), and

we do not offer an exhaustive recapitulation here. In its broadest outlines, the literature can be crudely summarized by saying that even very young children (i.e., 3- to 4-year-olds) can provide quite detailed and accurate accounts of past autobiographical events under some conditions but that even older children and adults often provide impoverished and inaccurate accounts under others. The aim of the current research was to provide additional insight into factors that compromise or enhance the amount and accuracy of the information interviewers gain from young children. Borrowing terms from Wells's (1993) analysis of eyewitness suspect identification, our research examined both "system variables" (i.e., factors that are under the control of investigators in forensic cases, such as the way questions are phrased) and "estimator variables" (i.e., factors that may affect the amount or accuracy of information children report but that cannot be

Figure 35.3. First page of an online journal article.

19. Online journal article with a Digital Object Identifier (DOI)

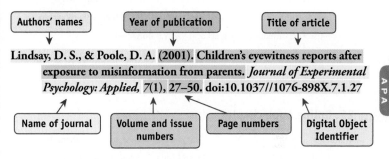

Authors' names · Year of publication · Title of article

Lindsay, D. S., & Poole, D. A. (2001). Children's eyewitness reports after exposure to misinformation from parents. *Journal of Experimental Psychology: Applied, 7*(1), 27–50. doi:10.1037//1076-898X.7.1.27

Name of journal · Volume and issue numbers · Page numbers · Digital Object Identifier

20. Online journal article without a DOI

Tuladhar-Douglas, W. (2007). Leaf blowers and antibiotics: A Buddhist stance for science and technology. *Journal of Buddhist Ethics, 14,* 200–238. Retrieved from http://www.buddhistethics.org

If there is no DOI, use the URL for the journal's home page instead of the URL for the article.

21. Online magazine article based on a print source

Acocella, J. (2008, May 26). A few too many. *The New Yorker, 84*(15), 32–37. Retrieved from http://www.newyorker.com

22. Online magazine article not found in print

Saletan, W. (2008, August 27). Unfinished race: Race, genes, and the future of medicine. *Slate.* Retrieved from http://www.slate.com

23. Article in an online newspaper

McGrath, C. (2002, June 15). Father time. *The New York Times.* Retrieved from http://nytimes.com

24. Online book

Stevens, K. (n.d.). *The dreamer and the beast*. Available from http://www
.onlineoriginals.com/showitem.asp?itemID=321&action=setvar&vartype
=history&varname=bookmark&v1=1&v2=46&v3=1

If access to an online book is not free, use "Available from"
instead of "Retrieved from."

25. Online book chapter

Wallner, F., & Durnwalder, K. (1994). Sciences, psychology and realism. In
V. Shen, R. Knowles, & T. Van Doan (Eds.), *Psychology, phenomenology
and Chinese philosophy. Chinese philosophical studies: Vol. 6.* Retrieved
from http://www.crvp.org/book/Series03/III-6/chapter_i__science.htm

If a DOI has been provided, use the DOI instead of the URL.

26. Web log posting

Chatham, C. (2008, August 29). Action without intention: Parietal damage
alters attention awareness. [Web log message]. Retrieved from
http://scienceblogs.com/developingintelligence/2008/08/action
_without_intention_parie.php

27. Lecture notes posted online

Wolfe, J. (2004). *Lecture 18: Freud and fairy tales* [Lecture notes]. Retrieved
from http://ocw.mit.edu/OcwWeb/Brain-and-Cognitive-Sciences
/9-00Fall-2004/LectureNotes/index.htm

28. Authored document from a Web site

Darling, C. (2002). *Guide to grammar and writing*. Retrieved from Capital

    Community College Web site: http://cctc2.commnet.edu/grammar

    /modifiers.htm

Provide the name of the host organization before the URL only when the document is from a large Web site, such as one sponsored by a university or government body.

29. Online document with no identified author

American School Counselor Association. (2006). *Position statement:*

    Equity for all students. Retrieved from http://asca2.timberlakepublishing

    .com/content.asp?contentid=503

Use the name of the organization hosting the Web site as the author of the document. If a date for the document is provided, place it in parentheses. If no date is listed, use the abbreviation *n.d.* The URL is located at either the top or the bottom of a printout.

30. Personal communication

Personal communications such as e-mail messages, letters, interviews, and telephone conversations are not included in the reference list but should be cited in the text as follows: (S. L. Johnson, personal communication, September 3, 2003).

31. Online encyclopedia

Dowe, P. (2007). Causal processes. In E. N. Zalta (Ed.), *The Stanford*

    encyclopedia of philosophy (Fall 2008 ed.). Retrieved from

    http://plato.stanford.edu/archives/sum2007/entries/cognitive-science/

32. Online consumer brochure

American Psychological Association. (2008). Elder abuse and neglect: In search

    of solutions. Retrieved from http://www.apa.org/pi/aging/eldabuse.html

33. Online report from a professional organization

Yones, M. (n.d.). Psychology of happiness and unhappiness. Retrieved

from International Institute of Management: http://www.iim-edu

.org/executivejournal/index.htm

OTHER SOURCES

34. Motion picture

Smith, M. (Producer/Writer), & Gaviria, M. (Producer/Director). (2001).

Medicating kids [Motion picture]. United States: Public Broadcasting

Service.

Begin with the primary contributor(s), identifying the nature
of the contribution. Then provide the release date, the title,
and the descriptive label in square brackets. End by indicating
the country where the movie was produced and the name of
the studio.

35. Television program

Holt, S. (Producer). (2002, October 1). *The mysterious lives of caves*

[Television broadcast]. Alexandria, VA: Public Broadcasting Service.

Give the title of the program in italics. If citing an entire series
(e.g., *Nova*), cite the producer for the series as a whole. Use the
descriptive label *Television series* in the square brackets.

35c   **Sample APA-style paper**

The APA recognizes that a paper may have to be modified so
that it adheres to an instructor's requirements. The following
boxes offer tips for preparing a title page, an abstract page, and

the body of a typical student paper. For tips on preparing a reference list, see page 376.

TIPS FOR PREPARING THE TITLE PAGE OF AN APA-STYLE PAPER

- The title page includes both the full title of the paper and a shortened version of it. The shortened version, along with a page number, is placed in the header. On the left side of the header, include the words "Running head:" (note the colon) and a version of your title that consists of no more than fifty characters. Use all uppercase letters for this title. On the right side of the header, insert the page number. The title page is page 1 of your paper.

- Place the full title in the upper half of the page, with your name below it. You may include your affiliation or a course name or number if your instructor requests one. Double-space these lines.

TIPS FOR PREPARING THE ABSTRACT AND THE BODY OF AN APA-STYLE PAPER

- The header for the remaining parts of the paper (including the abstract page) is similar to the header on the title page. It should have the shortened title on the left and the page number on the right; the body of the paper begins on page 3.

- Center the word "Abstract" one inch from the top of the page.

- Be sure that the abstract is no more than 250 words. For advice on summarizing, see page 263.

- Double-space throughout the body of the abstract. Do not indent the first line of the abstract.

- Center the title of the paper one inch from the top of the page.

- Use one-inch margins on both the left and right sides of all pages.

- Double-space throughout the body of the paper, indenting each paragraph one-half inch or five to seven spaces.

The running
head should
consist of
no more
than 50
characters.

APA

Use 1-inch
margins on both
sides of the
page.

The Social Status of an Art:

Historical and Current Trends in Tattooing

Rachel L. Pinter and Sarah M. Cronin

Central Washington University

If required by
the instructor,
the course name
and number
replace the
affiliation.

SOCIAL STATUS OF AN ART   2

Abstract

Current research demonstrates that the social practice of tattooing has changed greatly over the years. Not only have the images chosen for tattoos and the demographic of people getting tattoos changed, but the ideology behind tattooing itself has evolved. This paper first briefly describes the cross-cultural history of the practice. It then examines current social trends in the United States and related ideological issues.

Center the heading one inch from the top of the page.

An abstract generally contains between 150 and 250 words.

APA

1 inch

The Social Status of an Art:

Historical and Current Trends in Tattooing

Center the
title.

Tattoos have existed throughout history in countless

cultures. Currently, tattoos are considered popular art forms.

They can be seen on men and women from all walks of life

in the United States, ranging from a trainer at the local gym

to a character on a television show. Due to an increase in the

popularity of tattooing, studies of tattooing behavior have

proliferated as researchers attempt to identify trends. This paper

seeks to explore both the history of tattooing and its current

practice in the United States.

Tattooing can be found in the histories of people worldwide,

though its origin is currently unknown. Krcmarik (2003) provides

a helpful geographical overview. In Asia, tattooing has existed

for thousands of years in Chinese, Japanese, Middle Eastern, and

Indian cultures. In Europe, tattooing flourished during the 19th

century, most notably in England. Many of the sailors traveling

with Captain James Cook returned with tales of exotic tattooing

practices and sometimes with tattoos themselves. The Samoans

in the South Pacific are famous for their centuries old

tattooing practice, known as *tatau*—the word from which

tattoo is said to have originated. The Maori of New Zealand

Use 1-inch
margins on
both sides
of the page.

The writers'
thesis
statement
forecasts the
content of
the essay.

The writers
provide
historical
and cultural
information
about
tattooing.

APA

SOCIAL STATUS OF AN ART   4

are also well known for
their hand-carved facial
tattoos, known as *Moko*
(see Figure 1).

   In Africa, tattoos
can be found on Egyptian
and Nubian mummies,
which date back to
approximately 2000 BCE.
The tattooing history of
South America is noted
in the written accounts

Figure 1. A Maori man with a facial
tattoo. *Note.* Photo © Tim Graham/
Getty Images.

of Spanish explorers' encounters with tattooed Mayans. Finally, in
North America, tattooing became popular during the 1900s and has
experienced advances and retreats in social acceptance since then.
Starting in the 1960s, its popularity rose dramatically and continues
to rise.

   The practice of tattooing has gained and lost popularity,
often as a result of rather extreme changes in the ideologies
supporting or discouraging it. This roller-coaster pattern
of acceptance is well demonstrated in the United States.
Since the 19th century, the wearing of tattoos has allowed for

SOCIAL STATUS OF AN ART   5

The writers discuss changing perspectives on the appropriateness of tattoos.

subculture identification by such persons as sailors, bikers, circus "freak" performers, and prison inmates (DeMello, 1995). As a collective group behavior indicating deviant subculture membership, tattooing flourished during this time but remained plagued by negative associations. In the last 10 years, however, the practice has represented a more individualistic yet mainstream means of body adornment (Kosut, 2006). A wide range of Americans now wear tattoos.

Citation of a work by one author

The trend toward acceptance of tattoos may be a result of how American society views the people who wear them. Earlier, tattoos were depicted in mainstream media as worn by people with marginal status; now, they are considered to be an artful expression among celebrities as well as educated middle and upper classes, as Figure 2 illustrates (Kosut, 2006). This shift in the symbolic status of tattoos—self-expression among the social elite rather than deviant expression among the working class—has allowed tattoos to be obtained in greater numbers. Even in the workplace, where employees were often forbidden to display tattoos, employers now "take advantage of the open-mindedness and innovation that younger [tattooed] employees bring into the workplace" (Org, 2003, p. D1).

To clarify a direct quotation from a source, the writers insert a word in square brackets.

As the acceptability of tattoos has increased, tattooing has

SOCIAL STATUS OF AN ART   6

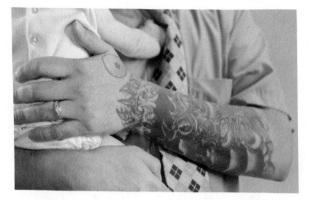

Figure 2. Tattoos are becoming more common among middle-class professionals. *Note.* Photo © Eric Anthony Photography/Monsoon Images/PhotoLibrary.

undergone the process of commercialization that frequently occurs in American society. Tattoos are now acquired as embodied status symbols and are used to sell tattoo maintenance products, skateboards, and fashion items (Kosut, 2006). This introduction into the consumer culture allows tattoos to gain even more popularity.

Researchers have been tracking the popularity of tattoos, though no one seems able to agree on a number. In 2000, MSNBC aired a documentary called "Skin Deep," which cited the tattooing rate at 20% of the population (Rosenbaum, 2000). In 2003, citing

SOCIAL STATUS OF AN ART   7

The writers list statistics to support a claim.

lower number, Harris Interactive reported that 16% of all adults in the United States have at least one tattoo (Sever, 2003). The actual number of individuals with tattoos is unknown, but most researchers believe the trend has been consistently gaining ground since the 1960s. Within the context of the larger population, statistics on the frequency of tattooing among specific age groups show a similar increase (Armstrong, Owen, Roberts, & Koch, 2002). However, due to the limitations of the various research designs, more research on a national level is needed to obtain truly representative figures.

The increase in acquisition of tattoos has resulted in trends concerning the images and locations of tattoos, which appear to be divided down lines of gender. Many of the tattoo images commonly found on men include, but are not limited to, death themes, military insignia, tribal armbands, and family crests. During the 1980s, cartoon images such as Bugs Bunny and the Tasmanian Devil were also popular for males. Males choose various locations for tattoos, but the most popular male sites are the upper back, back of the calves, and the upper arm, according to tattoo artist Ben Reames (personal communication, July 12, 2007). Conversely, females often obtain tattoos that symbolize traditional femininity, such as flowers, stars, and butterflies. A noticeable trend for females in the 1980s was the rose tattoo. Stars and butterflies now rival the rose in popularity.

Citation of an interview with tattoo artist

SOCIAL STATUS OF AN ART   8

Popular spots for tattoos
include the hip, foot
(see Figure 3), and lower
back.

The art of tattooing
has existed in many
culturally determined
forms throughout human
history, and its current
manifestations are as
varied as the cultures
themselves. However,

Figure 3. Many females who get a
tattoo choose to have it on the foot.
Note. Photo © Color-Blind Images/
Blend Images/Corbis.

based on the current literature, the social behavior of tattooing is
experiencing unparalleled growth in the United States. In fact, Kosut
(2006) argues, "New generations of American children are growing
up in a cultural landscape that is more tattoo-friendly and tattoo-
flooded than any other time in history" (p. 1037). Because today's
children see tattoos and tattoo-related products everywhere, usually
in neutral or positive situations, they will likely be more accepting
of tattoos than earlier generations were. Certainly, the tattooing trend
shows no signs of leveling off.

Conclusion

SOCIAL STATUS OF AN ART   9

References

Armstrong, M. L., Owen, D. C., Roberts, A. E., & Koch, J. R. (2002). College students and tattoos: Influence of image, identity, and family. *Journal of Psychosocial Nursing, 40*(10), 20–30.

DeMello, M. (1995). Not just for bikers anymore: Popular representations of American tattooing. *Journal of Popular Culture, 29*(3), 37–53.

Kosut, M. (2006). An ironic fad: The commodification and consumption of tattoos. *Journal of Popular Culture, 39*(6), 1035–1049.

Krcmarik, K. L. (2003). *History of tattooing*. Retrieved from Michigan State University: http://www.msu.edu/~krcmari1/individual/history.html

Org, M. (2003, August 28). The tattooed executive. *The Wall Street Journal*. Retrieved from http://online.wsj.com

Rosenbaum, S. (Executive Producer). (2000, August 20). *MSNBC investigates: Tattoos—skin deep* [Television broadcast]. New York, NY: MSNBC.

Sever, J. (2003, October 8). *A third of Americans with tattoos say they make them feel more sexy*. Retrieved from http://www.harrisinteractive.com/harris_poll/index.asp?PID=868

Center the heading.

Alphabetize the entries according to the first or only author's last name.

Indent second and subsequent lines of each entry one-half inch or five spaces.

Identification of the type of medium is placed in square brackets.

No period follows a URL at the end of an entry.

36 Writing in the Humanities

The humanities include disciplines such as philosophy, art history, history, foreign languages, religion, comparative literature, cultural studies, women's and gender studies, and English. Scholars in the humanities study the artifacts of human culture (works of art, novels, plays, architecture, musical compositions and forms, philosophical treatises, and handicrafts, as well as popular media) in order to better understand the wide variety of human experience, both past and present.

In courses in the humanities, you will write in a variety of ways and for various purposes. It is therefore important to analyze your rhetorical situation and identify an exigence before you begin drafting.

36a Audience, purpose, and the research question

Before writing a paper for a humanities course, you need to determine your exigence, your intended audience, and your purpose. Thinking about your exigence (what you are writing in response to, and why) will help you shape your research question, narrow your purpose, and identify your audience. Knowing who comprises your audience helps you determine how much background information on your topic to provide, how technical your language should be, and what kinds of evidence will be most persuasive.

Most researchers in the humanities write to convey a particular interpretation of a cultural artifact to a specific audience or to inform readers about the history of a particular event, individual, artifact, or social movement. They may also write to evaluate a work of art or a performance. Once you have determined your purpose for writing, you can develop a research question that will help you find and evaluate sources and use those sources responsibly. Research papers in the humanities often focus on texts or cultural products that help the researcher answer a specific question. The following are some research questions that scholars in the humanities might pose about the experience of African Americans during the civil rights movement:

Question about causes or purposes

What events stimulated the Montgomery bus boycott during the civil rights movement?

Question about consequences

How did jazz musician John Coltrane contribute to the success of the civil rights movement?

Question about process

What did civil rights workers do to gain national attention for their cause?

Question about definitions or categories

What kinds of protest tactics did different African American leaders, such as Martin Luther King and Malcolm X, advocate during the civil rights movement?

Question about values

What does the struggle for equal rights for African Americans reveal about the values of white Americans during the 1960s?

36b Evidence, sources, and reasoning

The aim of writers in the humanities is to understand human experience by observing and interpreting cultural artifacts; therefore, most claims in the humanities are not put forth as statements of absolute fact. Instead, researchers in the humanities often seek to demonstrate the validity of their interpretations through detailed analyses of texts, relying on textual evidence, logical reasoning, and the work of other scholars in a particular field to present a compelling argument for an interpretation. After considering the available evidence, researchers in the humanities advance a claim, or **thesis,** that expresses their interpretation of a work of art, a performance, or some other object or event.

(1) Using primary sources

Most researchers in the humanities begin their studies by working directly with a **primary source,** which can be a person, an object, or a text. For art historians, this primary source might be a drawing, a painting, or a sculpture, which they analyze in terms of the formal qualities of the work (line, color, shape, texture, composition, and so forth) and elements or themes that might have symbolic importance. They then write an explanation of how these features work together to create meaning in the work. For instance, in a classic analysis of Jan van Eyck's *Arnolfini Portrait* in his book *Early*

Jan van Eyck's *Arnolfini Portrait*, from the fifteenth century, has been the subject of many analyses by art historians.

Netherlandish Painting, art historian Erwin Panofsky argues that the elaborate details of the scene, such as the dog (representing fidelity), the two additional figures reflected in a mirror on the wall who may have served as witnesses, and van Eyck's signature on the wall indicate that the scene documents a wedding. More recently, art historians have challenged this interpretation: in her article "In the Name of God and Profit: Jan van Eyck's *Arnolfini Portrait,*" Margaret Carroll argues that the painting does not portray a wedding but is an important document that gives the wife power of attorney; in "The Arnolfini Double Portrait: A Simple Solution," Margaret Koster suggests instead that the painting is a memorial for Arnolfini's wife, painted after her death. Each of these different interpretations draws on formal and stylistic evidence from the painting itself as well as on expert knowledge of the cultural context in which it was created.

For historians, primary sources include letters, government documents, newspapers, pamphlets, and other materials produced during a particular time period about some person, group, or event. For example, when writing her biography of nineteenth-century Paiute activist Sarah Winnemucca, Sally Zanjani used letters written by Winnemucca, transcriptions of her public speeches, newspaper accounts of her activities, photographs, diaries, and other first-hand accounts to reconstruct Winnemucca's personal life and motivations. Like other historians, Zanjani analyzed these sources by comparing what they say, evaluating the reliability of their creators, and then generating her own interpretation of the information they present.

(2) Using secondary sources

Researchers in the humanities also use **secondary sources,** or works written by other scholars on their topic, to understand what these scholars think about the topic and to help establish the social and historical context for the topic. For instance, Zanjani referred to earlier biographies of Winnemucca

hum

and then demonstrated how her work offers new evidence about Winnemucca's life. Zanjani also relied on other historians for historical context that was not explicitly discussed in her primary sources, such as information about nineteenth-century American Indian reservations, government military policies regarding Indians, and so forth.

36c Conventions of language and organization

(1) Following conventions of style

When writing in the humanities, you will use the language and formatting prescribed by the style manual of the particular discipline. Some writers in the humanities, particularly those who write about languages and literature, use MLA style. Other writers in the humanities, including historians and art historians, follow the conventions outlined in *The Chicago Manual of Style* (CMS) or in Kate Turabian's *A Manual for Writers of Term Papers, Theses, and Dissertations*, which is based on CMS style.

Unlike writers in the sciences, who strive for objectivity in their writing, most writers in the humanities recognize that an interpretation is colored by the perspective of the person expressing it. Thus, writers in the humanities often acknowledge their own position on a topic, especially if it has a clear effect on their interpretation. In particular, many writers in the humanities use the first-person pronoun *I* as well as the active voice, which focuses readers' attention on the agent performing the action.

(2) Organizing information in particular ways

Nearly all humanities papers include a thesis statement that indicates the author's position on the topic, evidence that supports the thesis statement, and a conclusion that restates the major claim and explains why the topic is important.

(Specific formats for organizing papers in the humanities are discussed in the next section.)

Headings can help you organize your writing. Most short humanities papers do not require headings, but for longer papers, Turabian's style manual suggests the following levels of headings:

- First-level headings are centered and boldfaced (or italicized), with major words capitalized.

A First-Level He

- Second-level headings are centered and not boldfaced (or italicized), with major words capitalized.

A Second-Level Heading

- Third-level headings are flush with the left margin and boldfaced (or italicized), with major words capitalized.

A Third-Level Heading

(3) Including a bibliography

Include any sources you have cited in your paper in a bibliography at the end of the paper. A bibliography not only demonstrates that you have done sufficient research but also allows your readers to obtain any of the sources that interest them.

36e Examples of Writing in the Humanities

(1) Historical research paper

A historical research paper tries to reconstruct a past event or era or to profile an individual. Most historians use a combination of primary sources (newspapers, diaries, cookbooks, medical guides, and so forth, put out at the time of the event or during the lifetime of the person being profiled) and secondary sources (writings by later historians about the event or person or about the primary sources) to explain or interpret some feature of the past. A historical research paper allows you to place your interpretation in the context of others that have been offered, using some sources to support your interpretation and other sources to refute the alternative interpretations.

The introduction to a historical research paper explains the importance of the topic and provides the thesis. Following the introduction and thesis, the body of the paper provides evidence from both primary and secondary sources to support the thesis. Finally, the conclusion of a historical research paper should reconsider the major claim of the paper in terms of its overall significance and implications (for research, teaching, practice, and so forth).

(2) Critical review

Students in humanities courses, as well as professional writers, are often asked to write reviews of various creative works, including films, literary works, exhibits of artwork, musical performances, theatrical performances, and dance performances. The purpose of a critical review is to evaluate the quality of the work for an audience that wants to know what the work is about and to determine whether it would be worthwhile to experience it themselves. Accordingly, when you write a critical review, begin with some basic information about the work (the title and the artist, composer, or director and perhaps the location where the work can be seen or heard) and some kind of evaluative statement, or thesis, that gives readers your general opinion of the work. Following this introduction, provide a brief description of the work that helps readers unfamiliar with it to understand the review. As you evaluate the strengths and weaknesses of the work, be sure to provide examples from it to support your evaluation. Finally, most reviews conclude with a summary statement that drives home the final evaluation of the work. (See Matthew Marusak's critical review in 36e.)

(3) Critical analysis

Many researchers in the humanities write critical analyses—of visual arts, musical and theatrical performances, literary works, and other works—in which they argue for a specific interpretation of the work in question and aim at deepening an audience's understanding of and appreciation for that work. If your assignment is to write a critical analysis, your instructor is likely interested in assessing both your understanding of the work and your ability to think critically about it. Critical analyses usually focus on formal, stylistic, and/or symbolic features of a work and explain how these elements work together to create meaning. (See pages 402–405 for more information on evidence in critical analyses.) Such analyses sometimes explore the ways in which class, gender, or racial relationships are expressed in a work.

Most critical analyses include the following sections:

- **Introduction.** The introduction provides a brief historical context for the work. It may also explain why the work ought to be reexamined—perhaps scholars have overlooked the work's significance or have not considered other possible meanings of the work. At the end of the introduction, the **thesis,** a clearly focused claim, states the writer's interpretation of the work.
- **Body.** The body of the paper provides the evidence—the formal, stylistic, symbolic, or contextual details that support the writer's interpretation. Many analyses also address differing interpretations of the work, explaining why the writer's interpretation is more convincing. This section can be organized in a number of ways—for example, through comparison and contrast of data or artifacts or with chronological, thematic, or emphatic (from less to more familiar or from less to more contestable) arrangement.

■ **Conclusion.** The conclusion should review the thesis as well as the most important evidence supporting the writer's interpretation. Frequently, the conclusion also addresses implications—in other words, the writer explains to readers why his or her interpretation is so important, what effect the work may have had on other works or the cultural context, and/or what the writer's interpretation may mean to readers today.

36e Critical review of a theater production

In the following critical review, student Matthew Marusak makes an argument for his negative response to a production of Tennessee Williams's play *Suddenly Last Summer*.

1

Not So *Suddenly Last Summer*

Matthew Marusak

Theatre 464

March 15, 2008

The writer used a format based on Turabian's style manual for the title and header.

The writer introduces the performance and gives a brief evaluation of the production.

I began to nod off halfway through Carla Gugino's ardent, over-the-top, twenty-minute monologue at the end of Tennessee Williams's *Suddenly Last Summer* (Roundabout at Laura Pels Theatre, Harold and Miriam Steinberg Center for Theatre; November 4, 2007). It's not that there is anything inherently wrong with the material: Williams's stark, deeply ambiguous play about the dangers of sexual repression, denial, and deception remains as potent as ever. Rather, Roundabout's production turns an urgent and emotionally explosive work into an uncomfortably dull, embarrassingly archaic exercise in trying an audience's patience.

This paragraph describes the basic plot of the play for readers.

In theory, any revival of this play should be utterly and wholly riveting. In its production at the Laura Pels theatre, however, something has gone inexplicably awry. Violet Venable (an imposing Blythe Danner) is a wealthy widow—mannered and shrouded in a contradictory haze of unrelenting misery and dreamy-eyed

2

Gale Harold and Carla Gugino perform in
Tennessee Williams's play *Suddenly Last
Summer.* (Photo © Joan Marcus.)

idealism—suffering from the great loss of her son, Sebastian
(discussed but never seen), who perished under a veil of mystery
the previous summer. As her story unfolds, Mrs. Venable does her
best to cloud Sebastian's implicit homosexuality and the events
surrounding his death by praising him as a great artist—the way she
wants him to be remembered. Mrs. Venable sends the sophisticated
yet suspicious Dr. Cukrowicz (a debonair Gale Harold) to evaluate
her niece, Catharine Holly (a woefully miscast Carla Gugino), who,
having allegedly witnessed Sebastian's death, was sent away to a
psychiatric hospital after her experience. The decision is made to
perform a lobotomy on the young woman, against her will and at the

3

wishes of her clandestinely cruel, manipulative aunt. Only under the influence of a powerful truth serum does Catharine finally reveal the shocking circumstances of her cousin's death.

Suddenly Last Summer is a staggering achievement of drama; but this revival, directed with a heavy hand by Mark Brokaw, has no life. Noteworthy, though, is Santo Loquasto's dazzling set design. Sebastian's magical greenhouse garden is wonderfully staged, and scenes in the interior of the house are simple yet elegant. Loquasto's costume design is also impressive, while Peter Golub's original score is by turns lovely and haunting. A baffling technical aspect, however, is David Weiner's lighting design, which seems both inappropriate from scene to scene and peculiarly inconsistent.

Unfortunately, there are problems with the cast as well. Blythe Danner, while giving a respectable performance, is nowhere near as good as she could have been. She speaks in a distracting, maddeningly uneven dialect and gives the character far more nervous tics than are necessary. Lost is the nuance of the character, as is her caustic wit (as seen in Katharine Hepburn's superior portrayal in the 1959 film version). Danner's polished poise works for the character in many ways, but too often she seems overly rehearsed. Moreover, Carla Gugino should never have been cast as

The writer cites both positive and negative features of the production as he continues his evaluation.

4

Catharine. She has neither the presence nor the charm to pull off the role convincingly, and Catharine's fiery passion is lost in what seems to be little more than a bid for a Tony nomination in the monologue. Rounding out the leads is Gale Harold, who does his best with the play's most underwritten role, making Dr. Cukrowicz at once both charismatic and calculating.

Roundabout's revival of *Suddenly Last Summer,* while technically robust, leaves its audience exhausted and bored. Everyone involved tries too hard to make an impression, instead of allowing genuine talent and Williams's wonderful material to speak for themselves. I cannot rightfully recommend this production, though it might be worth seeing for Gale Harold alone. He's an underrated, underused actor, and watching him is an unmitigated pleasure.

The conclusion summarizes the major strengths and weaknesses of the production and indicates why the weaknesses outweigh the strengths.

37 CMS Documentation

The Chicago Manual of Style (CMS), published by the University of Chicago Press, provides guidelines for writers in history and other subject areas in the humanities. Its humanities style documents sources by using either footnotes or endnotes and, for most assignments, a bibliography. CMS also has an author-date citation style used in the sciences and social sciences.

37a CMS note and bibliographic forms

According to CMS humanities style, in-text citations take the form of sequential numbers that refer to **footnotes** (notes at the bottom of each page) or **endnotes** (notes at the end of the paper). The information in these notes may be condensed if a bibliography lists all the sources used in the paper. The condensed, or short, form for a note includes only the author's last name, the title (shortened if longer than four words), and the relevant page number(s): Eggers, *Court Reporters,* 312–15.

When a paper has no bibliography, the full note form is used for the first citation of each source. For either footnotes or endnotes, place a superscript number in the text wherever documentation of a source is necessary. The number should be as close as possible to whatever it refers to, following most punctuation that appears at the end of the direct quotation or paraphrase but preceding a dash.

TIPS FOR PREPARING FOOTNOTES

- Most word-processing programs will footnote your paper automatically. In Microsoft Word, pull down the Insert menu and choose Footnote. A superscript number will appear in the cursor's position. A box will also appear at the bottom of your page, in which you can insert the requisite information.
- Each note begins with a full-size number followed by a period and a space.
- Indent the first line of a note five spaces.
- Single-space lines within a footnote.
- Double-space between footnotes when more than one appears on a page.
- Use the abbreviation *Ibid.* (not italicized) to indicate that the source cited in an entry is identical to the one in the preceding entry. Include page numbers if they differ from those in the preceding entry: Ibid., 331–32.
- No bibliography is necessary when the footnotes provide complete bibliographic information for all sources.

TIPS FOR PREPARING ENDNOTES

- Place endnotes on a separate page, following the last page of the body of the paper and preceding the bibliography (if one is included).
- Center the word *Notes* (not italicized) at the top of the page.
- Use the abbreviation *Ibid.* (not italicized) to indicate that a source cited in an entry is identical to the one in the preceding entry. Include page numbers if they differ from those in the preceding entry: Ibid., 331–32.

(Continued on page 416)

(Continued from page 415)

- Indent the first line of a note five spaces.
- Single-space within an endnote and leave one blank line between endnotes.
- No bibliography is necessary when the endnotes provide complete bibliographic information for all sources used in the paper.

TIPS FOR PREPARING A BIBLIOGRAPHY

- Start the bibliography on a separate page, following the last page of the body of the paper if footnotes are used or following the last page of endnotes.
- Center the word *Bibliography* (not italicized) at the top of your paper.
- Alphabetize entries in the bibliography according to the author's last name.
- If a source has more than one author, alphabetize by the last name of the first author.
- For a work without an author, alphabetize the entry according to the first important word in the title.
- To indicate that a source has the same author(s) as in the preceding entry, begin an entry with a three-em dash (————) instead of the name(s) of the author(s). (If you do not know how to create this mark, search for *em dash,* using the Help function of your word processor.)
- Indent the second and subsequent lines of an entry five spaces (that is, use a hanging indent).
- Single-space within an entry and leave one blank line between entries.

Directory of CMS Note and Bibliographic Forms

BOOKS

ARTICLES

OTHER SOURCES

The following list contains entries for the full note form and the bibliographic form. The short note form is provided only for the first example.

BOOKS

1. Book with one author

Full note form

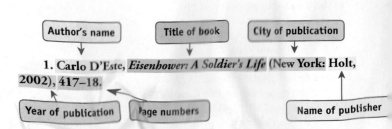

Provide the author's full name, in normal order, followed by a comma. The city of publication, publisher, and date of publication are all within parentheses. Italicize the titles of books, magazines, journals, and films. Capitalize all major words.

Short note form

1. D'Este, *Eisenhower*, 417–18.

Bibliographic form

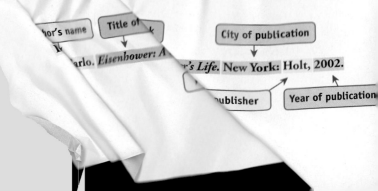

Provide the author's full name, last name first, followed by a comma and the first name. Provide either the full name of the publisher or an abbreviated version. The style chosen must be used consistently throughout the notes and the bibliography. End the entry with a period.

2. Book with two authors

Full note form

2. Cathy Scott-Clark and Adrian Levy, *The Stone of Heaven* (Boston: Little, Brown, 2001), 28.

Use the word *and* between the authors' names.

Bibliographic form

Scott-Clark, Cathy, and Adrian Levy. *The Stone of Heaven.* Boston: Little, Brown, 2001.

Invert the first author's name and follow it with a comma, the word *and* (not italicized), and the second author's name in normal order. The second and subsequent lines of an entry are indented five spaces.

3. Book with three authors

Full note form

3. Karen A. Foss, Sonja K. Foss, and Cindy L. Griffin, *Feminist Rhetorical Theories* (Thousand Oaks, CA: Sage, 1999).

Bibliographic form

Foss, Karen A., Sonja K. Foss, and Cindy L. Griffin. *Feminist Rhetorical Theories.* Thousand Oaks, CA: Sage, 1999.

Only the first author's name is inverted. If the city of publication is not widely known, include a two-letter state abbreviation.

4. Book with more than three authors

Full note form

4. Mike Palmquist et al., *Transitions: Teaching Writing in Computer-Supported and Traditional Classrooms* (Greenwich, CT: Ablex, 1998), 153.

In a note use the first person's name followed by the Latin phrase *et al.* or *and others,* its English translation. Neither phrase is italicized. Include all authors' names in the bibliographic form.

Bibliographic form

Palmquist, Mike, Kate Kiefer, James Hartvigsen, and Barbara Goodlew.
Transitions: Teaching Writing in Computer-Supported and Traditional Classrooms. Greenwich, CT: Ablex, 1998.

5. Book with an editor

Full note form

5. Hanna Schissler, ed., *The Miracle Years* (Princeton, NJ: Princeton Univ. Press, 2001).

Place the abbreviation *ed.* after the editor's name.

Bibliographic form

Schissler, Hanna, ed. *The Miracle Years.* Princeton, NJ: Princeton Univ. Press, 2001.

6. Book with an author and an editor

Full note form

6. Ayn Rand, *The Art of Fiction,* ed. Tore Boeckmann (New York: Plume, 2000).

Use the abbreviation *ed.* for "edited by."

Bibliographic form

Rand, Ayn. *The Art of Fiction.* Edited by Tore Boeckmann. New York: Plume, 2000.

Write out the words *Edited by.*

7. Translated book

Full note form

7. Murasaki Shikibu, *The Tale of Genji,* trans. Royall Tyler (New York: Viking, 2001).

Use the abbreviation *trans.* for "translated by."

Bibliographic form

Shikibu, Murasaki. *The Tale of Genji.* Translated by Royall Tyler. New York: Viking, 2001.

Write out the words *Translated by.*

8. Edition after the first

Full note form

8. Edward O. Wilson, *On Human Nature,* 14th ed. (Cambridge: Harvard Univ. Press, 2001).

Bibliographic form

Wilson, Edward O. *On Human Nature.* 14th ed. Cambridge: Harvard Univ. Press, 2001.

9. One volume in a multivolume work

Full note form

9. Thomas Cleary, *Classics of Buddhism and Zen,* vol. 3 (Boston: Shambhala Publications, 2001), 116.

Bibliographic form

Cleary, Thomas. *Classics of Buddhism and Zen.* Vol. 3. Boston: Shambhala Publications, 2001.

C M S

10. Government document

Full note form

10. US Bureau of the Census, *Statistical Abstract of the United States,* 120th ed. (Washington, DC, 2001), 16.

Bibliographic form

US Bureau of the Census. *Statistical Abstract of the United States.* 120th ed. Washington, DC, 2001.

11. Selection from an anthology

Full note form

11. Elizabeth Spencer, "The Everlasting Light," in *The Cry of an Occasion,* ed. Richard Bausch (Baton Rouge: Louisiana State Univ. Press, 2001), 171–82.

If you are citing information from a specific page or pages of a book or an article, place the page number(s) at the end of the note.

Bibliographic form

Spencer, Elizabeth. "The Everlasting Light." In *The Cry of an Occasion,* edited by Richard Bausch, 171–82. Baton Rouge: Louisiana State Univ. Press, 2001.

Use quotation marks to enclose the titles of selections from anthologies. The title is followed by a comma in the note form or by a period in the bibliographic form.

When only one selection from an anthology is used, inclusive page numbers precede the publication data in the bibliographic entry.

12. Published letter

Full note form

12. Lincoln to George McClellan, Washington, DC, 13 October 1862, in *This Fiery Trial: The Speeches and Writings of Abraham Lincoln,* ed. William E. Gienapp (New York: Oxford Univ. Press, 2002), 178.

Bibliographic form

Lincoln, Abraham. Abraham Lincoln to George McClellan, Washington DC, 13 October 1862. In *This Fiery Trial: The Speeches and Writings of Abraham Lincoln,* ed. William E. Gienapp, 178. New York: Oxford Univ. Press, 2002.

13. Indirect source

Full note form

13. Toni Morrison, *Playing in the Dark* (New York: Vintage, 1992), 26, quoted in Jonathan Goldberg, *Willa Cather and Others* (Durham, NC: Duke Univ. Press, 2001), 37.

Bibliographic form

Goldberg, Jonathan. *Willa Cather and Others*. Durham, NC: Duke Univ. Press, 2001.

Morrison, Toni. *Playing in the Dark.* New York: Vintage, 1992, 26. Quoted in Goldberg, *Willa Cather and Others*, 37.

In the note cite both the original work and the secondary source in which it is quoted. In the bibliography cite the secondary source in full and the original work in a separate citation with a cross-reference.

ARTICLES

14. Article in a journal

Full note form

14. A. Schedler, "The Menu of Manipulation," *Journal of Democracy* 13, no. 2 (2002): 48.

Use initials for an author's first and middle names only when they are used in the original publication.

Bibliographic form

Schedler, A. "The Menu of Manipulation." *Journal of Democracy* 13,

no. 2 (2002): 36–50.

15. Article in a popular (general-circulation) magazine

Full note form

15. John O'Sullivan, "The Overskeptics," *National Review,* June 17, 2002, 23.

Bibliographic form

O'Sullivan, John. "The Overskeptics." *National Review,* June 17,

2002, 22–26.

For a magazine published monthly, include only the month and the year, with no comma inserted between them.

16. Article from an online journal

Full note form

16. Zina Peterson, "Teaching Margery and Julian in Anthropology-Based Survey Courses," *College English* 68, no. 5 (2006): 481–501, accessed May 5, 2010, doi:10.2307/25472167.

Give the DOI (digital object identifier), a permanent identifying number, when citing electronic sources you used online.

If the source does not have a DOI, list the URL (see page 426). If the material is time-sensitive or if your discipline or instructor requires it, include the access date before the DOI or URL.

Bibliographic form

Peterson, Zina. "Teaching Margery and Julian in Anthropology-Based Survey
    Courses." *College English* 68, no. 5 (2006): 481–501. Accessed May 5,
    2010. doi:10.2307/25472167.

17. Article from a journal database

Full note form

    17. Samuel Guy Inman, "The Monroe Doctrine and Hispanic America,"
Hispanic America Historical Review 4, no. 4 (1921): 635, http://www.jstor.org
/stable/2505682.

If there is no DOI, give the stable URL for the article on the online database.

Bibliographic form

Inman, Samuel Guy. "The Monroe Doctrine and Hispanic America." *Hispanic
    America Historical Review* 4, no. 4 (1921): 635–76. http://www.jstor.org
    /stable/2505682.

18. Article from an online magazine

Full note form

    18. Mark Frank, "Judge for Themselves: Why a Supreme Court
Ruling on Sentencing Guidelines Puts More Power Back on the Bench,"
Time, January 24, 2005, http://www.time.com/time/magazine
/printout/0,8816,1018063,00.html.

Bibliographic form

Frank, Mark. "Judge for Themselves: Why a Supreme Court Ruling on

Sentencing Guidelines Puts More Power Back on the Bench."

Time, January 24, 2005. http://www.time.com/time/magazine

/printout/0,8816,1018063,00.html.

If the source has no DOI, cite the URL. A URL or DOI continued on a second line may be broken *after* a colon or double slash or *before* a single slash, a comma, a period, a hyphen, a question mark, a percent symbol, a number sign (#), a tilde (~), or an underscore (_). It can be broken either before or after an ampersand (&) or equals sign.

19. Newspaper article

Full note form

19. Rick Bragg, "An Oyster and a Way of Life, Both at Risk," *New York Times,* June 15, 2002, national edition, sec. A.

Omit the initial *The* in the newspaper's name. If the city of publication is not part of the name, add it at the beginning (italicized) as part of the name: *St. Paul Pioneer Press.* If the city is not well known or could be confused with another city of the same name, add the state name or abbreviation in parentheses after the city's name. If the paper is a well-known national one, such as the *Wall Street Journal,* it is not necessary to add the city.

Bibliographic form

Bragg, Rick. "An Oyster and a Way of Life, Both at Risk." *New York Times.*

June 15, 2002, national edition, sec. A.

If the name of the newspaper and the date of publication are mentioned in the text of the paper, no bibliographic entry is needed.

OTHER SOURCES

20. Interview

Full note form

20. Yoko Ono, "Multimedia Player: An Interview with Yoko Ono," interview by Carolyn Burriss-Krimsky, *Ruminator Review,* no. 10 (Summer 2002): 28.

Bibliographic form

Ono, Yoko. "Multimedia Player: An Interview with Yoko Ono." By Carolyn
    Burriss-Krimsky. *Ruminator Review,* no. 10 (Summer 2002): 26–29.

If you are required to list interviews, each entry should include the name of the person being interviewed, the title of the interview, the name of the person who conducted it, and any available publication data, online identifier, or audiovisual medium information.

21. Videocassette or DVD

Full note form

21. *Araby,* produced and directed by Dennis J. Courtney (Los Angeles: American Street Productions, 1999), videocassette (VHS).

Bibliographic form

Araby. Produced and directed by Dennis J. Courtney. Los Angeles: American
    Street Productions, 1999. Videocassette (VHS).

Place *Videocassette (VHS)* or *DVD* at the end of the entry.

37b   Sample CMS-style paper

The following student paper by Nicole Hester addresses an important development in the civil rights movement. Because it includes a full bibliography, the endnotes are written in short form. Only the first two pages of her paper and the first pages of the notes and the bibliography appear here.

1

Race in the U.S. Army:

An Executive Order for Hope

While students of the civil rights movement are often familiar with the Supreme Court decision *Brown v. Board of Education,* which acknowledged the inherent inequality in separate but equal practices, that decision would not happen until 1955, nearly eight years after President Harry S. Truman issued an executive order to integrate the federal government and, in particular, the United States military. Although the earlier Thirteenth (1865), Fourteenth (1868), and Fifteenth (1870) Amendments redefined freedom, citizenship, and voting, these amendments were diluted by Supreme Court decisions in the nineteenth and early twentieth centuries. In cases like *Plessy v. Ferguson,* the court established the precedent of "separate but equal," which legally allowed the separation of races in public facilities.[1] Thus, Truman's executive order in 1948 became an important step in the long-term struggle for civil rights.

Like American schools, the United States Army was segregated, and this segregation remained in place until after the Second World War (1941–45). In July of 1948, by executive order, President Truman demanded equal treatment and equal opportunity in the armed forces, thereby setting into motion

2

a series of events that would force change, however slow it
might be:

> It is hereby declared to be the policy of the
> President that there shall be equality of treatment
> and opportunity for all persons in the armed
> services without regard to race, color, religion or
> national origin. This policy shall be put into effect
> as rapidly as possible, having due regard to the
> time required to effectuate any necessary changes
> without impairing efficiency or morale.[2]

With such language as "all persons" and "as rapidly as
possible," Truman showed that his statement was more than a
publicity stunt. While understanding the scale of the change he
was demanding, Truman was also aware of the sentiment of the
American people and numerous government officials. Examining
the desegregation of the Army from the viewpoints of those
who sought to keep the races segregated and those who wanted
integration leads to understanding how the law can begin to
secure the pathways to justice and freedom.[3] Truman's executive
order in 1948 illustrates how the government can be a vehicle for
social change.

[Paper continues.]

11

Notes

1. Plessy v. Ferguson, 163 U.S. 537 (1896).

2. Merrill, *Documentary History,* 11:741.

3. It is beyond the scope of my paper to discuss all the non-Whites who were affected by Truman's order. In this essay, I focus on the effect of Truman's order on people whom I refer to as Black.

4. Lee, *Employment of Negro Troops*, 4.

5. Ibid., 73–74.

6. Mershon and Schlossman, *Foxholes and Color Lines*, 44–45.

7. Ibid., 73–77.

8. Nalty and MacGregor, *Blacks in the Military*, 108.

9. Ibid.

10. Lee, *Employment of Negro Troops,* 141.

11. Reddick, "Negro Policy," 12.

12. Gallup, *Public Opinion 1935–1971,* 2:782–83.

13. Nalty and MacGregor, *Blacks in the Military,* 114–15.

14. Merrill, *Documentary History,* 11:741.

15. Gardner, *Truman and Civil Rights*, 114.

16. Billington, "Freedom to Serve," 273.

17. Mershon and Schlossman, *Foxholes and Color Lines,* 209.

18. Nalty and MacGregor, *Blacks in the Military,* 289.

19. Ibid., 269.

[Notes continue.]

13

Bibliography

Billington, Monroe. "Freedom to Serve: The President's Committee
on Equality of Treatment and Opportunity in the Armed
Forces, 1949–1950." *Journal of Negro History* (1966): 262–74.
doi:10.2307/2716101.

Gallup, George H. *The Gallup Poll: Public Opinion 1935–1971.*
Vol. 2. New York: Random House, 1972.

Gardner, Michael R. *Harry Truman and Civil Rights: Moral
Courage and Political Risks.* Carbondale: Southern Illinois
Univ. Press, 2002.

Humphrey, Hubert H. *Beyond Civil Rights: A New Day of Equality.*
New York: Random House, 1968.

Lee, Ulysses. *The Employment of Negro Troops.* Washington, DC:
Center of Military History, 1963.

Mayer, Kenneth. *With the Stroke of a Pen: Executive Orders and
Presidential Power.* Princeton: Princeton Univ. Press, 2001.

McCullough, David. *Truman.* New York: Simon & Schuster, 1992.

Merrill, Dennis, ed. *Documentary History of the Truman Presidency.*
Vol. 11. Bethesda, MD: University Publishers of America, 1996.

Mershon, Sherie, and Steven Schlossman. *Foxholes and Color
Lines.* Baltimore: Johns Hopkins Univ. Press, 1998.

[Bibliography continues.]

38 Writing in the Natural Sciences

The **natural sciences** include mathematics, the biological sciences (biology, botany, and zoology), the physical sciences (chemistry and physics), and the earth sciences (geology and astronomy). They also include **applied sciences** such as medicine and allied health studies, engineering, and computer science. The natural sciences are problem-solving disciplines that report or analyze results derived from meticulous observation and experimentation. Writing assignments you can expect to receive in natural science courses include literature reviews, field reports, and laboratory reports.

38a Audience, purpose, and the research question

Before you start working on a writing assignment for a course in the natural sciences, be sure to consult with your instructor as you determine your audience and your purpose. Your instructor will always be one of your readers, but he or she may ask you to share your work with other readers as well. By knowing who constitutes your audience(s), you will be able to gauge how much background information is adequate, how much technical language is appropriate, and what types of evidence and reasoning are necessary.

After you have determined your purpose and audience, formulate a research question that will guide you to sources and help you to use them responsibly. The following example research questions focus on global warming:

Question about cause

What causes global warming?

Question about consequences

What are the effects of global warming?

Question about process

How can global warming be stopped?

Question about definitions or categories

What types of greenhouse gases are responsible for global warming?

Question about values

What are a scientist's responsibilities concerning the public in the face of global warming?

Research questions in the sciences are often narrowed to enable precise measurements:

Question about length, distance, frequency, and so on

How far has Mendenhall Glacier receded each year for the past decade, and do the values show any trend?

Question about comparisons and correlations

How are emission intensities related to the total amount of emissions?

38b Evidence, sources, and reasoning

Researchers in the natural sciences attempt to quantify phenomena in the world around them. They look for **empirical evidence**—facts that can be measured or tested—to support their claims. Most of their investigations, then, are set up as experiments. If you conduct an experiment for a course in the natural sciences, you will be expected to start with a **hypothesis,** a prediction that serves as a basis for experimentation. To test the hypothesis, you will follow a procedure—one designed by yourself, established in another study, or specified by your instructor. The results of your experiment will either validate your hypothesis or show it to be in error. This systematic way of proceeding from a hypothesis to verifiable results is called the **scientific method.** Consisting of six steps, this method helps ensure the objectivity and accuracy of experimental findings.

THE SCIENTIFIC METHOD

1. *State a problem*. When you recognize and then state a problem, you establish your exigence (the reason for your writing).

2. *Collect evidence*. Close observation is the key technique for collecting evidence. Be sure to record all details as accurately as you can. Alternatively, you may read the reports of other researchers who have addressed a problem similar to yours. If you draw on observations or experiments, you are using primary sources; if you use scientific articles and statistical charts, you are using secondary sources.

3. *Form a hypothesis*. A hypothesis is a tentative claim, or prediction, about the phenomenon you are studying.

4. *Test the hypothesis*. Although you will have conducted some research before formulating the hypothesis, you continue that research through additional observation or experimentation.

5. *Analyze the results*. Look at your results in light of your hypothesis. Attempt to find patterns, categories, or other relationships.

6. *State the conclusion*. If you have validated your hypothesis, explain why it accounts for *all* of your data. If your hypothesis is disproved, suggest revisions to it or offer a new one.

Reports based on the six steps of the scientific method are **quantitative studies,** because their results are presented as numerical data. Another type of study performed by scientists, especially those working in the field, is a **qualitative study.** The data in qualitative studies are produced through observation and analysis of natural phenomena. It is not uncommon, however, for studies to have both quantitative and qualitative features.

Regardless of the type of study they perform, scientists depend on previous research to place their work in context. They draw from both primary sources (experiments, observations, surveys, and so on) and secondary sources (books and articles already published on a topic).

38c Conventions of language and organization

(1) Style guidelines

The conventions that most writers in the sciences follow are presented in a manual titled *Scientific Style and Format,* compiled by the Council of Science Editors (CSE). However, you may sometimes be asked to use another manual, such as that published by the American Chemical Society, the American Institute of Physics, the American Mathematical Society, the American Medical Association, or the United States Geological Society. Before starting any writing project, check with your instructor to see which style manual you should use.

The CSE manual says that effective scientific prose has the qualities of accuracy, clarity, conciseness, and fluency. The following tips can help you write in the style recommended by the manual.

TIPS FOR PREPARING A PAPER IN THE NATURAL SCIENCES

- Select words that convey meaning precisely.
- Avoid gender bias.
- If two different wordings are possible, choose the more succinct alternative.
- Clarify noun strings by placing modifiers after the main noun.

  the system for measuring frequency
  NOT the frequency measuring system

- When using an introductory participial phrase, be sure that it modifies the subject of the sentence. Participial phrases that begin with *based on* are particulary troublesome, so double-check to make sure that such a phrase modifies the subject.

  Based on the promising results, the decision to approve the new medication seemed reasonable.

  NOT Based on the promising results, the new medication was approved.

---

(2) Organization

The most frequent writing assignments in the natural sciences are various types of reports—literature reviews, field reports, and laboratory reports. The specific formats for these reports are presented in the next section.

All scientific reports include headings and often subheadings to help readers find and understand information. Writers in the natural sciences also use tables and figures (such as graphs, drawings, and maps) to organize information. Essential for presenting numerical data, tables should be numbered and titled. Each table should be introduced in the text so that readers will understand its purpose. Alyssa Jergens includes two tables in her field report: one to summarize her data and one to report the results of a statistical test. She introduces her first table in this way: "Data from our observational study can be found in Table 1 and Figure 2." Alyssa also uses two figures in her report. The first is a diagram depicting the method used for recording data. The second provides a visual representation of the data in the corresponding table. Like tables, figures should be numbered, titled, and introduced in the text. For an example of a map used as a figure, see Kayla Berg's paper on the tsunami that hit Thailand in 2004 (39c).

(3) Reference lists

CSE provides three options for citing sources and listing them at the end of a paper: the citation-sequence system, the citation-name system, and the name-year system. You can find specific guidelines for creating a reference list in chapter 39.

38d   Examples of writing in the natural sciences

(1) Literature review

A **literature review** is essentially an evaluative overview of research directly related to a specific topic. It focuses on both strengths and weaknesses of previous research—in methodology or interpretation—with the goal of establishing what steps need to be taken to advance research on the topic. A literature review may be assigned as part of a longer paper, in which case the information it contains appears in the introductory section of the paper. In a paper on agate formation, student Michelle Tebbe included the following paragraphs, which provide, respectively, a historical account of research on her topic and a review of relevant current studies:

> Scientific interest in agate dates back at least to the 18th century when Collini (1776) contemplated the source of silica for agate formation and suggested a mechanism for producing repetitive banding. In the mid-19th

century, Noeggerath (1849) hypothesized that the repetitive banding of agate is indicative of natural, external (to the agate-bearing cavity), rhythmic processes such as bedrock leaching of silica by a fluid that enters into cavities via infiltration canals, forming agate after many separate infiltrations. Other processes such as variation in water-table height (Bauer 1904) and alternating wet-dry seasons (Linck and Heinz 1930) have been credited as responsible for rhythmic infilling of cavities by silica-rich solutions.

These now traditional ideas on agate formation imply fluid-rock interaction at low temperatures (<250 °C). Empirical support for low formation temperatures comes from several published studies. Based on hydrogen and oxygen isotope data, Fallick et al. (1985) estimated the temperature of formation of Devonian and Tertiary basalt-hosted Scottish agate to be approximately 50 °C. Using the same methods, Harris (1989) inferred the temperature of formation for basalt-hosted agate from Namibia to be approximately 120 °C. Lueth and Goodell (2005) performed fluid-inclusion analyses for agate from the Paraná Basalts, Rio do Sul, Brazil, and inferred the temperature of formation to be <50 °C for darker-colored samples and 140–180 °C for lighter-colored samples.

(2) Field report

Field work is research done in a natural environment rather than in a laboratory. Examples of field work range from recording beach erosion to studying avalanche patterns. To record their observations and analyses, researchers working in the field write **field reports**. These reports consist mainly of description and analysis, which may be presented together or in separate sections. A field report sometimes includes a reference list of sources mentioned in the text.

(3) Laboratory report

The most common writing assignment in the natural sciences is a **laboratory report**. The purpose of a lab report is to describe an experiment, including the results obtained, so that other researchers understand the procedure used and the conclusions drawn. When writing a lab report, you should explain the purpose of your research, recount the procedure you followed, and discuss your results. The format of this type of report follows the steps of the scientific method by starting with a problem and a hypothesis and concluding with a statement proving, modifying, or disproving the hypothesis.

- The **abstract** states the problem and summarizes the results. (You may not have to include an abstract if your report is short or if your instructor does not require it.)
- The **introduction** states the research question or hypothesis clearly and concisely, explains the scientific basis for the study, and provides brief background material on the subject of the study and the techniques to be used. The introduction usually includes citations referring to relevant sources.
- The **methods and materials** section is a narrative that describes how the experiment was conducted. It lists the materials that were used, identifies where the experiment was conducted, and describes the procedures that were followed. (Your lab notes should help you remember what you did.) Anyone who wants to repeat your work should be able to do so by following the steps described in this section.
- **Results** are reported by describing (but not interpreting) major findings and supporting them with properly labeled tables or graphs showing the empirical data.
- The **discussion** section includes an analysis of the results and an explanation of their relevance to the goals of the study. This section also reports any problems encountered and offers suggestions for further testing of the results.
- **References** are listed at the end of the paper. The list includes only works that are referred to in the report. The comprehensiveness and the accuracy of this list allow readers to evaluate the quality of the report and put it into a relevant context.

Alyssa Jergens wrote the following field report for a biology course. Her assignment was to form and test a hypothesis on the density and positioning of lichen growth on tree trunks. She worked as a member of a research group, but all the members wrote their own reports. Following the guidelines she was given by her instructor, Alyssa describes the observational study in the Methods section and analyzes the findings in the Results section.

1

Lichen Distribution on Tree Trunks

Alyssa Jergens

General Biology I

October 1, 2009

Method

Our group formulated the hypothesis that lichens grow more densely on higher parts of tree trunks than on lower parts of tree trunks. Our null hypothesis was as follows: there will be no difference in lichen density at various heights on tree trunks. Our hypothesis on lichen density led us to predict that the largest clusters of lichens would be found predominately on higher portions of tree trunks.

We conducted our study by sampling 20 trees in a designated area of the Central Washington University campus. Each tree trunk was divided into three sections based on height: from ground level to 0.5 m above the ground; from 0.5 m to 1.0 m above the ground; and from 1.0 m to 1.5 m above the ground. Data were recorded on a diagram (Figure 1). To the right in the diagram are the height ranges of the sections of tree trunks. The tick marks indicate how many trees had most of their lichens in that section of trunk.

The writer describes the observational research.

2

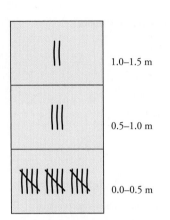

Figure 1   Method for recording lichen density

A diagram
used for data
collection is
presented in
the Method
section.

Results

The Results
section presents
the findings.

Our observations of lichen growth revealed that lichens are more commonly found on the lower parts of tree trunks. Data from our observational study can be found in Table 1 and Figure 2. Note that 15 of 20 trees had the densest lichen growth on the lowest section of the trunk (ground level to 0.5 m above the ground).

Table 1   Summary of data

Section of tree trunk	0.0–0.5 m	0.5–1.0 m	1.0–1.5 m
Number of trees with highest lichen density in given trunk section	15	3	2

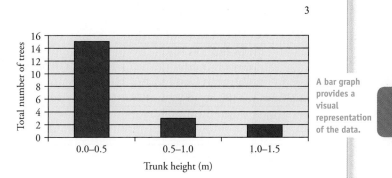

3

Figure 2   Association of trunk height with lichen distribution

To ensure that the pattern of lichen growth we found was not random, we performed a chi-square test. The observed number, f_o, was determined by counting the total number of trees having the most lichens in each height division. The expected number, f_e, was calculated by taking the total number of trees observed (20) and dividing it by the total number of height divisions (3), to arrive at an expected value of 6.67. The chi-square test results are summarized in Table 2; the calculated value is 15.69.

The critical value for the chi-square test given to us in class was 5.99. Our calculated chi-square value, 15.69, is greater than the critical value. Therefore, because the data from this observational study do not exhibit a random pattern, it can be concluded that a nonrandom pattern is present. The results of the chi-square test

4

Table 2   Results of chi-square test

	Observed number (f_o)	Expected number (f_e)	$f_o - f_e$	$(f_o - f_e)^2$	$\dfrac{(f_o - f_e)^2}{f_e}$
0.0–0.5 m	15	6.67	8.33	69.39	10.40
0.5–1.0 m	3	6.67	−3.67	13.47	2.02
1.0–1.5 m	2	6.67	−4.67	21.81	3.27
Total	20	20			15.69

show that our null hypothesis can be refuted. Although a pattern does exist in the sample of trees we observed, it was not the result we hypothesized. Our hypothesis stated that lichens would grow more densely on the upper portions of tree trunks rather than on the lower portions. Contrary to our expectations, our data and the results of the chi-square test indicate that lichens grow more densely on the lower portions of tree trunks than on the upper portions.

39 CSE Documentation

The Council of Science Editors (CSE) has established guide-lines for writers in the life and physical sciences. *Scientific Style and Format: The CSE Manual for Authors, Editors, and Publishers* presents three systems for citing and documenting research sources: the citation-sequence system, the name-year system, and the citation-name system.

39a CSE citation-sequence, name-year, and citation-name systems

(1) Citing material from other sources

As you prepare to write your paper, find out which system your instructor prefers—the citation-sequence system, the name-year system, or the citation-name system. Once you know your instructor's preference, use the guidelines in one of the following boxes for formatting your in-text references.

TIPS FOR FORMATTING CITATION-SEQUENCE IN-TEXT REFERENCES

- Place a superscript number after each use of information from a source. This number corresponds to the number assigned to the bibliographic entry for the source in the reference list.

- Insert the superscript number after the information taken from the source or after the word or phrase indicating the source; a single space precedes the number:

  Herbert's original method [1] was used.

- Insert the same number each time you use information from the source.

(Continued on page 446)

(Continued from page 445)

■ Order the numbers according to the sequence in which you introduce the sources:

Both Li [1] and Holst [2] have shown . . .

■ When referring to more than one source in the same in-text reference, use commas to separate the superscript numbers corresponding to the sources; notice that there is no space after each comma. Use an en dash between two numbers to indicate a sequence of sources:

The early studies [1,2,4–7] found . . .

TIPS FOR FORMATTING NAME-YEAR IN-TEXT REFERENCES

■ Place the author's last name and the year of publication in parentheses after mentioning the source or information from it:

In a more recent study (Karr 2011), these findings were not replicated.

Using the author's last name, the reader will be able to find the corresponding entry in the reference list, which is arranged alphabetically.

■ Omit the author's name from the in-text reference if the name appears in the text preceding it:

In Karr's study (2011), these findings were not replicated.

■ If the source has two authors, use both of their last names:

(Phill and Richardson 2011)

If there are three or more authors, use the first author's last name and the abbreviation *et al.*:

(Drake et al. 2010)

■ Use semicolons to separate multiple in-text references within a single set of parentheses. Order references chronologically when the years differ but alphabetically when the years are the same:

(Li 2010; Holst 2011)   BUT   (Lamont 2010; Li 2010)

TIPS FOR FORMATTING CITATION-NAME IN-TEXT REFERENCES

- Arrange your bibliographic list of references alphabetically. Then assign each reference a number. Use the superscript form of this number in the text immediately after the information taken from the source or after the word or phrase indicating the source:

  Stress-related illnesses are common among college students. [1]

  According to Li's study [6] of such illnesses . . .

- Use the same number each time you use material from or refer to the source.

- When referring to more than one source in the same in-text reference, use commas to separate the superscript numbers corresponding to the sources; note that there is no space after each comma. Use an en dash between two numbers to indicate a sequence of sources:

  Recent studies of posttraumatic stress disorder [1,2,4–7] show . . .

(2) Guidelines for quotations and headings

(a) Direct quotations

If a quotation is brief, incorporate it into a sentence. A comma or period at the end of a quotation is placed inside the quotation marks. A lengthy quotation should be set off as a block quotation.

(b) Headings

Headings and subheadings indicate how the various sections of a research paper or report are related. The CSE manual recommends that levels of headings be readily distinguishable and presents the following style as an illustration:

First level	**Boldfaced Uppercase and Lowercase Letters**
Second level	Uppercase and Lowercase Letters
Third level	*ITALICIZED SMALL UPPERCASE LETTERS*
Fourth level	*Italicized Uppercase and Lowercase Letters*

Two or three levels of subheadings are usually sufficient for most college-level assignments.

39b CSE-style reference list

All of the works you cite should be listed at the end of your paper, beginning on a separate page with the heading *End References*, *References,* or *Reference List*. The following tips will help you prepare such a list.

TIPS FOR PREPARING A REFERENCE LIST

- Place the heading (*End References*, *References*, or *Reference List*, not italicized) at the upper left of the page.

- If you are using the citation-sequence system, list the entries for your sources in the order in which they were introduced in the text. If your paper employs the citation-name system, your list of bibliographic entries should be ordered alphabetically according to the first author's last name and then numbered. If your paper employs the name-year system, your list should be ordered alphabetically. See page 457 for an example of a reference list in alphabetical order.

- CSE-style reference lists differ in overall organization: With the citation-sequence system, the entries in the reference list follow the order in which the sources were introduced in the text. With the citation-name or the name-year system, entries are listed alphabetically by the first author's last name.

- The name-year system differs from both the citation-sequence and the citation-name systems in the placement of the date of publication within entries: the name-year system calls for the date to be placed after the author's name; the citation-sequence and the citation-name systems call for the date to be placed after the publisher's name in entries for books and after the name of the periodical in entries for articles.

The following directory guides you to sample bibliographic entries for the citation-sequence system or the citation-name system.

BOOKS

1. Book with one author

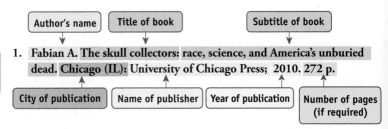

| Author's name | Title of book | Subtitle of book |

1. Fabian A. The skull collectors: race, science, and America's unburied dead. Chicago (IL): University of Chicago Press; 2010. 272 p.

| City of publication | Name of publisher | Year of publication | Number of pages (if required) |

2. Book with two or more authors

2. Easley D, Kleinberg J. Networks, crowds, and markets: reasoning about a highly connected world. Cambridge (GB): Cambridge University Press; 2010.

3. Book with an organization (or organizations) listed as author

3. Seattle Times. Natural wonders: the flora, fauna & formations of Washington. Seattle (WA): Seattle Times; 2003.

4. Book with editor(s)

4. Lund B, Hunter P, editors. The microbiological safety of food in healthcare settings. Malden (MA): Blackwell; 2007.

5. Chapter or part of an edited book

5. Martin DJ. Social data. In: Wilson J, Fotheringham AS, editors. The handbook of geographic information science. Malden (MA): Blackwell; 2008. p. 35–48.

ARTICLES

6. Article in a scholarly journal

6. Hilli S, Stark S, Derome J. Litter decomposition rates in relation to litter stocks in boreal coniferous forests along climatic and soil fertility gradients. Appl Soil Ecol. 2010;46(2):200–208.

7. Article in a popular (general-circulation) magazine

7. McKibben B. Carbon's new math. Natl Geogr Mag. 2007;212(4):33–37.

8. Article in a newspaper

8. O'Connor A. Heart attack risk linked to time spent in traffic. New York Times. 2004 Oct 26;Sect. F:9 (col. 4).

ELECTRONIC SOURCES

9. Online book

9. Committee on Planetary and Lunar Exploration. National Research Council. The quarantine and certification of Martian samples [Internet]. Washington (DC): National Academy Press; 2002 [cited 2007 Oct 31]. Available from: http://www.nap.edu/openbook.php?isbn=0309075718

10. Article in an online journal

10. Thom DH, Wong ST, Guzman D, Wu A, Penko J, Miaskowski C. Physician trust in the patient: development and validation of a new measure. Ann Fam Med [Internet]. 2011 [cited 2011 Apr 20]; 9(2):142–147. Available from: http://www.annfammed.org/cgi/content/full/9/2/142

11. Article in an online magazine

11. Shermer M. Weirdonomics and quirkology: how the curious science of the oddities of everyday life yields new insights. Sci Am [Internet]. 2007 [cited

2007 Nov 1]; 1297(5):45. Available from: http://www.sciam.com/issue.cfm after clicking on the article link.

12. Article in an online newspaper

12. Singer N. Making ads that whisper to the brain. New York Times [Internet]. 2010 Nov 13 [cited 2010 Nov 29]; [1 p.]. Available from: http://www.nytimes.com/2010/11/14/business/14stream.html?ref=health

13. Web site content

13. Corvus corax [Internet]. Bay Shore (NY): Long Island Ravens MC; c2000–2002 [updated 2001 Dec 3; cited 2003 Jan 3]. Available from: http://www.liravensmc.org/About/about_ravens.htm

14. Database

14. Honey Bee Genome Project [Internet]. Houston (TX): Baylor College of Medicine. [date unknown] -   [updated 2005 Jan 27; cited 2007 Nov 1]. Available from: http://www.hgsc.bcm.tmc.edu/projects/honeybee/

If you do not know the date of publication, place the words *date unknown* (not italicized) in square brackets; then add a space, a hyphen, and three more spaces.

Name-year system

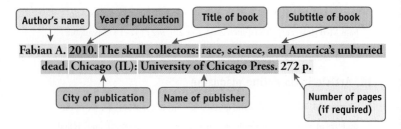

Author's name   Year of publication   Title of book   Subtitle of book

Fabian A. 2010. The skull collectors: race, science, and America's unburied dead. Chicago (IL): University of Chicago Press. 272 p.

City of publication   Name of publisher   Number of pages (if required)

The following sample entries for a reference list in the name-year format correspond to those listed as items 1 through 8 for the citation-sequence or citation-name system. (Because the CSE manual provides only one format for online sources, the entries for those sources are not repeated in this list.) The individual entries for books and articles differ from those in the citation-sequence and citation-name formats only in the placement of the date. In the name-year system, the date follows the author's name. For more examples of entries in name-year format, see page 457.

References

Easley D, Kleinberg J. 2010. Networks, crowds, and markets: reasoning about a highly connected world. Cambridge (GB): Cambridge University Press.

Fabian A. 2010. The skull collectors: race, science, and America's unburied dead. Chicago (IL): University of Chicago Press.

Hilli S, Stark S, Derome J. 2010. Litter decomposition rates in relation to litter stocks in boreal coniferous forests along climatic and soil fertility gradients. Appl Soil Ecol. 46(2):200–208.

Lund B, Hunter P, editors. 2007. The microbiological safety of food in healthcare settings. Malden (MA): Blackwell.

Martin DJ. 2008. Social data. In: Wilson J, Fotheringham AS, editors. The handbook of geographic information science. Malden (MA): Blackwell. p. 35–48.

McKibben B. 2007. Carbon's new math. Natl Geogr Mag. 212(4):33–37.

O'Connor A. 2004 Oct 26. Heart attack risk linked to time spent in traffic. New York Times. Sect. F:9 (col. 4).

Seattle Times. 2003. Natural wonders: the flora, fauna & formations of Washington. Seattle (WA): Seattle Times.

39c CSE-style research paper

Writing assignments in the natural sciences range from literature reviews to laboratory reports. Kayla Berg, portions of whose paper follow, was asked to review the causes and impacts of a natural disaster for a geology course. Kayla applied the guidelines in the CSE manual in formatting her paper. However, those guidelines do not cover all features of undergraduate papers, and Kayla's title page was formatted according to her instructor's directions. Kayla used the CSE name-year system to cite and document her sources.

Thailand Tsunami

Kayla Berg

Geology 380: Environmental Geology

November 5, 2009

1

Abstract

In 2004, an earthquake off the coast of Sumatra caused a tsunami that struck the coasts of several countries, causing not only a great deal of human suffering but also much environmental damage. This paper reports on various types of damage caused by the tsunami and the safety precautions that have been put into place to avoid similar destruction in the future.

2

Introduction

In December 2004, an earthquake with a magnitude of 9.0 occurred about 250 km off the west coast of Sumatra (in Indonesia) (Figure 1). The epicenter of the earthquake was located in the Indian Ocean at 3.3°N and 95.9°E. (Lukkunprasit and Ruangrassamee 2008). This earthquake caused a series of tsunami waves that struck the coasts of Thailand, Indonesia, Sri Lanka, India, Somalia, Madagascar, Kenya, Tanzania, Malaysia, Myanmar, and Bangladesh (At-a-glance 2005) damaging property and ecosystems.

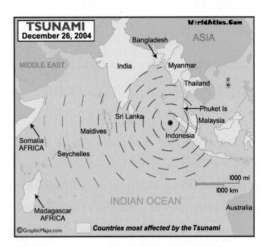

Figure 1. Epicenter of the earthquake and the areas affected by the tsunami (© GraphicMaps.com)

10

References

At-a-glance: countries hit. 2005 Dec 22. BBC News [Internet]. [cited 2011 Jan 9]; [1 p.] Available from: http://news.bbc.co.uk/2/hi/4126019.stm

Boszke, L, Astel A. 2007. Fractionation of mercury in sediments from coastal zone inundated by tsunami and in freshwater sediments from the rivers. J Environ Sci Health, Pt A: Toxic/Hazard Subst Environ Eng. (42)7:847–858.

Geist, EL, Titov, VV, Synolakis, CE. 2006. Tsunami: wave of change. Sci Am. (294)1:56–63.

Lukkunprasit P, Ruangrassamee, A. 2008. Building damage in Thailand in the 2004 Indian Ocean tsunami and clues for tsunami-resistant design. IES J Part A: Civ & Struct Eng. 1(1):17–30.

Szczucinski W, Chaimanee N, Niedzielski G, Rachlewicz G, Saisuttichai D, Tepsuwan T, Lorenc S, Siepak J. 2006. Environmental and geological impacts of the 26 December 2004 tsunami in coastal zone of Thailand—overview of short- and long-term effects. Polish J of Environ Stud. 15(5):793–810.

Yanagisawa H, Koshimura S, Goto K, Miyagi T, Imamura F, Ruangrassamee A, Tanavud C. 2009. Damage to mangrove forest by 2004 tsunami at Pakarang Cape and Namkem, Thailand. Polish J of Environ Stud. 18(1):35–42.

40 Writing in Business

Writing in business, like writing in any other environment, requires close attention to the rhetorical situation: exigence, audience, purpose, message, and context. It differs from other writing, however, in the nature of authorship: as a business writer, you need to present yourself and your employer as credible and reliable. One way to project that positive image is to follow the conventions and formats expected by the business community, whether you are writing letters, memos and e-mails, PowerPoint presentations, oral reports, or business reports.

40a Conventions of language and organization

In any business environment, you will face both anticipated and unexpected deadlines. The following strategies for effective business communication will help you produce comprehensive, concise, and well-organized documents on time.

STRATEGIES FOR EFFECTIVE BUSINESS COMMUNICATION

Be direct.

- Know who your audience members are and consider their needs.
- State the purpose of your document in your opening sentence or paragraph.
- Write straightforward sentences, beginning with a subject and including an active verb.
- Use technical language sparingly, unless the document is intended for a specialized audience.

Be concise.

- Compose direct, uncomplicated sentences.
- Include only necessary details.
- Use numbers, bullets, or descriptive headings that guide readers to information.
- Use graphs, tables, and other visual elements that convey information succinctly.

Use conventional formatting.

- Follow the standard formats that have been established within a business or industry or use the formats outlined in this chapter.
- Avoid informal language unless you know that a casual tone is acceptable.
- Edit and proofread your documents carefully. Typos, grammatical mistakes, sentence fragments, and missing words detract significantly from your ethos.

40b Business letters

Business letters serve a variety of purposes—to inquire, to inform, to complain, or to respond, for example. Regardless of its purpose, a business letter is usually single-spaced and fits on one sheet of paper. It also follows a standard block format: each element is aligned flush with the left margin, with double spacing between paragraphs.

ELEMENTS OF A STANDARD BUSINESS LETTER

- **Return address.** Your employer may require you to use stationery with a letterhead. If not, type your mailing address one inch from the top of the paper, flush left on a one-inch margin, and single-spaced.

(Continued on page 460)

(Continued from page 459)

- **Date.** Type the date beneath your return address. If you are using letterhead stationery, type the date one or two lines below the letterhead's last line.

- **Recipient's name and address.** Provide the full name and address of the recipient. Single-space these lines, and allow an extra line space above them. If you do not know the person's name, try to find it by checking the company's Web site or phoning the company. If you cannot find the recipient's name, use an appropriate title such as *Personnel Director* or *Customer Service Manager* (not italicized).

- **Greeting.** Type your greeting two lines below the last line of the recipient's address. The conventional greeting is *Dear* (not italicized) followed by the recipient's name and a colon. If you and the recipient use first names to address each other, use the person's first name. Otherwise, use *Mr., Ms., Mrs.,* or *Miss* and the last name. (Choose *Ms.* when you do not know a woman's preference.) Avoid the sexist *Dear Sir, Gentlemen,* or *Dear Madam* and the stilted *To Whom It May Concern* or *Dear Sir or Madam.*

- **Body of the letter.** Begin the first paragraph two lines below the greeting. Single-space lines within a paragraph; double-space between paragraphs. If your letter must continue on a second page, include the recipient's last name, the date, and the page number in three single-spaced lines at the top left on the second page.

- **Closing.** Close your letter two lines after the end of the body with an expression such as *Sincerely* or *Cordially* (not italicized) followed by a comma.

- **Signature.** Type your full name four lines below the closing. Then, in the space above your typed name, sign your full name, using blue or black ink. If you have addressed the recipient by his or her first name, sign just your first name.

■ **Additional information.** If you are enclosing extra material such as a résumé, type the word *Enclosure* or the abbreviation *Encl.* (not italicized) two lines below your name. You may also note the number of enclosures or the identity of the document(s): for example, *Enclosures (3)* or *Encl.: 2002 Annual Year-End Report*. If you would like the recipient to know the names of people receiving copies of the letter, use the abbreviation *cc* (for "carbon copy") and a colon followed by the other recipients' names. Place this element on the line directly below the enclosure line or, if there is no enclosure, two lines below your name.

The sample **letter of inquiry** (a letter intended to elicit information) in fig. 40.1 illustrates the parts of a typical business letter.

40c   Business memos and e-mails

A **memo** (short for *memorandum*) is a brief, single-topic document sent within a business to announce a meeting, explain an event or situation, set a schedule, or request information or action (see fig. 40.2). E-mail messages are also used for these purposes as well as for external communication with clients, prospective employees, or people at other companies. The basic guidelines for writing memos also apply to e-mail messages.

Because it is circulated internally, a memo or e-mail is usually less formal than a letter. Nonetheless, it should still be direct and concise: a memo should be no longer than a page, and an e-mail no longer than a screen. The guidelines for formatting these kinds of documents that appear on pages 463 and 464 are fairly standard, but a particular company or organization may establish its own format.

Return
address
and date

550 First Avenue
Ellensburg, WA 98926
February 4, 2009

Name and
address of
recipient

Mr. Mark Russell
Bilingual Publications
5400 Sage Avenue
Yakima, WA 98907

Greeting

Dear Mr. Russell:

Body of letter

I am a junior in the Bilingual Education Program at Central
Washington University. For my coursework, I am investigating
positions in publishing that include the use of two languages. Your
name and address were given to me by my instructor, Marta Cole,
who worked for you from 2003 through 2007.

I have learned something about your publications on your Web site.
I am most interested in dual documents—those in both English and
Spanish. Could you please send me samples of such documents
so that I can have a better idea of the types of publications you
produce?

I am also interested in finding out what qualifications I would need
to work for a business like yours. I am fluent in both Spanish and
English and have taken a course in translation. If possible, I would
like to ask you a few questions about your training and experience.
Would you have time for an interview some day next week?

Closing

Sincerely,

Signature

Chris Humphrey

Chris Humphrey

Figure 40.1. A sample letter of inquiry.

To: Intellectual Properties Committee
From: Leo Renfrow, Chair of Intellectual Properties Committee
Date: March 15, 2010
Subject: Review of Policy Statement

Heading

At the end of our last meeting, we decided to have our policy
statement reviewed by someone outside our university. Clark Beech,
chair of the Intellectual Properties Committee at Lincoln College,
agreed to help us. Overall, as his review shows, the format of our
policy statement is sound. Dr. Beech believes that some of the
content should be further developed, however. It appears that we
have used some ambiguous terms and included some conditions that
would not hold up in court.

Body of
memo

Early next week, my assistant will deliver a copy of Dr. Beech's
review to each of you. Please look it over before our next meeting,
on March 29. If you have any questions or comments before then,
please call me at ext. 1540. I look forward to seeing all of you at the
meeting.

Figure 40.2. A sample business memo.

ELEMENTS OF A STANDARD BUSINESS MEMO OR E-MAIL

■ **Heading.** On four consecutive lines, type *To* (not italicized)
   followed by a colon and the name(s) of the recipient(s), *From*
   followed by a colon and your name and title (if appropriate),
   Date followed by a colon and the date, and *Subject* followed by
   a colon and a few words identifying the memo's subject. (The
   abbreviation *Re*, for "regarding," is sometimes used instead of
   Subject.) This information should be single-spaced. If you are
   sending copies to individuals whose names are not included in

(Continued on page 464)

(Continued from page 463)

the *To* line, place those names on a new line beginning with *cc* ("carbon copy") and a colon. Most e-mail software supplies these header lines on any new message.

■ **Body.** Use the block format, single-spacing lines within each paragraph and double-spacing between paragraphs. Double-space between the heading and the body of the memo. Open your memo with the most important information and establish how it affects your audience. Use your conclusion to establish goodwill.

The effectiveness of memos and e-mails depends on several essential features: tone, length, and directness. A conversational tone is acceptable for an internal message to a coworker, but a more formal tone is required for a memo or an e-mail to a supervisor or a larger group of associates. One way to enhance the professional tone of your e-mails is to use an e-mail signature: a set of information that identifies you and your institution and is appended to the end of all your outgoing messages. Tone also includes the content of a message, so take care not to mention, let alone forward, any information that you or other correspondents might prefer to keep private. Keep in mind that anything you send in an e-mail can easily be forwarded by others.

People tend to read only one rhetorical unit, so keep your messages to just that: one page for a memo, one screen (or twenty lines) for an e-mail. Your memo or e-mail should fit on a single page or screen but retain enough white space to allow for easy reading.

Regular e-mail users receive a large volume of messages every day, most of which they scan, delete, or respond to quickly. To ensure that your e-mail receives attention, announce your topic in the subject line and then arrange and present your message in concise, readable chunks (perhaps bulleted or numbered lists) that incorporate white space and guide recipients to important information. Short paragraphs also allow for white space, which helps readers to maintain their attention and absorb the key points.

TIPS FOR SENDING ATTACHMENTS WITH E-MAIL MESSAGES

- Before you send any attachment, consider the size of the file—many inboxes have limited space and cannot accept large files or multiple files (totalling over 1000 KB) or files that contain streaming video, photographs, or sound clips. If you plan to send a large file, call or e-mail the recipient to ask permission before doing so.

- When you do not know the type of operating system or software installed on a recipient's computer, send text-only documents in rich text format (indicated by the file suffix **.rtf**), which preserves most formatting and is recognized by many word-processing programs.

- Because attachments are notorious for transmitting computer viruses, never open an attachment sent by someone you do not know or any attachment if your computer does not have active antivirus software.

40d Résumés

A **résumé** is essentially an argument designed to emphasize a person's job qualifications by highlighting his or her experience and abilities. Therefore, writing an impressive résumé requires smart choices about what to include, exclude, and emphasize. Start by placing all your contact information at the top center of the page, including your name, address, phone number(s), and e-mail address. Then, briefly state your career objective, including short-term as well as long-term goals, if appropriate. In the next section, establish a strong link between you and the organization to which you are applying, leading with your work or educational experience, whichever one is more suitable. (No matter what you decide to present first, you need to include information about both kinds of experience.) Many college students showcase their educational background, including their degrees or diplomas, special honors, participation in advanced programs, grade point average (either in general or in their major), and relevant courses. List your extracurricular activities if they relate directly to the position for which you are applying or demonstrate distinctive leadership, athletic, or artistic abilities. When describing your work experience, include all your jobs (paying, volunteer, and internships, as well as military service). Include dates, places of employment, and job titles, describing your duties with active verbs that emphasize your initiative and your sense of responsibility.

The next step is to decide how to organize your résumé. A **chronological résumé** lists positions and activities in *reverse* chronological order; that is, your most recent experience comes first. This format works well if you have a steady job history and want to emphasize your most recent experience. A **functional résumé**, which lists job skills rather than jobs held, is especially useful when you have the required skills, but your work history in the particular field is modest or you are just starting your career.

Remember that your résumé is, in effect, going to someone's office for a job interview. Make sure that it is dressed for success. Effective résumés are brief, so try to design your résumé to fit on a single page. Use good-quality paper (preferably white or off-white) and a laser printer. Choose a standard format and a traditional typeface, applying them consistently throughout. Use boldface or italic type only for headings. Resist the impulse to make the design unnecessarily complicated: when in doubt, opt for simplicity.

Joe Delaney's résumé (fig. 40.3) incorporates features of both the chronological and the functional formats.

Joseph F. Delaney III
138 Main Street, Apt. 10D
Cityville, PA 16800
(555) 544-9988   JoeDel4@psu.edu

OBJECTIVE   To obtain a position in project and risk management

EDUCATION
Pennsylvania State University, University Park, PA, 2003–2007
Majors: IST BS (Information Context Option), Psychology BS
Dean's List: Summer 2006, Fall 2006, and Spring 2007
Cumulative GPA: 3.60
Relevant Classes:
- Project Management in Technology—learned to apply basic concepts of project management to the information sciences
- Database Management—managed a project team that applied MySql, PHP, and HTML in completing Rabble Mosaic Creator, described at www .schoolproject.psu.edu/~100

COMPUTER AND TECHNICAL SKILLS
- MySql, PHP, GD Library, C++, Java
- TCP/IP, network security, LANs and WANs
- HTML, XML, and project and risk management

CLUBS/ACTIVITIES
IST Student Government:
- Regular participation in the student government's Academic Committee
- Student resource for the IST Student Executive Board
IST Academic Committee:
- Participated in regularly scheduled meetings with the dean, Henry C. Foley, and the professor in charge, John Yen
- Worked with the administration to address students' problems

WORK EXPERIENCE
Penn State Pollock Library, University Park, PA, May–July 2006
- Assisted patrons of the library in using computers, printers, and the Internet via a wireless network using VPN
- Coordinated computers in my designated area and assisted with defragmenting, rebooting, reformatting, charging, and normal maintenance of laptops

HONORS
- 2005 scholarship student in the College of IST; recipient of the Cingular Wireless Trustee Scholarship
- Pollock Library 2006 student employee of the year

Figure 40.3. Sample résumé.

TIPS FOR RÉSUMÉ WRITING

- Include your name, address, telephone number, e-mail address, and a fax number, if available.

- Identify your career or job objective, but only if you have a compelling one. You can provide details about your future plans when you are asked about them during an interview.

- Whenever possible, establish a clear relationship between your qualifications and the employer's needs.

- List your college or university degree and any pertinent areas in which you have had special training.

- Do not include personal data such as age, marital status, race, religion, or ethnicity.

- Even if an advertisement or posting asks you to state a salary requirement, defer that conversation until you are given an interview or a job offer.

- The names and addresses of **references** (people who have agreed to speak or write on your behalf) are not usually listed on a résumé. Instead, take a list of references to interviews. The list should include their names and addresses as well as their telephone numbers and/or e-mail addresses.

- To show that you are well organized and thoughtful, use a clean, clear format (see fig. 40.3).

- Meticulously proofread your résumé before sending it and have others read it carefully as well. Errors in business writing always detract from your credibility, but errors in a résumé or letter of application can destroy your chances of getting an interview.

40e Letters of application

Writing a letter of application, or cover letter, is an essential step in applying for a job. Your letter of application provides you with the chance to sound articulate, interesting, and professional, and to put a personal face on the factual content of the résumé. Letters of application follow the general format of all business letters; see fig. 40.4 for a sample letter of application.

TIPS FOR WRITING LETTERS OF APPLICATION

- Address your letter to a specific person. If you are responding to an ad that mentions a department without giving a name, call the company and find out who will be doing the screening. If you cannot obtain a specific name, use an appropriate title such as Human Resources Director (not italicized).

- Be brief. You can assume that the recipient will be screening many applications, so keep your letter to one easy-to-read page.

- Mention that you are enclosing a résumé or refer to it, but do not summarize it. Your goal is to attract the attention of a busy person (who will not want to read the same information in both your letter and your résumé).

- Indicate why you are interested in working for the company or organization to which you are applying. Demonstrating that you already know something about the company and the position, that you can contribute to it, indicates your seriousness and motivation. If you want more information about the company, locate an annual report and other information by searching the Web.

- In your closing, be sure to specify how and where you can be reached and emphasize your availability for an interview.

Return address and date

Joseph F. Delaney III
138 Main Street, Apt 10D
Cityville, PA 16800
June 4, 2007

Name and address of recipient

Mr. Jim Konigs, Human Resource Director
E. G. Hickey Technical Enterprise
333 Cumberville State Road, Suite 110
West Cumberville, PA 19428-2949

Greeting

Dear Mr. Konigs:

Body of letter

I am applying for the position of project manager advertised on Monster.com. I graduated on May 15 with a B.S. degree in information sciences and technology from Pennsylvania State University. I believe that my in-depth research and education in information technology make me an ideal candidate for this position.

I have completed the required coursework and an internship in information technology, consulting, and security, working under such distinguished professors as James Wendle and David Markison. I am currently a teaching instructor with Dr. Markison, responsible for student evaluation and advising. I have served as a project team leader in database management; my team created Rabble Mosaic Creator, a website that allows users to create mosaics out of images.

In addition, I have applicable experience as a member of the student government's Academic Committee, which analyzes students' problems in light of policy before presenting the issues to the dean and professor in charge. I have also worked in the Penn State libraries.

I would appreciate the opportunity to talk with you about the position and my interest in risk and project management. I am available for an interview and can be reached at the phone number or e-mail address at the top of my résumé.

Closing

Sincerely,

Signature

Joseph F. Delaney

Joseph F. Delaney III

Enclosure line

Encl.: résumé

Figure 40.4. Model letter of application.

40f Oral presentations with PowerPoint

Oral reports accompanied by PowerPoint presentations are commonplace in business. Such reports can be either internal (for supervisors and colleagues) or external (for clients or investors). They may take the form of project status reports, demonstrations of new equipment or software, research reports, or recommendations.

Keep in mind the following guidelines as you compose an oral report and create PowerPoint slides to accompany it.

ELEMENTS OF A STANDARD ORAL PRESENTATION

- **Introduction.** Taking no more than one-tenth of your overall presentation time (for example, one minute of a ten-minute presentation), your introduction should indicate who you are, your qualifications, your topic, and the relevance of that topic to your audience. The introduction provides an outline of your main points so that listeners can easily follow your presentation.

- **Body.** Make sure the organization of your presentation is clear through your use of transitions. You can number each point, use cause-and-consequence transitions, or use chronological transitions. Provide internal summaries to remind your listeners where you have been and where you are going and offer comments to help your audience sense the weight of various points.

- **Conclusion.** Rather than restating the main ideas, make your conclusion memorable by ending with a proposal for action, a final statistic, recommendations, or a description of the benefits of a certain course of action. Conclusions should be even shorter than introductions.

TIPS FOR INCORPORATING POWERPOINT INTO AN ORAL PRESENTATION

- Design your slides for your audience, not for yourself. If you need speaking notes for your talk, write them on note cards or type them into the notes section provided below each slide in the PowerPoint program.

- Use text and visuals on the PowerPoint slides that complement the oral part of your presentation and do not repeat what you plan to say.

- Be aware of the limitations of PowerPoint. Use no more than five lines of 16-point type per slide. PowerPoint tends to encourage oversimplification, so tell your audience where they can find more details.

- In general, keep text and visuals separate. Alternating predominantly visual slides with slides of text will keep your audience's attention. Let visuals (charts, pictures, or graphs) stand alone with just a heading or a title. Use text slides to define terms, to present block quotes that might be difficult to follow orally, and to list the main points you will be making.

- Time your speaking with your presentation of the slides so that the two components are synchronized.

Student Emily Cohen and fellow group members created PowerPoint slides to accompany an oral presentation in a business class in which they were writing a business plan. Figure 40.5 shows two of those slides.

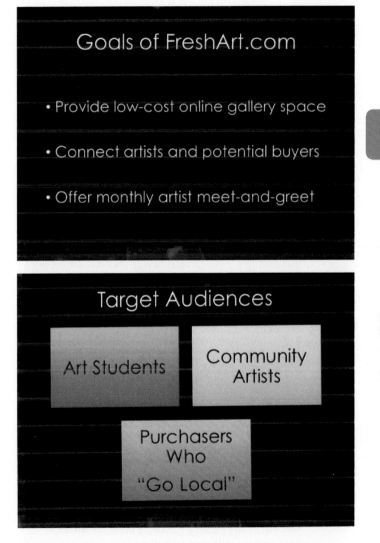

Figure 40.5. A precise title and concise bulleted points help audience members skim the upper slide, letting them focus more on what the presenter is saying. Using contrasting colors makes slides easier to read.

40g Business reports

Business reports take many forms, including periodic reports, sales reports, progress reports, incident reports, and longer reports that assess relocation plans, new lines of equipment or products, marketing schemes, and so on. The following box describes elements of such reports.

ELEMENTS OF A STANDARD BUSINESS REPORT

- **Front matter.** Depending on the audience, purpose, and length of a given report, the front matter materials may include a letter of transmittal, a title page, a table of contents, a list of illustrations, and/or an abstract.

- **Introduction.** This section identifies the problem addressed by the report (the rhetorical opportunity), presents background information, and includes a purpose statement and a description of the scope of the report (a list of the limits that framed the investigation). An introduction should not take up more than ten to fifteen percent of the length of a report.

- **Body or discussion.** This, the longest section of the report, presents the research findings. It often incorporates charts and graphs to help make the data easy to understand. This section should be subdivided into clear subsections by subheadings or, for a shorter report, paragraph breaks.

- **Conclusion(s).** This section summarizes any conclusions and generalizations deduced from the data presented in the body of the report.

- **Recommendation(s).** Not always necessary, this section outlines what should be done with or about the findings.

- **Back matter.** Like the front matter, the back matter of a report depends on the audience, purpose, and length of the report. Back matter may include a glossary, a list of the references cited, and/or one or more appendixes.

Glossary of Usage

By learning about usage in this glossary, you will increase your ability to use words effectively.

Agreement on usage occurs slowly–often after a period of debate. An asterisk (*) before an entry indicates that a new usage has been reported by dictionary editors. This usage, however, might not yet be accepted by everyone.

a lot of   *A lot of* is conversational for *many, much,* or *a great deal of:* They do not have ~~a lot of~~ much time. *A lot* is sometimes misspelled as *alot.*

a while, awhile   *A while* means "a period of time." It is often used with the prepositions *after, for,* and *in:* We rested for **a while.** *Awhile* means "a short time." It is not preceded by a preposition: We rested **awhile.**

accept, except   The verb *accept* means "to receive": I **accept** your apology. The verb *except* means "to exclude": The policy was to have everyone wait in line, but mothers and small children were **excepted.** The preposition *except* means "other than": All **except** Joe will attend the conference.

advice, advise   *Advice* is a noun: They asked their attorney for **advice.** *Advise* is a verb: The attorney **advised** us to save all relevant documents.

affect, effect   *Affect* is a verb that means "to influence": The lobbyist's pleas did not **affect** the politician's decision. The noun *effect* means "a result": The **effect** of his decision on the staff's morale was positive and long lasting. When used as a verb, *effect* means "to produce" or "to cause": The activists believed that they could **effect** real political change.

all ready, already   *All ready* means "completely prepared": The rooms are **all ready** for the conference. *Already* means "by or before the time specified": She has **already** taken her final exams.

* **all right**   *All right* means "acceptable": The students asked whether it was **all right** to use dictionaries during the exam. *Alright* is not yet a generally accepted spelling of *all right,* although it is becoming more common in journalistic writing.

all together, altogether   *All together* means "as a group": The cast reviewed the script **all together.** *Altogether* means "wholly, thoroughly": That game is **altogether** too difficult.

allude, elude   *Allude* means "to refer to indirectly": The professor **alluded** to a medieval text. *Elude* means "to evade" or "to escape from": For the moment, his name **eludes** me.

allusion, illusion   An *allusion* is a casual or indirect reference: The **allusion** was to Shakespeare's *Twelfth Night.* An *illusion* is a false idea or an unreal image: His idea of college is an **illusion.**

alot   See **a lot of.**

already   See **all ready, already.**

alright   See **all right.**

altogether   See **all together, altogether.**

* **among, between**   To follow traditional usage, use *among* with three or more entities (a group): The snorklers swam **among** the fish. Use *between* when referring to only two entities: The rivalry **between** the two teams is intense. Current dictionaries also note the possibility of using *between* to refer to more than two entities, especially when these entities are considered distinct: We have strengthened the lines of communication **between** the various departments.

amount of, number of   Use *amount of* before nouns that cannot be counted: The **amount of** rain that fell last year was insufficient. Use *number of* with nouns that can be counted: The **number of** students attending college has increased.

and/or   This combination denotes three options: one, the other, or both: a parent **and/or** a teacher. These options can also be presented separately with *or:* The student's application should be signed by a parent, a teacher, **or** both.

* **angry at, angry with**   Both *at* and *with* are commonly used after *angry,* although according to traditional guidelines, *with* should be used when a person is the cause of the anger: She was **angry with** me because I was late.

another, other, the other   *Another* is followed by a singular noun: **another** book. *Other* is followed by a plural noun: **other** books. *The other* is followed by either a singular or a plural noun: **the other book, the other books.**

anymore, any more   *Anymore* meaning "any longer" or "now" most frequently occurs in negative sentences: Sarah doesn't work here **anymore.** Its use in positive sentences is considered conversational; *now* is generally used instead: All he ever does ~~anymore~~ now is watch television. As two words, *any more* appears with *not* to mean "no more": We do not have **any more** time.

anyone, any one   *Anyone* means "any person at all": We did not know **anyone.** *Any one* refers to one of a group: **Any one** of the options is better than the current situation.

* **anyplace, everyplace, someplace**   These words are becoming increasingly common in academic writing. However, according to traditional usage rules, they should be replaced by *anywhere, everywhere,* and *somewhere.*

as   Conversational when used after such verbs as *know, say,* and *see.* Use *that, if,* or *whether* instead: I do not know ~~as~~ whether my application is complete. Also considered conversational is the use of *as* instead of *who, which,* or *that:* Many of the performers ~~as~~ who have appeared on our program will be giving a concert this evening.

* **as, like**   According to traditional usage, *as* begins either a phrase or a clause; *like* begins only a phrase: My brother drives too fast, just ~~like~~ as my father did. Current dictionaries note the informal use of *like* to begin clauses after verbs such as *look* and *sound.*

assure, ensure, insure   *Assure* means "to state with confidence, alleviating any doubt": The flight attendant **assured** us that our flight would arrive on time. *Ensure* and *insure* are usually interchangeable to mean "make certain," but only *insure* means "to protect against loss": The editor **ensured** [OR **insured**] that the reporter's facts were accurate. Physicians must **insure** themselves against malpractice suits.

awhile   See **a while, awhile.**

bad   Unconventional as an adverb; use *badly* instead. The team played **badly.** However, the adjective *bad* is used after sensory verbs such as *feel, look,* and *smell:* I feel **bad** that I forgot to return your book yesterday.

being as, being that   Unconventional; use *because* instead. ~~Being as~~ Because the road was closed, traffic was diverted to another route.

* **beside, besides**   According to traditional usage, these two words have different meanings. *Beside* means "next to": The president sat **beside** the prime minister. *Besides* means "in addition to" or "other than": She has written many articles **besides** those on political reform. Current dictionaries report that professional writers regularly use *beside* to convey this meaning, as long as there is no risk of ambiguity.

better, had better   *Better* is conversational. Use *had better* instead: We ~~better~~ had better finish the report by five o'clock.

between   See **among, between.**

* **can, may**   *Can* refers to ability, and *may* refers to permission: You **can** [are able to] drive seventy miles an hour, but you **may** not [are not permitted to] exceed the speed limit. Current dictionaries report that in contemporary usage *can* and *may* are used interchangeably to denote possibility or permission, although *may* is used more frequently in formal contexts.

capital, capitol   *Capital* means either "a governing city" or "funds": The **capital** of Minnesota is St. Paul. An anonymous donor provided the **capital** for the project. As a modifier, *capital* means "chief" or "principal": This year's election is of **capital** importance. It may also refer to the death penalty: **Capital** punishment is legal in some states. A *capitol* is a statehouse; the *Capitol* is the U.S. congressional building in Washington, DC.

cite, site, sight   *Cite* means "to mention": Be sure to **cite** your sources. *Site* is a location: The president visited the **site** for the new library. As a verb, *site* also means "to situate": The builder

sited the factory near the freeway. *Sight* means "to see": The crew **sighted** land. *Sight* also refers to a view: What an incredible **sight!**

climactic, climatic *Climactic* refers to a climax, or high point: The actors rehearsed the **climactic** scene. *Climatic* refers to the *climate:* Many environmentalists are worried about the recent **climatic** changes.

coarse, course *Coarse* refers to roughness: The jacket was made of **coarse** linen. *Course* refers to a route: Our **course** to the island was indirect. *Course* may also refer to a plan of study: I want to take a **course** in nutrition.

compare to, compare with *Compare to* means "to regard as similar," and *compare with* means "to examine for similarities and/or differences": She **compared** her mind **to** a dusty attic. The student **compared** the first draft **with** the second.

complement, complementary, compliment, complimentary *Complement* means "to complete" or "to balance": Their personalities **complement** each other. They have **complementary** personalities. *Compliment* means "to express praise": The professor **complimented** the students on their first drafts. Her remarks were **complimentary.** *Complimentary* may also mean "provided free of charge": We received **complimentary** tickets.

* **compose, comprise** *Compose* means "to make up": That collection **is composed** of medieval manuscripts. *Comprise* means "to consist of": The anthology **comprises** many famous essays. Dictionary editors have noted the increasing use of *comprise* in the passive voice to mean "to be composed of."

conscience, conscious, consciousness *Conscience* means "the sense of right and wrong": He examined his **conscience** before deciding whether to join the protest. *Conscious* means "awake": After an hour, the patient was fully **conscious.** After an hour, the patient regained **consciousness.** *Conscious* may also mean "aware": We were **conscious** of the possible consequences.

continual, continually, continuous, continuously *Continual* means "constantly recurring": **Continual** interruptions kept us from completing the project. Telephone calls **continually** interrupted us. *Continuous* means "uninterrupted": The job applicant had a record of ten years' **continuous** employment. The job applicant worked **continuously** from 2000 to 2009.

could of   *Of* is often mistaken for the sound of the unstressed *have:* They **could ~~of~~ have** [OR might **have,** should **have,** would **have**] gone home.

couldn't care less   *Couldn't care less* expresses complete lack of concern: She **couldn't care less** about her reputation. *Could care less* is considered unconventional in academic writing.

council, counsel   A *council* is an advisory or decision-making group: The student **council** supported the new regulations. A *counsel* is a legal adviser: The defense **counsel** conferred with the judge. As a verb, *counsel* means "to give advice": She **counsels** people with eating disorders.

criteria, criterion   *Criteria* is a plural noun meaning "a set of standards for judgment": The teachers explained the **criteria** for the assignment. The singular form is *criterion:* Their judgment was based on only one **criterion.**

* **data**   *Data* is the plural form of *datum,* which means "piece of information" or "fact": When the **data are** complete, we will know the true cost. However, current dictionaries also note that *data* is frequently used as a mass entity (like the word *furniture*), appearing with a singular verb.

desert, dessert   *Desert* can mean "a barren land": Gila monsters live in the **deserts** of the Southwest. As a verb, *desert* means "to leave": I thought my friends had **deserted** me. *Dessert* refers to something sweet eaten at the end of a meal: They ordered apple pie for **dessert.**

device, devise   *Device* is a noun: She invented a **device** that measures extremely small quantities of liquid. *Devise* is a verb: We **devised** a plan for work distribution.

differ from, differ with   *Differ from* means "to be different": A bull snake **differs from** a rattlesnake in a number of ways. *Differ with* means "to disagree": Senator Brown has **differed with** Senator Owen on several issues.

different from, different than   *Different from* is generally used with nouns, pronouns, noun phrases, and noun clauses: This school was

different from most others. The school was **different from** what we had expected. *Different than* is used with adverbial clauses; *than* is the conjunction: We are no **different than** they are.

discreet, discrete   *Discreet* means "showing good judgment or self-restraint": His friends complained openly, but his comments were quite **discreet.** *Discrete* means "distinct": The participants in the study came from three **discrete** groups.

disinterested, uninterested   *Disinterested* means "impartial": A **disinterested** observer will give a fair opinion. *Uninterested* means "lacking interest": She was **uninterested** in the outcome of the game.

distinct, distinctive   *Distinct* means "easily distinguishable or perceived": Each proposal has **distinct** advantages. *Distinctive* means "characteristic" or "serving to distinguish": We studied the **distinctive** features of hawks.

* **due to**   Traditionally, *due to* was not synonymous with *because of:* ~~Due to~~ Because of holiday traffic, we arrived an hour late. However, dictionary editors now consider this usage of *due to* acceptable.

effect   See **affect, effect.**

elicit, illicit   *Elicit* means "to draw forth": He is **eliciting** contributions for a new playground. *Illicit* means "unlawful": The newspaper reported their **illicit** mishandling of public funds.

elude   See **allude, elude.**

emigrate from, immigrate to   *Emigrate* means "to leave one's own country": My ancestors **emigrated from** Ireland. *Immigrate* means "to arrive in a different country to settle": The Ulster Scots **immigrated to** the southern United States.

ensure   See **assure, ensure, insure.**

especially, specially   *Especially* emphasizes a characteristic or quality: Some people are **especially** sensitive to the sun. *Especially* also means "particularly": Wildflowers are abundant in this area, **especially** during May. *Specially* means "for a particular purpose": The classroom was **specially** designed for music students.

etc.   Abbreviation of *et cetera,* meaning "and others of the same kind." Use only within parentheses: Be sure to bring appropriate camping gear (tent, sleeping bag, mess kit, **etc.**). Because *and* is part of the meaning of *etc.,* avoid using the combination *and etc.*

everyday, every day   *Everyday* means "routine" or "ordinary": These are **everyday** problems. *Every day* means "each day": I read the newspaper **every day.**

everyone, every one   *Everyone* means "all": **Everyone** should attend. *Every one* refers to each person or item in a group: **Every one** of you should attend.

everyplace   See **anyplace, everyplace, someplace.**

except   See **accept, except.**

explicit, implicit   *Explicit* means "expressed clearly and directly": Given his **explicit** directions, we knew how to proceed. *Implicit* means "implied or expressed indirectly": I mistakenly understood his silence to be his **implicit** approval of the project.

farther, further   Generally, *farther* refers to geographic distance: We will have to drive **farther** tomorrow. *Further* means "more": If you need **further** assistance, please let me know.

* **feel**   Traditionally, *feel* was not synonymous with "think" or "believe": I ~~feel~~ think that more should be done to protect local habitat. Dictionary editors now consider this use of *feel* to be a standard alternative.

fewer, less   *Fewer* occurs before nouns that can be counted: **fewer** technicians, **fewer** pencils. *Less* occurs before nouns that cannot be counted: **less** milk, **less** support. *Less than* may be used with measurements of time or distance: **less than** three months, **less than** twenty miles.

* **first, firstly; second, secondly**   Many college instructors prefer the use of *first* and *second.* However, dictionary editors state that *firstly* and *secondly* are also well-established forms.

former, latter   Used together, *former* refers to the first of two; *latter* to the second of two. John and Ian are both English. The **former** is from Manchester; the **latter** is from Birmingham.

further   See **farther, further.**

get   Considered conversational in many common expressions: The weather ~~got better~~ improved overnight. I did not know what he ~~was getting at~~ meant.

good, well   *Good* is an adjective, not an adverb: He pitched ~~good~~ **well** last night. *Good* in the sense of "in good health" may be used interchangeably with *well:* I feel **good** [OR **well**] this morning.

had better   See **better, had better.**

half   *A half a* or *a half an* is unconventional; use *half a/an* or *a half:* You should be able to complete the questionnaire in **a half ~~an~~** hour.

hanged, hung   *Hanged* means "put to death by hanging": The prisoner was **hanged** at dawn. For all other meanings, use *hung:* He **hung** the picture above his desk.

has got, have got   Conversational; omit *got*: I **have ~~got~~** a meeting tomorrow.

he/she, his/her   As a solution to the problem of sexist language, these combinations are not universally accepted. Consider using *he or she* and *his or her.* See 12c.

herself, himself, myself, yourself   Unconventional as subjects in a sentence. Joe and ~~myself~~ I will lead the discussion. See 5a(3).

hopefully   Conversational to mean "I hope": ~~Hopefully,~~ I hope the game will not be canceled.

hung   See **hanged, hung.**

i.e.   Abbreviation of *id est,* meaning "that is." Use only within parentheses: All participants in the study ran the same distance (**i.e.**, six kilometers). Otherwise, replace *i.e.* with the English equivalent, *that is:* Assistance was offered to those who would have difficulty boarding, ~~i.e.,~~ that is, the elderly, the disabled, and parents with small children. Do not confuse *i.e.* with *e.g.,* meaning "for example."

illicit   See **elicit, illicit.**

illusion   See **allusion, illusion.**

immigrate   See **emigrate from, immigrate to.**

* **impact**   Though *impact* is commonly used as a verb in business writing, many college teachers still use it as a noun only: The new tax ~~impacts~~ affects everyone.

implicit   See **explicit, implicit.**

imply, infer   *Imply* means "suggest without actually stating": Though he never mentioned the statistics, he **implied** that they were questionable. *Infer* means "draw a conclusion based on evidence": Given the tone of his voice, I **inferred** that he found the work substandard.

in regards to   Unconventional; see **regard, regarding, regards.**

inside of, outside of   Drop *of* when unnecessary: Security guards stood **outside ~~of~~** the front door.

insure   See **assure, ensure, insure.**

irregardless   Unconventional; use *regardless* instead.

its, it's   *Its* is a possessive form: The committee forwarded **its** recommendation. *It's* is a contraction of *it is:* **It's** a beautiful day.

kind of a, sort of a   The word *a* is unnecessary: This **kind of ~~a~~** book sells well. *Kind of* and *sort of* are not conventionally used to mean "somewhat": The report was **~~kind of~~ somewhat** difficult to read.

later, latter   *Later* means "after a specific time" or "a time after now": The concert ended **later** than we had expected. *Latter* refers to the second of two items: Of the two versions described, I prefer the **latter.**

lay, lie   *Lay* (*laid, laying*) means "put" or "place": He **laid** the book aside. *Lie* (*lay, lain, lying*) means "rest" or "recline": I had just **lain** down when the alarm went off. *Lay* takes an object (to **lay** something), while *lie* does not. These verbs may be confused because the present tense of *lay* and the past tense of *lie* are spelled the same way.

lead, led   As a noun, *lead* means "a kind of metal": The paint had **lead** in it. As a verb, *lead* means "to conduct": A guide will **lead** a tour of the ruins. *Led* is the past tense of the verb *lead:* He **led** the country from 1949 to 1960.

less, less than   See **fewer, less.**

lie   See **lay, lie.**

like   See **as, like.**

literally   Conversational when used to emphasize the meaning of another word: I was **~~literally~~ nearly** frozen after I finished shoveling the sidewalk. *Literally* is conventionally used to indicate that an expression is not being used figuratively: My friend **literally** climbs the walls after work; his fellow rock climbers join him at the local gym.

lose, loose   *Lose* is a verb: She does not **lose** her patience often. *Loose* is chiefly used as an adjective: A few of the tiles are **loose.**

lots, lots of   Conversational for *many* or *much:* He has ~~lots of~~ many friends. We have ~~lots~~ much to do before the end of the quarter.

mankind   Considered sexist because it excludes women: All ~~mankind~~ humanity will benefit from this new discovery.

may   See **can, may.**

may of, might of   See **could of.**

maybe, may be   *Maybe* is an adverb: **Maybe** the negotiators will succeed this time. *May* and *be* are verbs: The rumor **may be** true.

* **media, medium**   According to traditional definitions, *media* is a plural word: The **media** have sometimes created the news in addition to reporting it. The singular form is *medium:* The newspaper is one **medium** that people seem to trust. Dictionary editors note the frequent use of *media* as a collective noun taking a singular verb, but this usage is still considered conversational.

might could   Conversational for "might be able to": The director **might** ~~could~~ be able to review your application next week.

most   Unconventional to mean "almost": We watch the news ~~most~~ almost every day.

myself   See **herself, himself, myself, yourself.**

nothing like, nowhere near   Unconventional; use *not nearly* instead: Her new book is ~~nowhere near~~ not nearly as mysterious as her previous novel.

number of   When the expression *a number of* is used, the reference is plural: **A number of** positions **are** open. When *the number of* is used, the reference is singular: **The number of** possibilities **is** limited. See also **amount of, number of.**

off of   Conversational; omit *of:* He walked **off** ~~of~~ the field.

on account of   Conversational; use *because of:* The singer canceled her engagement ~~on account of~~ because of a sore throat.

on the other hand   Use *however* instead or make sure that the sentence or independent clause beginning with this transitional phrase is preceded by one starting with *on the one hand.*

other   See **another, other, the other.**

passed, past   *Passed* is the past tense of the verb *pass:* Deb **passed** the other runners right before the finish line. *Past* means "beyond a time or location": We walked **past** the high school.

per   In ordinary contexts, use *a* or *an:* You should drink at least six glasses of water ~~per~~ a day.

percent, percentage   *Percent* (also spelled *per cent*) is used with a specific number: **Sixty percent** of the students attended the ceremony. *Percentage* refers to an unspecified portion: The **percentage** of students attending college has increased in recent years.

perspective, prospective   *Perspective* means "point of view": We discussed the issue from various **perspectives.** *Prospective* means "likely to become": **Prospective** journalists interviewed the editor.

phenomena, phenomenon   *Phenomena* is the plural form of *phenomenon:* Natural **phenomena** were given scientific explanations.

plus   *Plus* joins nouns or noun phrases to make a sentence seem like an equation: Her endless curiosity **plus** her boundless energy makes her the perfect camp counselor. Note that a singular form of the verb is required (e.g., *makes*). *Plus* is not used to join clauses: I telephoned ~~plus~~ and I sent flowers.

precede, proceed   To *precede* is to "go ahead of": A moment of silence **preceded** the applause. To *proceed* is to "go forward": After stopping for a short rest, we **proceeded** to our destination.

prejudice, prejudiced   *Prejudice* is a noun: They were unaware of their **prejudice.** *Prejudiced* is an adjective: She accused me of being **prejudiced.**

pretty   *Pretty* means "attractive," not "rather" or "fairly": We were ~~pretty~~ fairly tired after cooking all day.

principal, principle   As a noun, *principal* means "chief official": The **principal** greeted the students every day. It also means "capital": The loan's **principal** was still quite high. As an adjective, *principal* means "main": Tourism is the country's **principal** source of income. The noun *principle* refers to a rule, standard, or belief: She explained the three **principles** supporting the theory.

proceed   See **precede, proceed.**

prospective   See **perspective, prospective.**

quotation, quote   In academic writing, *quotation,* rather than *quote,* refers to a repeated or copied sentence or passage: She began her speech with a ~~quote~~ quotation from *Othello. Quote* expresses an action: My friend sometimes **quotes** lines from television commercials.

raise, rise   *Raise* (*raised, raising*) means "to lift or cause to move upward, to bring up or increase": Retailers **raised** prices. *Rise* (*rose, risen, rising*) means "to get up" or "to ascend": The cost of living **rose** sharply. *Raise* takes an object (to **raise** something); *rise* does not.

real, really   *Really* rather than *real* is used to mean "very": He is from a ~~real~~ really small town. To ensure this word's effectiveness, use it sparingly.

* **reason why**   Traditionally, this combination was considered redundant: No one explained **the reason** ~~why~~ the negotiations failed. [OR No one explained ~~the reason~~ **why** the negotiations failed.] However, dictionary editors report its use by highly regarded writers.

regard, regarding, regards   These forms are used in the following expressions: *in regard to, with regard to, as regards,* and *regarding* [NOT *in regards to, with regards to,* or *as regarding*].

* **relation, relationship**   According to traditional definitions, *relation* is used to link abstractions: We studied the **relation** between language and social change. *Relationship* is used to link people: The **relationship** between the two friends grew strong. However, dictionary editors now label as standard the use of *relationship* to connect abstractions.

respectfully, respectively   *Respectfully* means "showing respect": The children learned to treat one another **respectfully.** *Respectively* means "in the order designated": We discussed the issue with the chair, the dean, and the provost, **respectively.**

rise   See **raise, rise.**

should of   See **could of.**

sight   See **cite, site, sight.**

sit, set   *Sit* means "to be seated": Jonathan **sat** in the front row. *Set* means "to place something": The research assistant **set** the chemicals on the counter. *Set* takes an object (to **set** something); *sit* does not.

site   See **cite, site, sight.**

so   Instead of using *so* to mean "very," find a precise modifier: She was ~~so~~ intensely focused on her career. See 7g.

someplace   See **anyplace, everyplace, someplace.**

sometime, sometimes, some time   *Sometime* means "at an unspecified time": They will meet **sometime** next month. *Sometimes* means "at times": **Sometimes** laws are unfair. *Some time* means "a span of time": They agreed to allow **some time** to pass before voting on the measure.

sort of a   See **kind of a, sort of a.**

specially   See **especially, specially.**

stationary, stationery   *Stationary* means "in a fixed position": Traffic was **stationary** for an hour. *Stationery* means "writing paper and envelopes": The director ordered new department **stationery.**

supposed to, used to   Be sure to include the frequently unsounded *d* at the end of the verb form: We are **suppose**d **to** leave at 9:30 a.m. We **use**d **to** leave earlier.

than, then   *Than* is used in comparisons: The tape recorder is smaller **than** the radio. *Then* refers to a time sequence: Go straight ahead for three blocks; **then** turn left.

their, there, they're   *Their* is the possessive form of *they:* They will give **their** presentation tomorrow. *There* refers to location: I lived **there** for six years. *There* is also used as an expletive (see 14a(3)): **There** is no explanation for the phenomenon. *They're* is a contraction of *they are:* **They're** leaving in the morning.

theirself, theirselves   Unconventional; use *themselves.* The students finished the project by ~~theirself~~ themselves.

then   See **than, then.**

to, too, two   *To* is an infinitive marker: She wanted **to** become an actress. *To* is also used as a preposition, usually indicating direction: They walked **to** the memorial. *Too* means either "also" or "excessively": I voted for her **too.** They are **too** busy this year. *Two* is a number: She studied abroad for **two** years.

toward, towards   Although both are acceptable, *toward* is preferred in American English.

try and   Conversational for *try to:* The staff will **try ~~and~~ to** finish the project by Friday.

uninterested   See **disinterested, uninterested.**

* **unique**   Traditionally, *unique* meant "one of a kind" and thus was not preceded by a qualifier such as *more, most, quite,* or *very:* Her prose style is ~~quite~~ **unique.** However, dictionary editors note that *unique* is also widely used to mean "extraordinary."

use, utilize   In most contexts, *use* is preferred to *utilize:* We ~~utilized~~ used a special dye in the experiment. However, *utilize* may suggest an effort to employ something for a purpose: We discussed how to **utilize** the resources we had been given.

used to   See **supposed to, used to.**

very   To ensure this word's effectiveness, use it sparingly. Whenever possible, choose a stronger word: She was ~~very satisfied~~ delighted with her new digital camera.

ways   Conversational when referring to distance; use *way* instead: It's a long ~~ways~~ way from home.

well   See **good, well.**

where . . . at, where . . . to   Conversational; omit *at* and *to:* **Where** is the library ~~at?~~ **Where** are you moving ~~to?~~

with regards to   Unconventional; see **regard, regarding, regards.**

would of   See **could of.**

your, you're   *Your* is a possessive form: Let's meet in **your** office. *You're* is a contraction of *you are:* **You're** gaining strength.

yourself   See **herself, himself, myself, yourself.**

Credits

This page constitutes an extension of the copyright page. We have made every effort to trace the ownership of all copyrighted material and to secure permission from copyright holders. In the event of any question arising as to the use of any material, we will be pleased to make the necessary corrections in future printings. Thanks are due to the following authors, publishers, and agents for permission to use the material indicated.

Text

p. 274: "Prose Poem: Portrait" by Pinkie Gordon Lane. © 1991. Used by permission.

p. 309: (Fig. 33.1): Page from *American Literary History* 20: 1–2 (Spring/Summer 2008), by permission of Oxford University Press.

pp. 313, 314 (Figs. 33.2 and 33.3): *Skin: A natural history* by Nina Jablonsky. Copyright 2006 by University of California Press–Books. Reproduced with permission of University of California Press–Books in the format Textbook via Copyright Clearance Center.

p. 355 (Fig. 34.1): Excerpt from abstract to Matthew Gervais and David Wilson's article "The Evolution and Functions of Laughter and Humor" from *Quarterly Review of Biology* 80:4 (December 2005), 395.

p. 356 (Fig. 34.2): Higher Education Academy Psychology Network (2008). Case study from *Improving Provision for Disabled Psychology Students.* Available from http://www.psychology.heacademy. ac.uk/ipdps.

p. 379 (Fig. 35.1): Thomas and Woods (2003), *Working with People with Learning Disabilities,* Jessica Kingsley Publishers, London and Philadelphia. Reproduced with kind permission of Jessica Kingsley Publishers.

p. 383 (Fig. 35.2): Excerpt from "Tricksters and the Marketing of Breakfast Cereals" by Thomas Green, *The Journal of Popular Culture,* Vol. 40, No. 1, January 24, 2007, p. 49. Reprinted by permission of John Wiley through Rightslink.

p. 386 (Fig. 35.3): "Children's Eyewitness Reports After Exposure to Misinformation From Parents" by Debra Ann Poole and D. Stephen Lindsay, *Journal of Experimental Psychology: Applied,* Vol. 7, No. 1, p. 27. Copyright © 2001 by the American Psychological Association. Reproduced with permission.

Photos and Illustrations

p. 220 (Fig. 27.3): Courtesy of Canon USA, Inc. © 2005 Canon USA, Inc.

p. 239: © Danny Daniels/PhotoLibrary.

p. 259 (Fig. 31.1): © Michael & Patricia Fogden/Corbis.

p. 274: © Reuters/Michael Daniel/Landov.

p. 276: Image from the feature film "The Yellow Wallpaper," directed by Logan Thomas, starring Juliet Landau, Aric Cushing, Veronica Cartwright, Dale Dickey, Raymond J. Barry, and Michael Moriarty.

p. 323 (Fig. 33.4): © The Art Institute of Chicago.

p. 326 (Fig. 33.5): Copyright © 2005 ProQuest.

p. 395: © Tim Graham/Getty Images.

p. 397: © Eric Anthony Photography/Monsoon Images/PhotoLibrary.

p. 399: © Color-Blind Images/Blend Images/Corbis.

p. 403: © SuperStock/SuperStock

p. 411: © Joan Marcus

p. 456: © GraphicMaps.com.

p. 473 (Fig. 40.5): Courtesy of Heather Adams

* * Index *

Numbers and letters in color refer to chapters and sections in the handbook; other numbers refer to pages.

SPECIAL TOPICS FOR MULTILINGUAL WRITERS

CHECKLISTS